Virginia Real Estate: Practice & Law

SIXTH EDITION

Real Estate Education

This publication is designed to provide accurate and authoritative information in regard to the subject matter covered. It is sold with the understanding that a publisher is not engaged in rendering legal, accounting, or other professional service. If legal advice or other expert assistance is required, the services of a competent professional person should be sought.

Senior Vice President and General Manager: Roy Lipner
Publisher: Evan Butterfield
Development Editor: Anne Huston
Production Manager: Bryan Samolinski
Creative Director: Lucy Jenkins

©1978, 1989, 1995, 1999, 2002 by Dearborn Financial Publishing, Inc.®

Published by Dearborn™ Real Estate Education
a division of Dearborn Financial Publishing, Inc.®
a Kaplan Professional Company
155 North Wacker Drive
Chicago, Illinois 60606-1719
(312) 836-4400
http:\\www.dearbornRE.com

All rights reserved. The text of this publication, or any part thereof, may not be reproduced in any manner whatsoever without the written permission from the copyright holders.

Printed in the United States of America.

02 03 04 10 9 8 7 6 5 4 3 2

Library of Congress Cataloging-in-Publication Data
Virginia real estate : practice & law : – 6th ed.
   p.cm.
   Includes index.
   ISBN 0-7931-4847-2
   1. Vendors and purchasers–Virgina. 2. Real property–Virginia
I. Dearborn Real Estate Education (Firm)
KFV2526.Z9 V57 2002
346.75504'3–dc21   2002025967

Contents

Preface and Chapter Conversion Table   iv

1 Real Estate Brokerage and Agency   1
Questions   12

2 Listing Agreements and Buyer Representation   14
Questions   28

3 Interests in Real Estate   30
Questions   35

4 Forms of Real Estate Ownership   37
Questions   50

5 Legal Descriptions   53
Questions   57

6 Real Estate Taxes and Other Liens   58
Questions   65

7 Real Estate Contracts   66
Questions   79

8 Transfer of Title   80
Questions   85

9 Title Records   87
Questions   91

10 Virginia's Real Estate License Law   93
Questions   119

11 Real Estate Financing: Principles and Practice   124
Questions   131

12 Leases   133
Questions   141

13 Fair Housing and Ethical Practices   143
Questions   149

Appendix A: Information Sources   151
Appendix B: Purchase and Sale Documentation Review   154
Appendix C: Practice Examination   155
Answer Key: Chapter Quizes   161
             Practice Exam   162
Index   163

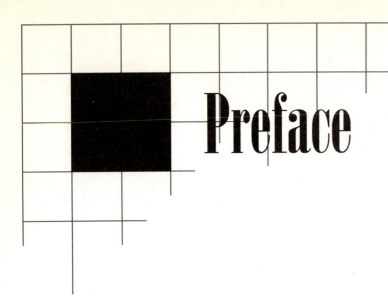

Preface

Although real estate activity in Virginia is subject to federal laws and regulations, it is controlled primarily by Virginia's laws, rules, and regulations and by state customs that prevail where no law covers a practice.

Each chapter in this book is followed by a quiz. These quizzes serve as both learning and teaching devices. As you finish each chapter, and before going on to the next, be sure that you can answer each question and that you understand all the material covered. There is an expanded 50-question examination in Appendix C. An answer key section for all the test questions is included at the end of the text.

Doris Barrell, CRB, GRI, DREI, Alexandria, Virginia, served as Consulting Editor for *Virginia Real Estate: Practice & Law*, Sixth Edition. Ms. Barrell has been in the real estate business for over 20 years, working first for a builder-developer, then as general brokerage agent, and for 9 years as managing broker for a 60-agent office in Alexandria, Virginia. She brings this wealth of real-life experience into her classes and seminars as she now devotes full-time to real estate instruction in the areas of Finance, Agency, Fair Housing, Ethics, and Legislative Issues. She is the author of two Dearborn Real Estate Education books, *Real Estate Finance Today* and *Ethics and Real Estate*. In addition, she is Consulting Editor for *Essentials of Real Estate Finance*, Tenth Edition.

Regarding the preparation of the new edition of *Virginia Real Estate: Practice & Law*, Ms. Barrell would like to extend her heartfelt thanks to the reviewers. Editing a book that includes so many different areas of real estate practice requires a true team effort. The reviewers who took the time to thoroughly review the material and submit comments, questions, and suggestions have made this sixth edition as accurate and useful as possible.

Thanks especially to Helen L. Grant, Mosely-Flint Schools of Real Estate; William C. League, Long & Foster Institute of Real Estate; Lem Marshall, general counsel, Virginia Association of REALTORS®; Allan R. Marteney, Dulles Area Real Estate School; Mary Otis, Northern Virginia Association of REALTORS®; and Roger W. Smith, Long & Foster Real Estate, Inc.

Thanks also to the Northern Virginia Association of REALTORS®, Inc. (NVAR), for providing the forms used in this book. *The forms have been reprinted with permission from NVAR for educational purposes only. Any other use of these forms without the express written consent of NVAR is strictly prohibited.*

Chapter Conversion Table

Virginia Real Estate: Practice & Law	Modern Real Estate Practice	Real Estate Fundamentals	Mastering Real Estate Principles	SuccessMaster™ Software, National	Guide to Passing the PSI Real Estate Exam
1. Real Estate Brokerage & Agency	4.5	9	13	13	8, 15
2. Listing Agreements & Buyer Representation	6	7	15	15	10
3. Interests in Real Estate	7	3	7	7	4
4. Forms of Real Estate Ownership	8	5	9	9	4
5. Legal Descriptions	9	2	6	6	4
6. Real Estate Taxes & Other Liens	10	10	5, 25	5, 26	5
7. Real Estate Contracts	11	7	14	14	10
8. Transfer of Title	12	4	10	10	11
9. Title Records	13	6	11	11	11
10. Real Estate License Laws	–	–	16	16	–
11. Real Estate Financing	14, 15	12	UNIT 7	20–23	7, 15
12. Leases	16	8	8	8	14
13. Fair Housing & Ethical Practices	20	15	17	17	12

Virginia Real Estate: Practice & Law may also be used with other tools from Dearborn™ Real Estate Education®. The conversion chart indicates which chapter, or chapters, in each of the national products corresponds with your Virginia specific text. We hope that this conversion chart will be helpful to you as you study for your real estate exam.

1 Real Estate Brokerage and Agency

The practice of real estate in the Commonwealth of Virginia is governed by Title 54.1, Chapter 21 of the Code of Virginia and Chapter 18 of the Virginia Administrative Code (VAC). The Virginia General Assembly is solely responsible for creating and amending the Code of Virginia. As part of the Department of Professional and Occupational Regulation (DPOR), the Real Estate Board (REB) is charged with issuing regulations that further describe what will be expected of both salespersons and brokers. All regulations must be consistent with the Code of Virginia.

The most current issue of the Real Estate Board Rules and Regulations, effective January 1, 1999, is available from the Department of Professional and Occupational Regulation, 3600 West Broad Street, Richmond, Virginia, 23230-4917. The rules and regulations are currently under review by the REB and new copies will be distributed to all licensees on or before January 1, 2003. All licensees, real estate brokers, and real estate salespersons are responsible to stay informed of licensing laws, regulations, and current changes.

The REB Rules and Regulations are further explained in Chapter 18 of the VAC. References may be made throughout this text to either the Code of Virginia, Title 54.1 (Chapter 21, Professions and Occupations) [§54.1 et seq.] or to the VAC, Title 18 [18 VAC 35-20 et seq.]. If you have questions about the laws or regulations to practice real estate in Virginia, you may write or call the REB at (804) 367-8500. Information is also available on the Internet; see Code of Virginia and Virginia Administrative Code at the following Web address.

WWWeb.Link
http://leg1.state.va.us

BROKERAGE DEFINITIONS

In Virginia, a real estate *broker* is defined by statute as

> ...any person or business entity, including, but not limited to, a partnership, association, corporation, or limited liability corporation, who, for compensation or valuable consideration (i) sells or offers for sale, buys or offers to buy, or negotiates the purchase or sale or exchange of real estate, including units or interest in condominiums, cooperative interest... or time shares in a time-share program... or (ii) who leases or offers to lease, or rents or offers for rent, any real estate or the improvements thereon for others. [§54.1-2100]

In practice the word *broker* may refer to a firm, a sole proprietor who transacts real estate business, a managing broker for a branch office of a larger firm, or a person who holds a broker's license but practices under the supervision of a principal broker. It is important to note that the brokerage relationship is established between the *broker*, principal broker or sole proprietor, as the *agent* and the *client* as the *principal*.

The statutory definition of a real estate *salesperson* is

> ...any person, or business entity of not more than two persons unless related by blood or marriage, who for compensation or valuable consideration is employed either directly or indirectly by, or affiliated as an independent contractor with, a real estate broker, to sell or offer to sell, or to buy or offer to buy, or to negotiate the purchase, sale, or exchange of real estate, or to lease, rent or offer for rent, any real estate, or to negotiate leases thereof, or of the improvements thereon. [§54.1-2101]

Although a salesperson may generally perform the same functions as a broker, the salesperson must be employed by or affiliated with a licensed real estate broker. Brokers are expected to supervise all activities of the salespersons affiliated with their company and are responsible for the actions of every salesperson. Salespersons are considered to be general agents of the brokers they represent.

Brokers and salespersons can be further defined according to their specific roles within a brokerage firm.

Firm—any sole proprietorship (nonbroker owned) partnership, association, limited liability company, or corporation, other than a sole proprietorship (principal broker owned), that is required by regulation to obtain a separate brokerage firm license.

Principal Broker—the individual broker designated by each firm to assure compliance with Chapter 21 of Title 54.1 of the Code of Virginia, and to receive all communications and notices from the REB which may affect the firm and/or its licensees. In the case of a sole proprietorship, the licensed broker who is the sole proprietor has the responsibilities of the principal broker. The principal broker shall have responsibility for the activities of the firm and all of its licensees.

Supervising Broker (or, *managing broker*)—an individual associate broker who shall be designated by the firm to supervise the activities of a branch office.

Associate Broker—any individual licensed as a broker who practices within a brokerage firm as a sales associate. An associate broker is required to meet the same educational, experience, and testing requirements as a principal broker but is subject to the same restrictions of brokerage activity as a salesperson.

Sole Proprietor—an individual, not a corporation, who is doing business either under his or her own name, or under a legally registered fictitious name. A licensed broker who is a sole proprietor shall have the same responsibilities as a principal broker. A sole proprietor who is not licensed must designate a licensed broker to perform the duties of a principal broker.

Licensee—any person, partnership, association, limited liability company or corporation that holds a license issued by the REB to act as a real estate broker or salesperson.

Standard Agent—a licensee, either broker or salesperson, who acts for or represents a client in an agency relationship according to the statutory duties later described on page 6 under "Duties of a Client."

Independent Contractor—a licensee who acts for or represents a client according to a written contract between the licensee and the client instead of as a standard agent. This is a specific distinction pertaining to agency law and is not related to the definition of "independent contractor" as used for tax purposes by the Internal Revenue Service (IRS).

Designated Agent (or *designated representative*)—a licensee designated by the principal or supervising broker to represent one party to a transaction when the broker is also representing another party in the same transaction.

Dual Agent (or *dual representative*)—a licensee who has a brokerage relationship with both seller and buyer, or both landlord and tenant, in the same real estate transaction. Because the brokerage relationship is established between the broker and the client, the principal broker, or supervising broker, would always remain in a dual agent position in the transaction even though the broker may designate one salesperson to represent one party to the transaction and another salesperson to represent the other party to the transaction.

Common Source Information Company—any person who or entity that compiles or provides information regarding real estate for sale or lease and other data, and includes but is not limited to a multiple listing service (MLS). No broker or salesperson license is required.

WHO MUST HAVE A LICENSE

Any person who or business entity that performs or advertises brokerage services must be licensed by the REB. Licenses are issued for individuals, partnerships, limited liability companies (LLCs), associations, corporations, and nonbroker-owned sole proprietorships. The license may be granted in a fictitious name, that is, a name other than that of the principal broker.

Individual licenses are issued to the business entity or firm, principal brokers, associate brokers, and salespersons. (See Chapter 10 for licensing requirements.) All broker and salesperson licenses are to be displayed at the main office of the brokerage firm and be available for public inspection.

An individual with a broker's license may operate as a sole proprietor without an additional firm license unless the firm is to operate under a fictitious name, in which case a separate brokerage firm license is required.

Additional regulations for business entities include the following:

1. Every member or officer who actively participates in brokerage business must hold a license as a broker.
2. Every employee or independent contractor who acts as a salesperson must hold a license as either salesperson or broker.

A separate branch office license must be issued for each branch office of a brokerage firm, including the name of the supervising broker. The branch office license is the only license that is displayed outside the main office and must be clearly visible to the public.

EXEMPTIONS

Not everyone who performs an act of real estate brokerage or related real estate activities is required to hold a Virginia real estate license. Following are a few examples of persons exempt from the state licensing requirement. These and other exemptions will be discussed in detail in Chapter 10.

- Individuals who are selling or renting their own property
- Persons selling or renting property owned by their employers
- Attorneys involved in real estate transactions in their normal role as attorneys
- Licensed auctioneers selling real estate at public auction.

AGENCY

The concept of common law of agency as it relates to real estate brokerage no longer exists in Virginia. In 1995, the Virginia General Assembly expressly abrogated the common law of agency in real estate transactions. [§54.1-2144] In its place, the legislature enacted an agency statute that codifies the agency relationships among brokers, buyers, sellers, landlords, and tenants. [§§54.1-2130 through 54.1-2144] This is referred to as "standard" or statutory agency.

In addition to establishing new rules and standards for agency relationships in real estate transactions, the statute provides that neither compensation nor use of a common source information company, such as an MLS, creates a brokerage relationship. [§54.1-2140]

Definitions [§54.1-2130]

Virginia's agency statute provides the following definitions:

Agency is defined as any relationship in which a real estate licensee acts for or represents a person by such person's express authority in a real estate transaction.

The parties are, however, free to enter into a written agreement that establishes some other sort of relationship—for instance, where the broker is an *independent contractor*, or where additional duties are imposed on the broker. In that case, the written agreement governs the relationship not the statute. The lack of a specific written agreement would impose the duties of standard agency.

A *brokerage relationship* is a contractual relationship between client and broker, in which the broker licensee has been engaged by the client to procure a seller, buyer, option, tenant or landlord, who is ready, willing, and able to sell, buy, option, exchange, or rent real estate. Note that although it is often the salesperson who initiates the brokerage relationship with the client, it is in fact the broker who has the brokerage relationship with the client. In this context, the "broker licensee" refers to the brokerage firm. For example: XYZ Realty as a nonbroker owned sole proprietor may have hired Mary Smith to act as principal broker of the firm. The broker/client relationship is with XYZ Realty not Mary Smith.

The brokerage relationship is limited to a broker and a client. A *client* is a person who has entered into a brokerage relationship with a broker licensee; any other party to the transaction with whom the licensee does not have a brokerage relationship but for whom the licensee may perform routine services, referred to as "ministerial acts", is a customer. *Ministerial acts* are routine acts that a licensee can perform for a person that do not involve discretion or the exercise of the licensee's own judgment.

The roles of "designated agent" or "dual agent" are very important under the law of agency. Although the principal broker remains in a dual agent position whenever the brokerage firm represents both parties to one transaction, the responsibilities of the salespersons may be different.

In Practice

J is the principal broker of ABC Realty. Through the actions of his agent, *M*, *J* has established a brokerage relationship with prospective buyer *S* by having her sign an Exclusive Right to Represent agreement. *S* decides to make an offer on a property that is listed with ABC Realty with *B* as listing agent. Broker *J* may now designate *M* to be the "designated agent" for the buyer and *B* to be the "designated agent" for the seller. Both *M* and *B* will be able to meet all of the statutory obligations of duties to their clients. *J*, as the principal broker, will remain in a "dual agency" position with equal responsibility to both clients.

If the buyer, *S*, wished to purchase a property listed by ABC Realty with *M* as listing agent, *M* could then enter into a disclosed "dual agent" role where he would have statutory responsibilities to both clients. ABC Realty would have brokerage relationships with both the buyer, through the signing of an Exclusive Right to Represent Agreement, and the seller, through the signing of a listing agreement.

Another alternative would be to withdraw from the buyer representation brokerage agreement with *S* and continue to only represent the seller. Buyer *S* would then be a "customer" instead of a "client." The statutory obligation would be to treat *S* honestly. *M* would also be able to perform "ministerial acts" for her, but his primary responsibility would be to the seller.

Duties to a Client [§§54.1-2131 to 54.1-2134]

The Virginia agency statute establishes specific duties for a licensee who is in an agency relationship with a seller, buyer, landlord, or tenant. These statutory duties for a client require licensees to

1. perform according to the terms of the brokerage relationship;
2. promote the best interests of the client by
   - *seeking a sale (or lease) at the price and terms established in the brokerage relationship*, or at some other price and terms acceptable to the client (once the property is under contract, the licensee is not expected to continue to pursue additional offers unless he or she is required to do so under the brokerage agreement or sales contract);
   - *presenting all written offers and counteroffers* in a timely manner, even after the property is under contract;
   - *disclosing* to the client all material facts, related to the property or concerning the transaction; of which the licensee has actual knowledge;
   - *accounting* in a timely manner for all money and property received in which the client has or may have an interest;
3. maintain *confidentiality* of all personal and financial information received from the client during the brokerage relationship, and all information characterized as confidential by the client, unless the seller consents in writing to its release or unless the licensee is required by law to release the information—under Virginia law, such confidential information is to remain confidential forever;
4. exercise ordinary care; and
5. comply with all applicable laws, including fair housing statutes and regulations and all other statutes and regulations required by the state.

The traditional "fiduciary" responsibilities that were a part of the common law of agency are basically included in the new statutory duties but with far less implied liability.

Duties to a Customer

Customers, the parties with whom the license does *not* have a brokerage relationship, must be treated honestly and may not knowingly be given false information. In addition, they must be informed of any material adverse facts regarding the property's physical condition of which the licensee has actual knowledge. No legal action may be brought against a licensee for making such required disclosures:

> A licensee will not be held liable for providing false information if the false information was provided to the licensee by the seller; and the licensee did not actually know that the information was false; or did not act in reckless disregard of the truth. [§54-2131B]

A licensee having a brokerage relationship with a client is permitted to assist customers by performing ministerial acts. The performance of ministerial acts does not violate the licensee's brokerage relationship with the client. Similarly, the brokerage relationship is not violated if the licensee shows alternative properties to prospective buyers or tenants or represents other sellers (or landlords).

Additional Disclosure Required by Buyer's Agent

In the case of a residential transaction, a licensee must disclose to the seller the buyer's *intent to occupy* the property as a principal residence. [§54.1-2132B] This disclosure is often stated in the body of a purchase agreement.

Property Management

Licensees who are engaged to manage real estate are required by Virginia law to perform according to the management agreement, exercise ordinary care, disclose all material facts concerning the property of which the licensee has actual knowledge, maintain confidentiality of information, account for all money and property received, and comply with all relevant real estate and fair housing laws and regulations. The licensee is expected to perform his or her services in accordance with the property management agreement. Licensees are permitted to represent other owners in the management of real property and to represent the owner as seller or landlord under a brokerage agreement. [§54.1-2135] The broker is a General Agent to the owner of the property under a Property Management Agreement.

Establishing the Brokerage Relationship [§54.1-2136]

Prior to entering into a brokerage relationship, the licensee is required to advise the prospective client of

- the type of brokerage relationship proposed by the broker;
- the broker's compensation; and
- whether the broker will share the compensation with a broker who may have a brokerage relationship with another party to the transaction.

Remember, compensation does not imply or create a brokerage relationship.

Although oral contracts are legal in Virginia, they are not enforceable, and it is highly recommended by legal counsel and the REB that all brokerage relationships be established in writing.

Commencement and Termination of Brokerage Relationship [§54.1-2137]

Under Virginia's agency statute, the brokerage relationship begins at the time a client engages a licensee. Ideally, the relationship terminates when the brokerage agreement's terms have been completely performed. However, the relationship may also be terminated by

- the expiration of the agreement;
- a mutual agreement to terminate;
- a default by any party; or
- the licensee's withdrawal when a client refuses to consent to disclosed dual agency. (Additional reference in [§54.1-2139D])

All brokerage relationships must have a definite termination date. If no date is specified, the statute establishes a mandatory termination date of 90 days after the commencement of the brokerage relationship. [§54.1-2137B]

Once a brokerage relationship has terminated or expired, the licensee owes no further duties to the client. However, the licensee is nonetheless required to account for all monies and property relating to the brokerage relationship and must *preserve the confidentiality* of information.

Disclosure Requirements

Virginia agency law requires full disclosure of any existing brokerage relationships. It is essential that the party to the transaction who is not the client of the licensee, and who is not represented by another licensee clearly understands that the licensee represents only his or her client. Although the licensee is required to treat a customer honestly and to disclose any material adverse facts about the physical condition of the property, the agent's primary responsibility is to protect and promote the best interest of his or her client.

At the time of the first substantive discussion about a specific property with an actual or prospective buyer, seller, landlord, or tenant who is not a client of the licensee and who is not represented by another licensee, a licensee is required to disclose any broker relationship he or she has with any other party to the transaction. The disclosure must be made orally no later than the time when specific real estate assistance is first provided and in writing at the earliest practical time for sales transactions and at the time of the application or lease, whichever is first, for rental transactions. Disclosure is not required for lease terms of less than two months.

The written disclosure must be in substantially the same form as that illustrated in Figure 1.1.

Figure 1.1 *Disclosure of Brokerage Relationship [§54.1-2138A]*

The undersigned do hereby acknowledge disclosure that:

The licensee _____
                          Name of Firm

represents the following party in a real estate transaction:

_____ Seller(s) or _____ Buyer(s)

_____ Landlord(s) or _____ Tenant(s)

_____   _____
    Date   Name

_____   _____
    Date   Name

Note: The Disclosure of Brokerage Relationship is only to be signed by the person who is *not* the client. The client will sign either an Exclusive Right to Represent, buyer agency agreement, or an Exclusive Right to Sell, listing agreement. The point of disclosure is for the person who is *not* a client to understand that the licensee represents the other party to the transaction.

If the required disclosure is given in combination with other disclosures or information, the disclosure must be conspicuous, printed in bold lettering, all capitals, underlined, or within a separate box. [§54.1-2139B] If the licensee's relationship with any party to the transaction changes, all clients and customers involved in the transaction must be informed—in writing—of the change. Copies of all disclosures must be kept for three years.

Disclosed Dual Representation [§54.1-2139]

In Virginia, a licensee may represent both parties in the same real estate transaction—seller and buyer or landlord and tenant—only with the written consent of all clients in the transaction. The client's signature on the written disclosure form is presumptive evidence of the brokerage relationship. The disclosure must be substantially in the same form as that illustrated in Figure 1.2.

A dual representative does not terminate any brokerage relationship by making the required disclosures of dual representation. [§54.1-2139C] As mentioned previously, a licensee may withdraw from representing a client who refuses to consent to disclosed dual agency. The licensee may withdraw under such circumstances without liability and may continue to represent the other client. Further, the licensee may continue to represent in other transactions the client who refused dual representation. [§54.1-2139D]

Designated Representation

A principal or supervising broker may assign different affiliated licensees as *designated representatives* to represent different clients in the same transaction. The appointment of designated representatives excludes other licensees in the firm from involvement in the transaction. *The use of designated representatives does not constitute dual representation if each designee represents only one client in a particular real estate transaction.* [§54.1-2139E] The designated representatives are pledged to maintain all confidential information received from their clients. Such information may be shared with the principal or supervising broker who remains in the position of a dual representative with equal responsibilities to both clients. The disclosure must be made in writing and must be similar to Figure 1.3.

Imputed Knowledge [§54.1-2142]

One aspect of the Virginia agency law that differs from the formerly used common law of agency with respect to real estate transactions is that there is no longer imputed liability on the part of either the client or the broker.

A client is not liable for misrepresentations made by a licensee, nor is a broker liable for misrepresentation on the part of another broker engaged to assist in a real estate transaction. In both cases, liability for another's actions would only occur if the client and/or broker knew, or should have known, of the misrepresentation or failed to take steps to correct it.

Knowledge or information between clients or brokers is not imputed. Each is responsible only for actual knowledge or information although liability may still occur in a case of unlawful housing discriminatory practices.

Figure 1.2   Disclosure of Dual Represenation

The undersigned do hereby acknowledge disclosure that:

The licensee(s) _____
                          Name of Broker, Firm or Salesperson(s)

represents more than one party in this real estate transaction as indicated below:

_____Seller(s) and Buyer(s)   _____Landlord(s) and Tenant(s)

The undersigned understands that the foregoing dual representative(s) may not disclose to either client or such client's designated representative any information that has been given to the dual representative by the other client within the confidence and trust of the brokerage relationship except for that information which is otherwise required or permitted by Article 3 (§54.1-2130 et seq.) of Chapter 21 of Title 54.1 of the Code of Virginia to be disclosed. The undersigned by signing this notice do hereby acknowledge their informed consent to the disclosed dual representation by the licensee.

| _____ | _____ |
| Date | Name (one party) |

| _____ | _____ |
| Date | Name (other party) |

| _____ | _____ |
| Date | Name (other party) |

| _____ | _____ |
| Date | Name (other party) |

Figure 1.3 Disclosure of the Use of Designated Representatives

The undersigned do hereby acknowledge disclosure that:

The licensee _____
                              Name of Broker and Firm

represents more than one party in this real estate transaction as indicated below:

_____ Seller(s) and Buyer(s) _____ Landlord(s) and Tenant(s)

The undersigned understands that the foregoing dual representative may not disclose to either client or such client's designated representative any information that has been given to the dual representative by the other client within the confidence and trust of the brokerage relationship except for that information which is otherwise required or permitted by Article 3 (§54.1-2130 et seq.) of Chapter 21 of Title 54.1 of the Code of Virginia to be disclosed. The undersigned by signing this notice do hereby acknowledge their informed consent to the disclosed dual representation by the licensee.

The principal or supervising broker has assigned _____
                                                          Licensee/Sales Associate

to act as Designated Representative for the one party as indicated below:

_____ Seller(s) or   _____ Buyer(s)

_____ Landlord(s) or   _____ Tenant(s)

and _____ to act as Designated Representative for
           Licensee/Sales Associate

the other party as indicated below:

_____ Seller(s) or   _____ Buyer(s)

_____ Landlord(s) or   _____ Tenant(s)

_____   _____
       Date   Name (one party)

_____   _____
       Date   Name (other party)

Questions

1. By Virginia statutory definition, a salesperson may perform all of the following functions **EXCEPT**:
   1. offer a residence for sale.
   2. negotiate an exchange.
   3. serve as a managing broker.
   4. lease rental apartments.

2. An individual wants to sell her own house. Which of the following statements is TRUE?
   1. She does not need a real estate license to sell her own property.
   2. In Virginia, anyone who sells real property must have a real estate license.
   3. An individual may obtain a temporary real estate license in order to legally sell her own house.
   4. She may sell her house without a real estate license because she is an attorney.

3. Any individual holding a broker's license in Virginia who is not a principal broker is a/an
   1. affiliate broker.
   2. supervising broker.
   3. managing broker.
   4. associate broker.

4. An "agency" relationship could BEST be described as one in which a licensee
   1. has a signed agreement establishing a brokerage relationship.
   2. has a separate independent contractor agreement with a buyer.
   3. performs ministerial acts for a seller.
   4. acts for or represents another person in a real estate transaction.

5. Routine services that do NOT create an agency relationship are referred to as
   1. transactional acts.
   2. routine brokerage
   3. ministerial acts.
   4. customer service.

6. All of the following are specific duties owed to a seller or buyer client **EXCEPT** to:
   1. perform to the terms of the contract.
   2. protect and promote the best interests of the client.
   3. always be obedient to the client's demands.
   4. maintain confidentiality forever.

7. P is a real estate licensee who has signed a brokerage agreement with H, who is looking for an apartment to rent. P does not charge a fee to prospective tenants; rather, P receives a commission from landlords. P tells a landlord that H could probably pay a somewhat higher rent than the landlord is asking. Which of the following statements is true?
   1. P owes statutory agency duties to the landlords who pay the commission.
   2. P's disclosure to the landlord was appropriate under these circumstances.
   3. P's disclosure violated the statutory duties owed to H.
   4. Because P is not charging a fee to prospective tenants, P has violated Virginia's agency statute.

8. A brokerage relationship may be terminated by any of the following **EXCEPT**
   1. one party unilaterally "firing" the other.
   2. expiration of the agreement.
   3. a default by either party.
   4. a licensee's withdrawal when the client refuses to consent to dual agency.

9. *G* is representing buyer *J* in the purchase of a townhouse listed with *S*. *G* has a signed Exclusive Right to Represent contract with *J*. Mark will need to have a Disclosure of Brokerage Relationship form signed by:
   1. *J*.
   2. sellers of the townhouse.
   3. both *J* and the sellers of the townhouse.
   4. no one because the sellers have their own agent.

10. *M* and *T* are licensed salespersons who are both affiliated with ABC Realty. *M* has listed a house, and *T* has a likely buyer. What should the supervising broker do?
    1. Nothing since neither *M* nor *T* wish to act as disclosed dual representatives.
    2. The broker's only legal option is to insist that either *M* or *T* sign a disclosed dual representation agreement with the buyers and sellers.
    3. The broker may assign *M* and *T* as designated representatives, and provide a disclosure form to the sellers only. The broker will be a subagent.
    4. The broker may assign *M* and *T* as designated representatives, and provide a disclosure form to both the sellers and the prospective buyers. The broker will be a dual agent.

2 Listing Agreements and Buyer Representation

LISTING AGREEMENTS

The standard types of listings—open, exclusive-agency, and exclusive-right-to-sell are all legal in Virginia. Many brokers will not accept open listings, however, since there would be no guarantee of payment for time and money spent on the listings. Also, open listings may not be allowed by many multiple listing service (MLS) systems. All listing agreements must include a definite termination date. The owner must be furnished a copy of the listing at the time it is signed.

Virginia Real Estate Board (REB) regulations specifically prohibit net listings [18 VAC 135-20-280(5)]. A *net listing* is an agreement in which an owner specifies a particular dollar amount that he or she must net from the sale or rental of a property; the broker may keep any amount over the seller's net that is generated by the transaction. Under a net listing, it is difficult to balance the broker's responsibility to the principal with the broker's own interest in making a profit. Because this practice is not permitted in Virginia, brokers must inform prospective clients that their fee will be a percentage of the selling price, a *commission*, or a flat fee for services.

FOR EXAMPLE *O*, a homeowner, called *D*, a Richmond real estate broker, and told her that he wanted to sell his house. "I don't have time to be bothered with percentages and bargaining and offers and counteroffers," *O* explained. "I just need to walk out of this deal with $150,000 in my pocket. If you sell this place for more than that, you can keep the rest." Broker *D* knew that homes such as *O*'s were selling for well over $200,000. On the other hand, *D* knew that net listings are illegal in Virginia. What should *D* do?

LISTING FORMS

There is no "standard" listing form used throughout the commonwealth of Virginia. Each local association or their independent MLS companies will develop forms for use by the licensees. Each MLS system will have its own set of rules and regulations that must be followed by licensees making entries into the particular system. Figure 2.1 illustrates a listing form used by the Northern Virginia Association of REALTORS®, whose website can be found at the following address.

www.nvar.com

In Practice   In a listing form, the blanks are rarely optional. *All blanks should be filled in.* If an item does not apply in a particular transaction, the notation N/A, not applicable, should be used. Finding accurate information for each item may require additional research.

Some items on the listing forms may have to be entered as approximations, such as the mortgage balance—until a payoff statement is available from the lender—or the exact age of the dwelling. Accurate figures should be used wherever possible. Any changes involving financial responsibility, such as a price change, dates, or other major seller commitments must be authorized in writing by the seller.

Line-By-Line Analysis of Virginia Listing Agreement

The following is a line-by-line analysis of the content of Figure 2.1:

Item 1: Selling price should be clearly written. Be careful not to confuse numbers. Commas and decimals points should be properly placed.

Each personal property item requires a yes or no response. There is also space in which to list any other items that are not preprinted on the form. A frequent issue of disagreement between buyers and sellers involves which personal property items convey with the property; by being clear about all possible items, licensees can avoid arguments later.

Item 1 also clarifies that the seller will sign a sales contract enforceable in the Commonwealth of Virginia in the event of a sale and that the property is to be delivered in substantially the same condition as on the contract date with all existing appliances, heating, cooling, plumbing, and electrical systems and equipment in normal working order. The key word here is "existing"; if the dishwasher is listed as being conveyed, it must work! If items on the "to be conveyed" list are questionable, they may be marked "as is."

Item 2: Virginia's agency law (discussed in Chapter 1) requires a full disclosure of agency options and issues. Licensees must be certain that their client clearly understands this important information. The specific duties of the broker are listed plus notice that all material adverse facts about the property must be disclosed to any potential buyer. Brief descriptions of Buyer, Designated, and Dual representation are given.

Item 3: Virginia law requires that all listing agreements have a definite expiration date. Such words as "90 days from the date of this agreement" are not sufficient. Failing to include a definite termination date is an act of "improper dealing" in violation of the REB rules and regulations as defined in [18 VAC 135-20-290(1)]

Item 4: This statement of the Fair Housing law puts the seller on notice that the licensee will show the property to any qualified buyer.

Item 5: The broker may use a MLS and related electronic databases and may distribute information about the property in print and electronic form during and after the expiration of the agreement. The seller's permission must be obtained for the broker to disclose the contract price of the property in an MLS prior to closing. Entry into the local MLS is to be made within 48 hours unless the seller instructs otherwise. Sellers occasionally want a few days to complete repairs, painting, etc., but any delay beyond the 48 hours should be put into writing. Note: These specific conditions may vary from one MLS system to another. Some MLS systems prohibit the entry of the listing into the system until the property and seller are actually ready for marketing and showing of the property.

Item 6: Broker's compensation must be clearly stated, for the broker's protection as well as for the seller's information. This item also clarifies the possible use of a retainer agreement or other fees and makes it clear that there are no antitrust violations involved in the transaction.

Item 7: The brokers, sales associates, MLSs, and REALTOR® associations are released from liability in case of vandalism, theft, or damage of any nature during the term of the agreement, unless they themselves were responsible. The seller further agrees to hold them harmless for any property damage or personal injury that might happen resulting from use or access to the property during the term of the agreement.

Item 8: The seller remains fully responsible for utilities, maintenance, and security of the property. Seller is obliged to permit the property to be shown, inspected, and appraised during reasonable hours. The broker must receive permission from the seller to place a "For Sale" sign and lockbox on the property.

Item 9: Additional seller disclosures are required if the property is a cooperative or condominium. It is important that the seller understand that the buyer has a legal right to cancel the contract if the buyer is not satisfied with the documents. [Title 55, Chapter 4.2 of Code of Virginia]

Item 10: If the property is located in a development subject to the Virginia Property Owners' Association Act (POA), a special disclosure packet must be obtained by the seller and presented to the buyer. By law, the buyer has a right to cancel the contract if not satisfied with the POA documents. [Title 55, Chapter 26 of Code of Virginia] Effective July 1, 2001, the POA packet can be ordered at the time the listing is taken and given to the buyer at the time of contract. The new law no longer requires the packet to be current within 30 days of the contract. The buyer will still have three days after receipt of the POA packet to cancel the contract.

Item 11: Unless exempt, sellers must comply with the Virginia Residential Property Disclosure Act providing either the Property Disclosure or Property Disclaimer statement to the buyer. Either form should be included in the listing package for the buyer's review prior to signing a contract. Otherwise, the buyer has certain rights to cancel the contract.

Item 12: If a property was built before 1978, required disclosures must be made regarding lead-based paint hazards.

Item 13: Property in Virginia is financed with a deed of trust rather than a mortgage. If the property is to be sold subject to an existing deed of trust, the amount of the unpaid balance must be disclosed.

Item 14: Although the item reads "shall provide," this is only applicable if the seller wishes to offer to hold the financing.

Item 15: The owner or broker may add any other terms, conditions, or contingencies under which the property will be sold.

Space is provided for signatures of seller(s) including whether or not seller is a licensed real estate agent or broker, and listing broker and sales associate.

BUYER REPRESENTATION

A buyer's agent establishes a brokerage relationship with a client through a *buyer representation agreement.* (See Chapter 1 on Brokerage and Agency.) A typical buyer's representation agreement used in Virginia is illustrated in Figure 2.2.

STATUTE OF FRAUDS

It should be noted that while an oral listing or buyer representation agreement may be legal in Virginia, such an agreement would not be enforceable.

SELLER DISCLOSURE

The Virginia Residential Property Disclosure Act [§55-517 et seq.] requires that sellers disclose all material information about the property being sold or allows the seller to file a disclaimer. The act applies to residential property consisting of one to four units, and to sales, options, installment sales, or leases with option-to-buy. The law applies to the sale of most residential property, whether or not a real estate professional is involved. If a licensee is involved, the disclosure should be obtained when the listing is taken. The disclosure must be made *prior* to acceptance of an offer. If the disclosure is not made *prior* to acceptance, the purchaser will have specified rights to terminate the contract.

Sellers must disclose certain known information about the property. (See Figure 2.3.) The information includes

- the property's age and physical condition, structural defects, termites, environmental hazards, and land use issues;
- the type of water and sewage, plumbing, electrical, heating, ventilation, and air conditioning (HVAC systems);
- the type of insulation, roof condition and material; and
- notification of the purchaser's responsibility to obtain information on registered sexual offenders.

Subsequent to the delivery of the disclosure statement to the buyer, the owner is required to disclose any material changes or certify to the buyer that the property is substantially the same as when the disclosure was provided. [§55-522].

Figure 2.1 Listing Agreement—Exclusive Right To Sell

VIRGINIA REGIONAL LISTING AGREEMENT - EXCLUSIVE RIGHT TO SELL

This Agreement is made on _____, _____, by and between _____
_____ ("Seller") and _____ ("Broker").
(Firm Name)

In consideration of providing the services and facilities described herein, the Broker is hereby granted the exclusive right to sell the Property known as:
_____, Virginia _____ ("Property").

Legal Description _____ Tax Map No./ ID# _____.

1. The Property is offered for sale at a selling price of $ _____, or such other price as later agreed upon, which price includes the Broker compensation. In the event of a sale, the Seller will sign a sales contract enforceable in the Commonwealth of Virginia.

The Sales Price includes the following personal property and fixtures which shall be transferred free of liens: A. Any existing built-in heating and central air conditioning equipment, plumbing and lighting fixtures, storm windows, storm doors, screens, installed wall-to-wall carpeting, window shades, blinds, smoke and heat detectors, tv antennas, exterior trees and shrubs and B. The items marked YES below as currently installed or offered:

YES	NO	ITEM	YES	NO	ITEM	YES	NO	ITEM	YES	NO	ITEM
☐	☐	Stove or Range	☐	☐	Disposer	☐	☐	Ceiling Fan(s) # ____	☐	☐	Alarm System
☐	☐	Cooktop	☐	☐	Freezer	☐	☐	Washer	☐	☐	Intercom
☐	☐	Wall Oven(s) # ____	☐	☐	Window Fan(s) # ____	☐	☐	Dryer	☐	☐	Storage Shed(s) # ____
☐	☐	Refrigerator(s) # ____	☐	☐	Window A/C Unit(s) # ____	☐	☐	Furnace Humidifier	☐	☐	Garage Opener(s) # ____
☐	☐	w/ ice maker	☐	☐	Pool, Equip. & Cover	☐	☐	Electronic Air Filter	☐	☐	w/ remote(s) # ____
☐	☐	Dishwasher	☐	☐	Hot Tub, Equip. & Cover	☐	☐	Central Vacuum	☐	☐	Playground Equipment
☐	☐	Built-in Microwave	☐	☐	Satellite Dish and Equip.	☐	☐	Water Treatment System	☐	☐	Wood Stove
☐	☐	Trash Compactor	☐	☐	Attic Fan(s)	☐	☐	Exhaust Fan(s)	☐	☐	Fireplace Screen/ Doors
☐	☐	Sump Pump	☐	☐	Window Treatments						

Other inclusions or exclusions: _____

WATER, SEWAGE, HEATING, AND CENTRAL AIR CONDITIONING: (Check all that apply)
Water Supply: ☐ Public ☐ Well ☐ Other _____ Hot Water: ☐ Oil ☐ Gas ☐ Elec.
Sewage Disposal: ☐ Public ☐ Septic # BR ____ Air Conditioning: ☐ Gas ☐ Elec. ☐ Heat Pump
Heating: ☐ Oil ☐ Gas ☐ Elec. ☐ Heat Pump ☐ Other _____

The Seller will deliver the Property in substantially the same condition as on the Contract Date and in broom clean condition with all trash and debris removed. The Seller warrants that the existing appliances, heating, cooling, plumbing and electrical systems and equipment and smoke and heat detectors (as required) will be in normal working order as of the possession date.

2. **The Broker and the Sales Associate(s) shall promote the interests of the Seller by:** (a) performing the terms of this Agreement; (b) seeking a buyer at a price and terms agreed upon herein or otherwise acceptable to the Seller. However, the Broker and the Sales Associate(s) shall not be obligated to seek additional offers to purchase the Property while the Property is subject to a contract of sale, unless stated herein or as the contract of sale so provides; (c) presenting in a timely manner all written offers or counteroffers to and from the Seller even when the Property is already subject to a contract of sale; (d) disclosing to the Seller all material facts related to the Property or concerning the transaction of which the Broker and Sales Associate(s) have actual knowledge; (e) accounting for in a timely manner all money and property received in which the Seller has or may have an interest. Unless otherwise provided by law or the Seller consents in writing to the release of the information, the Broker and the Sales Associate(s) shall maintain the confidentiality of all personal and financial information and other matters identified as confidential by the Seller, if that information is received from the Seller during the brokerage relationship. In satisfying these duties, the Broker and the Sales Associate(s) shall exercise ordinary care, comply with all applicable laws and regulations and treat all prospective buyers honestly and not knowingly give them false information; and the Broker and the Sales Associate(s) shall disclose to prospective buyers all material adverse facts pertaining to the physical condition of the Property which are actually known by them. In addition, the Broker and the Sales Associate(s) may provide assistance to a buyer or prospective buyer by performing ministerial acts that are not inconsistent with the Broker's and the Sales Associate's duties under this Agreement. The Seller acknowledges that the Broker and Sales Associate(s) and any cooperating brokers and sales associates may act on behalf of the Seller as the Seller's representatives.

Buyer representation occurs when buyers contract to use the services of their own broker (known as a buyer representative) to act on their behalf.

Designated representation occurs when a buyer and seller in one transaction are represented by different Sales Associate(s) affiliated with the same Broker. Each of these Sales Associates, known as a Designated Representative, represents fully the interests of a different client in the same transaction. Designated Representatives are not dual representatives if each represents only the buyer or only the seller in a specific real estate transaction. Except for disclosure of confidential information to the Broker, each Designated Representative is bound by the confidentiality requirements as above. The Broker remains a dual representative. ☐ The Seller consents to designated representation **OR** ☐ The Seller does not consent to designated representation which means the Seller does not allow the Property to be shown to a buyer represented by this Broker through another Designated Representative associated with the firm. The Broker will notify other associates within the firm via the MLS whether the Seller consents or does not consent.

Dual representation occurs when a buyer and seller in one transaction are represented by the same Broker and the same Sales Associate(s). When the parties agree to dual representation, the ability of the Broker and the Sales Associate(s) to represent either party fully and exclusively is limited. The confidentiality of all information of all clients shall be maintained as above. ☐ The Seller consents to dual representation **OR** ☐ The Seller does not consent to dual representation which means the Seller does not allow the Property to be shown to a buyer represented by this Broker through the same Sales Associate(s).

3. This Exclusive Right to Sell will expire at midnight on _____.

4. This Property shall be shown and made available without regard to race, color, religion, sex, handicap, familial status or national origin as well as all classes protected by the laws of the United States, the Commonwealth of Virginia and applicable local jurisdictions.

NVAR - 01 - Rev. 9/00   Page 1 of 2   Please Initial: Seller _____ / _____

Figure 2.1   Listing Agreement—Exclusive Right To Sell (Continued)

5. The Broker shall make a blanket unilateral offer of cooperation and compensation to other brokers in any Multiple Listing Service that the Broker deems appropriate. The Broker shall disseminate information regarding the Property, including the entry date, listing price(s), final price and all terms, and expired or withdrawn status, by printed form and/or electronic computer service during and after the expiration of this Agreement. The Broker shall enter the listing information into the MLS data base within 48 hours (unless otherwise instructed in writing by the Seller) after all Sellers' signatures have been obtained.

6. A. The Seller shall pay the Broker compensation of _____ in cash if, during the term of this Agreement, anyone produces a buyer ready, willing and able to buy the Property. The compensation is also earned if within _____ days after the expiration or termination of this Agreement, a contract is ratified with a ready, willing and able buyer to whom the Property has been shown during the term of this Agreement; provided, however, that the compensation need not be paid if a contract is ratified on the Property while the Property is listed with another real estate company. B. The Broker acknowledges receipt of a retainer fee in the amount of _____, which ❑ shall, OR ❑ shall not be subtracted from any compensation due the Broker under this Agreement. The retainer is non-refundable and is earned when paid. C. The Broker shall offer compensation to the selling broker as indicated: Subagency Compensation _____ Buyer Agency Compensation _____ Non Agency Compensation_____ *Note: Compensation shall be shown by a percentage of the gross selling price, a definite dollar amount or "N" for no compensation.* No Multiple Listing Service or Association of REALTORS® is a party to this Agreement and no Multiple Listing Service or Association of REALTORS® sets, controls, recommends or suggests the amount of compensation for any brokerage service rendered pursuant to this Agreement.

7. In consideration of the use of Broker's services and facilities and of the facilities of any REALTOR® Multiple Listing Service, the Seller and Seller's heirs and assigns hereby release the Broker, sales associates accompanying buyers or prospective buyers, any REALTORS® Multiple Listing Service and the directors, officers and employees thereof, including officials of any parent Association of REALTORS®, except for malfeasance on the part of such parties, from any liability to the Seller for vandalism, theft or damage of any nature whatsoever to the Property or its contents during the term of this Agreement, and that the Seller waives any and all rights, claims and causes of action against them and holds them harmless for any property damage or personal injury arising from the use or access to the Property by any person during the term of this Agreement.

8. The Seller retains full responsibility for the Property, including all utilities, maintenance, physical security and liability during the term of this Agreement and the sales contract period. Virginia licensed real estate salespersons and appraisers, inspectors and other persons shall be given access as needed to the Property to facilitate and/or consummate a sale. Authorization is granted to the Broker to show the Property during reasonable hours. Authority is granted to the Broker to: A. Place a "For Sale" sign on the Property and to remove all other such signs and B. Place a common keysafe/lockbox on the Property containing keys and information necessary to obtain full access to the Property.

9. The Seller represents that the Property ❑ is, OR ❑ is not located within a development which is a Condominium or Cooperative. Condominiums or Cooperatives being offered for sale are subject to the receipt by buyers of the required Disclosures, and the Seller is responsible for payment of appropriate fees and for providing these disclosure documents to prospective buyers as prescribed in the Condominium Act, Section 55-79.39 et seq., and the Cooperative Act, Section 55-424, et seq., of the Code of Virginia.

10. The Seller represents that the Property ❑ is, OR ❑ is not located within a development(s) which is subject to the Virginia Property Owners' Association Act, Sections 55-508 through 55-516 of the Code of Virginia. If the Property is within such a development, the Seller is responsible for payment of the appropriate fees and for providing these disclosure documents to the buyers.

11. The Seller acknowledges that the Broker has informed the Seller of the Seller's rights and obligations under the Virginia Residential Property Disclosure Act. This Property ❑ is, OR ❑ is not exempt from the Act. If not exempt, the Seller has completed and provided to the Broker: ❑ a Residential Property Disclosure Statement where the Seller is making representations regarding the condition of the Property on which the buyer may rely, OR ❑ a Residential Property Disclaimer Statement where the Seller is making no representations regarding the condition of the Property and is selling the Property "as is", except as may be provided otherwise in the sales contract.

12. The Seller represents that the residential dwelling(s) at the Property ❑ were, OR ❑ were not constructed before 1978. If the dwelling(s) were constructed before 1978, the Seller is subject to Federal law concerning disclosure of the possible presence of lead-based paint at the Property, and the Seller acknowledges that the Broker has informed the Seller of the Seller's obligations under the law. If the dwelling(s) were constructed before 1978, unless exempt under 42 U.S.C. 4852d, the Seller has completed and provided to the Broker the form, "Sale: Disclosure And Acknowledgment Of Information On Lead-Based Paint And/Or Lead-Based Paint Hazards" or equivalent form.

13. The Property may be sold subject to existing Deed(s) of Trust, having a total unpaid balance of approximately $ _____.

14. The Seller shall provide a _____ Deed of Trust Loan in the amount of $ _____ with further terms to be negotiated.

15. Other terms: _____
_____
_____

The terms and conditions of this Agreement must be used as a basis for presenting the Property to prospective buyers, and, unless amended in writing, contain the final and entire Agreement between the parties hereto. The parties shall not be bound by any terms, conditions, oral statements, warranties or representations not herein contained. Seen and agreed and receipt of a signed copy of this Agreement is hereby acknowledged.

_____ Date _____ Seller   _____ Broker
                                                                                    (Firm)
_____ Date _____ Seller   _____
The Seller ❑ is, OR ❑ is not a licensed (active/inactive) real estate agent/broker   (Address)

_____   _____, VA _____
          (Seller's Mailing Address)

_____   Date_____ By: _____
          (City, State, Zip)   (Broker/Sales Manager)
                                                                 Sales Associate _____
                                                                                    (Designated Representative)
Phone (O)_____ Phone (H)_____   Phone (O)_____ Phone (H)_____
Fax #_____ Email _____   Fax #_____ Email _____

© 2000 Northern Virginia Association of REALTORS®, Inc.

This is a suggested form of the Northern Virginia Association of REALTORS®, Inc. ("NVAR"). This form has been created and printed exclusively for the use of REALTORS® and Non-Resident members of NVAR, who may copy or otherwise reproduce this form in identical form with the addition of their company logo. Any other use of this form by REALTORS® and Non-Resident members of NVAR, or any use of this form whatsoever by non-members of NVAR, is prohibited without the prior written consent of NVAR. Notwithstanding the above, no REALTOR® or Non-Resident member of NVAR, or any other person, may copy or otherwise reproduce this form for purposes of resale.

Figure 2.2 Buyer Representation Agreement

EXCLUSIVE RIGHT TO REPRESENT BUYER AGREEMENT

This Agreement is made on _____, _____ between _____
_____("Buyer") and _____ ("Broker").
                                                                    (Name of brokerage firm)

In consideration of services and facilities, the Broker is hereby granted the right to represent the Buyer in the acquisition of real property. (As used in this Agreement, "acquisition of real property" shall include any purchase, option, exchange or lease of property or an agreement to do so.)

1. **BUYER'S REPRESENTATIONS.** The Buyer represents that as of the commencement date of this Agreement, the Buyer is not a party to a buyer representation agreement with any other brokerage firm. The Buyer further represents that the Buyer has disclosed to the Sales Associate information about any properties that the Buyer has previously visited at any new homes communities or resale "open houses", or that the Buyer has been shown by any other real estate sales associate(s) in any area where the Buyer seeks to acquire property under this Agreement.

2. **TERM.** This Agreement commences when signed and, subject to Paragraph 7, expires at _____ a.m./p.m. on _____, _____.

3. **RETAINER FEE.** The Broker, _____, acknowledges receipt
                                          (Name of brokerage firm)
of a retainer fee in the amount of _____, which ☐ shall OR ☐ shall not be subtracted from any compensation due the Broker under this Agreement. The retainer is non-refundable and is earned when paid.

4. **BROKER'S DUTIES.** The Broker and the Sales Associate shall promote the interests of the Buyer by: (a) performing the terms of this Agreement; (b) seeking property at a price and terms acceptable to the Buyer; (c) presenting in a timely manner all written offers or counteroffers to and from the Buyer; (d) disclosing to the Buyer all material facts related to the property or concerning the transaction of which they have actual knowledge; (e) accounting for in a timely manner all money and property received in which the Buyer has or may have an interest. Unless otherwise provided by law or the Buyer consents in writing to the release of the information, the Broker shall maintain the confidentiality of all personal and financial information and other matters identified as confidential by the Buyer, if that information is received from the Buyer during the brokerage relationship. In satisfying these duties, the Broker shall exercise ordinary care, comply with all applicable laws and regulations, treat all prospective sellers honestly and not knowingly give them false information, and disclose whether or not the Buyer's intent is to occupy the property as a principal residence. In addition, the Broker may: show the same property to other buyers; represent other buyers on the same or different properties; represent Sellers relative to other properties; or provide assistance to a seller or prospective seller by performing ministerial acts that are not inconsistent with the Broker's duties under this Agreement.

5. **BUYER'S DUTIES.** The Buyer shall: (a) work exclusively with the Broker during the term of this Agreement; (b) pay the Broker, directly or indirectly, the compensation set forth below; (c) comply with the reasonable requests of the Broker to supply any pertinent financial or personal data needed to fulfill the terms of this Agreement; (d) be available during the Broker's regular working hours to view properties.

6. **PURPOSE.** The Buyer is retaining the Broker to acquire the following type of property: _____
_____.

7. **COMPENSATION.** In consideration of the time and effort expended by the Broker on behalf of the Buyer, and in further consideration of the advice and counsel provided to the Buyer, the Buyer shall pay compensation ("Broker's Fee") to the Broker as described below. The Broker's Fee, less the retainer fee, if any, shall be earned, due and payable under any of these circumstances whether the transaction is consummated through the services of the Broker or otherwise:

   (a) If the Buyer enters into a contract to acquire real property during the term of this Agreement and goes to settlement on that contract any time thereafter: **OR**
   (b) If, within _____ days after expiration or termination of this Agreement, the Buyer enters into a contract to acquire real property that has been described to or shown to the Buyer by the Broker during the term of this Agreement, unless the Buyer has entered into a subsequent "Exclusive Right to Represent Buyer" agreement with another real estate broker; **OR**
   (c) If, having entered into a enforceable contract to acquire real property during the term of this Agreement, the Buyer defaults under the terms of that contract.
   The Broker's Fee shall be _____.
If the seller or the seller's representative offers compensation to the Broker, then the Buyer authorizes the Broker to receive such compensation and the amount of such compensation shall be credited against the Buyer's obligation to pay the Broker's Fee.
   In addition to the Broker's Fee, an Administrative Fee of _____ will be collected from the Buyer payable to the Broker, at the time of settlement.
   Any obligation incurred under this Agreement on the part of the Buyer to pay the Broker's Fee shall survive the term of this Agreement.

NVAR - 1121 - 10/01   Page 1 of 2   Initials: Buyer _____ / _____

Figure 2.2   Buyer Representation Agreement (Continued)

8. **DISCLOSED DUAL REPRESENTATION.** The Buyer acknowledges that in the normal course of business the Broker may represent sellers of properties in which the Buyer is interested. If the Buyer wishes to acquire any property listed with the Broker, then the Buyer will be represented in one of the two ways that are permitted under Virginia law in this situation. The written consent required from the parties in each case will be accomplished via execution of the appropriate disclosure form at the time of the contract offer.

   Dual representation occurs when a buyer and seller in one transaction are represented by the same Broker and the same Sales Associate. When the parties agree to dual representation, the ability of the Broker and the Sales Associate to represent either party fully and exclusively is limited. The confidentiality of all clients shall be maintained as in paragraph 4 above.

   Designated representation occurs when a buyer and seller in one transaction are represented by different Sales Associates affiliated with the same Broker. Each of these Sales Associates, known as a Designated Representative, represents fully the interests of a different client in the same transaction. Designated Representatives are not dual representatives if each represents only the buyer or only the seller in a specific real estate transaction. Except for disclosure of confidential information to the Broker, each Designated Representative is bound by the confidentiality requirements in paragraph 4 above. The Broker remains a dual representative.

   CHECK ONE CHOICE IN EACH SECTION:
   Dual representation: The Buyer ☐ does OR ☐ does not consent to be shown and to consider acquiring properties listed with the Broker through the Sales Associate.
   Designated representation: The Buyer ☐ does OR ☐ does not consent to be shown and to consider acquiring properties listed with the Broker through another Designated Representative associated with the firm.

9. **DISCLAIMER.** The buyer acknowledges that the Broker is being retained solely as a real estate agent and not as an attorney, tax advisor, lender, appraiser, surveyor, structural engineer, home inspector or other professional service provider. The Buyer is advised to seek professional advice concerning the condition of the property or concerning legal and tax matters. The Buyer should exercise whatever due diligence the Buyer deems necessary with respect to information on any sexual offenders registered under Chapter 23 (§19.2-387 et. seq.) of Title 19.2. Such information may be obtained by contacting your local police department or the Department of State Police, Central Criminal Records Exchange, at (804)674-2000 or www.state.va.us/vsp/vsp.html.

10. **EQUAL OPPORTUNITY.** Properties shall be shown and made available to the Buyer without regard to race, color, religion, sex, handicap, familial status or national origin as well as all classes protected by the laws of the United States, the Commonwealth of Virginia and applicable local jurisdictions.

11. **OTHER PROVISIONS.** _____

12. **MISCELLANEOUS.** This Agreement, any exhibits and any addenda signed by the parties constitute the entire agreement between the parties and supersedes any other written or oral agreements between the parties. This Agreement can only be modified in writing when signed by both parties. In any action or proceeding involving a dispute between the Buyer, the seller and/or the Broker, arising out of this Agreement, or to collect the Broker's Fee, the prevailing party shall be entitled to receive from the other party reasonable attorney's fees to be determined by the court or arbitrator(s).

(NOTE: The Buyer should consult with the Sales Associate before visiting any resale or new homes or contacting any other REALTORS® representing sellers, to avoid the possibility of confusion over the brokerage relationship and misunderstandings about liability for compensation.)

_____ _____ (SEAL)
Date   Buyer's Signature

_____ _____ (SEAL)
Date   Buyer's Signature

The Buyer ☐ does OR ☐ does not hold an active or inactive Virginia real estate license.

_____
Address

_____
City, State, Zip Code

Telephone: _____ _____
                Work   Home

Fax _____   Email _____

_____
Brokerage Firm (Broker)

_____
Address

_____
City, State, Zip Code

_____ (SEAL)
Date   Broker/Sales Manager's Signature

_____
Sales Associate's/Designated Representative's Printed Name

Telephone: _____ _____
                Work   Home

Fax _____   Email _____

© 2000 Northern Virginia Association of REALTORS®, Inc.

This is a suggested form of the Northern Virginia Association of REALTORS®, Inc. ("NVAR"). This form has been exclusively printed for the use of REALTOR® and Non-Resident members of NVAR, who may copy or otherwise reproduce this form in identical form with the addition of their company logo. Any other use of this form by REALTOR® and Non-Resident members of NVAR, or any use of this form whatsoever by non-members of NVAR is prohibited without the prior written consent of NVAR. Notwithstanding the above, no REALTOR® or Non-Resident member of NVAR, or any other person, may copy or otherwise reproduce this form for purposes of resale.

NVAR - 1121 - 7/99   Page 2 of 2

SELLER DISCLAIMER

A seller may choose to file a *disclaimer* instead of the disclosure. (See Figure 2.4.) In choosing a disclaimer over the disclosure statement, the seller makes no representations or warranties as to the condition of the property. In other words, the buyer accepts the property "as is" with all existing defects, except as provided for in the contract. It is important that the sellers realize that they are still responsible for all items listed in the contract unless they have been specifically deleted. For example: The contract states that all existing appliances must be in normal working order. The property disclaimer form does not negate that statement. The disclosure or disclaimer may be included in the contract itself, in an addendum to the contract or as a separate document.

Time for Disclosure

The disclosure/disclaimer is required *prior* to contract ratification by the seller and buyer. If the disclosure or disclaimer is received *after* contract ratification, the sole remedy for the purchaser is to terminate the contract by giving written notice to the seller. Once the disclosure or disclaimer is received by the buyer, notice to terminate must be given to the seller

- within three days if the notice is hand carried;
- within five days of postmark, if the notice is mailed;
- prior to settlement;
- prior to occupancy if occupancy occurs before settlement; *or*
- prior to loan application where the loan application discloses that the right of contract terminations ends when the loan application is taken.

The purchaser may allow the contract to remain valid if he or she

- provides a notice of waiver of rights to terminate the contract, or
- remains silent and does nothing.

If the purchaser elects to terminate the contract in accordance with the disclosure law, he or she may do so without any penalty. Any monies already paid by the purchaser, such as earnest money deposits, must be returned.

The purchaser will lose the right to terminate the contract if the termination right is not exercised

- at the time the purchaser makes a written application to obtain a mortgage loan, and the loan application conatins a disclosure that the right to terminate shall end; *or*
- at settlement or occupancy, in the event of a sale; *or*
- at the time of occupancy in the event of lease with option to buy.

Builders of new homes must only disclose known material defects that would constitute a violation of local building codes. Builders are required to disclose defects before acceptance of an offer for purchase of an already completed house or after issuance of an occupancy permit if the offer is accepted before or during construction.

The issuance of the disclosure does not relieve the builder of any other new home warranties or contractual obligations. While the disclosure may be in any form, the builder may *not* satisfy the disclosure requirement by the use of the disclaimer statement.

Figure 2.3 Disclosure Statement

RESIDENTIAL PROPERTY DISCLOSURE STATEMENT
THIS IS NOT A WARRANTY OF CONDITION OF THE PROPERTY

NOTE TO OWNER(S): Complete and sign this statement only if you elect to disclose defects in the conditions of the property actually known by you; otherwise, sign the RESIDENTIAL PROPERTY DISCLAIMER STATEMENT. You may wish to obtain professional advice or inspection of the property, or obtain information from the Department of Environmental quality which identifies confirmed releases or discharges of oil which may affect the property, but you are not required to undertake or provide any independent investigation or inspection of the property in order to make the disclosures set forth below.

NOTE TO PURCHASER(S): This statement is based upon the owner's actual knowledge of the condition of the property as of the date noted. You may wish to obtain professional advice or inspections of the property. The information contained in this statement is the representation of the owner and not the representation of the broker or salesperson, if any.

Property Address/Legal Description: _____

How long have you owned the property? _____ Dates lived in property? _____

Property Systems: Water, Sewage, Heating & Air Conditioning (Answer all that apply)

Water Supply	☐ Public	☐ Well	☐ Other		
Sewage Disposal	☐ Public	☐ Septic System approved for ____ (#) BR	Garbage Disposal ☐ Yes ☐ No	Dishwasher ☐ Yes ☐ No	
Heating	☐ Oil	☐ Natural Gas	☐ Electric	☐ Heat Pump Age_____	Other_____
Air Conditioning	☐ Oil	☐ Natural Gas	☐ Electric	☐ Heat Pump Age_____	Other_____
Hot Water	☐ Oil	☐ Natural Gas	☐ Electric	Capacity_____ Age_____	Other_____

Please indicate your actual knowledge with respect to the following:

1. **Structural Systems, including Roof, Walls, Floors, Foundation and any Basement:** Any Known defects (structural or otherwise)?
   ☐ Yes ☐ No ☐ Unknown
   Comments:_____

2. **Basement:** Any leaks or evidence of moisture?
   ☐ Yes ☐ No ☐ Unknown ☐ Does Not Apply
   Comments:_____

3. **Roof:** Any Leaks or evidence of moisture?
   ☐ Yes ☐ No ☐ Unknown
   Type of roof:_____ Age_____
   Is there any existing fire retardant treated (FRT) plywood?
   ☐ Yes ☐ No ☐ Unknown ☐ Does Not Apply

4. **Fireplace/Chimney(s):** In working condition?
   ☐ Yes ☐ No ☐ Unknown ☐ Does Not Apply
   Comments:_____

5. **Plumbing System:** Is the system in working condition?
   ☐ Yes ☐ No ☐ Unknown
   Comments:_____

6. **Septic/Sewer Systems:** Is the system functioning properly?
   ☐ Yes ☐ No ☐ Unknown ☐ Does Not Apply
   If septic, when was the system last pumped?_____

7. **Water Supply:** Any problems with water quality or supply?
   ☐ Yes ☐ No ☐ Unknown
   Is the system in working condition?
   ☐ Yes ☐ No ☐ Unknown
   Comments:_____

8. **Heating System:** Is heat supplied to all finished rooms?
   ☐ Yes ☐ No ☐ Unknown
   Is the system in working condition?
   ☐ Yes ☐ No ☐ Unknown
   Comments:_____

9. **Air Conditioning System:** Is cooling supplied to all finished rooms?
   ☐ Yes ☐ No ☐ Unknown ☐ Does Not Apply
   Is the system in working condition?
   ☐ Yes ☐ No ☐ Unknown ☐ Does Not Apply
   Comments:_____

10. **Electric Systems:** Are there any problems with electrical fuses/circuit breakers, outlets or wiring?
    ☐ Yes ☐ No ☐ Unknown
    Comments:_____
    Does the electrical system meet existing code requirements?
    ☐ Yes ☐ No ☐ Unknown
    Comments:_____

11. **Insulation:**
    In exterior walls? ☐ Yes ☐ No ☐ Unknown
    In ceiling/attic? ☐ Yes ☐ No ☐ Unknown
    In other areas? ☐ Yes ☐ No ☐ Unknown
    Comments:_____

12. **Exterior Drainage:** Does water stand on the property for more than 24 hours after a heavy rain?
    ☐ Yes ☐ No ☐ Unknown
    Are gutters and downspouts in working condition?
    ☐ Yes ☐ No ☐ Unknown ☐ Does Not Apply
    Comments:_____

13. **Wood-destroying organisms:** Any infestation and/or prior damage?
    ☐ Yes ☐ No ☐ Unknown
    Any treatments or repairs?
    ☐ Yes ☐ No ☐ Unknown
    Comments:_____

14. Are there any substances, materials or environmental hazards (including but not limited to asbestos, radon gas, lead-based paint, underground storage tanks, or other contamination) on or affecting the property?
    ☐ Yes ☐ No ☐ Unknown
    Comments:_____

15. Are there any additions, structural modifications or other alterations or repairs made without required permits or not in compliance with building codes?
    ☐ Yes ☐ No ☐ Unknown
    Comments:_____

16. Are there any zoning violations, nonconforming uses, violations of building restrictions or setback requirements, or any recorded or unrecorded easements, except for utilities, on or affecting the property?
    ☐ Yes ☐ No ☐ Unknown
    Comments:_____

17. Are there any defects in the following, if installed in the property?
    Water treatment system
    ☐ Yes ☐ No ☐ Unknown ☐ Does Not Apply
    Comments:_____
    Lawn sprinkler system
    ☐ Yes ☐ No ☐ Unknown ☐ Does Not Apply
    Comments:_____
    Security system
    ☐ Yes ☐ No ☐ Unknown ☐ Does Not Apply
    Comments:_____

18. Are there any other material defects affecting the physical condition of the property?
    ☐ Yes ☐ No ☐ Unknown
    Comments:_____

19. Is the property subject to covenants and restrictions, the VA Condominium Act, VA Property Owners Association Act or Real Estate Cooperative Act?
    ☐ Yes ☐ No ☐ Unknown
    Comments:_____

Note: Owner(s) may wish to disclose the condition of other buildings on the property on a separate RESIDENTIAL PROPERTY DISCLOSURE STATEMENT.

Note: Purchaser(s) should exercise whatever due diligence they deem necessary with respect to information on any sexual offenders registered under Chapter 23 (§19.2-387 et seq.) of Title 19.2, whether the owner proceeds under subdivision 1 or 2 of subsection A of §55-519. Such information may be obtained by contacting your local police department or the Department of State Police, Central Criminal Records Exchange, at 804-674-2000 or www.vsp.state.va.us/vsp.html

✦✦✦✦✦✦✦✦✦✦✦✦✦✦✦✦✦✦✦✦✦✦✦✦✦✦✦✦✦✦✦✦✦✦✦✦✦✦✦

The owner(s) acknowledge having carefully examined this statement, including any comments continued on the reverse side, and state that this statement is complete and accurate as of the date signed. At or before settlement, the owner(s) will be required to disclose any material change in the physical condition of the property. The owner(s) further acknowledge that they have been informed of their rights and obligations under the Virginia Residential Property Disclosure Act.

_____ _____   _____ _____
Owner   Date   Owner   Date

The purchaser(s) acknowledge receipt of a copy of this disclosure statement and further acknowledge that they have been informed of their rights and obligations under the Virginia Residential Property Disclosure Act. The purchaser(s) acknowledge that the owner(s) make no representation with respect to any matters which may pertain to parcels adjacent to the subject property and should exercise whatever due diligence deemed necessary with respect to adjacent parcels in accordance with terms and conditions as may be contained in the real estate purchase contract, buy in any event, prior to settlement.

_____ _____   _____ _____
Purchaser   Date   Purchaser   Date

Reprinted with permission from the Virginia Department of Professional and Occupational Regulation (DPOR) and Northern Virginia Association of REALTORS®, Inc. (NVAR), for educational purposes only. Any other use of these forms without the express written consent of DPOR and NVAR is strictly prohibited.

Figure 2.3   Disclosure Statement (Continued)

ANNOTATED SUMMARY OF "RIGHTS AND OBLIGATION" OF SELLERS AND PURCHASERS UNDER VIRGINIA'S RESIDENTIAL PROPERTY CONDITION DISCLOSURE ACT

[Virginia Code Sections 55-517 et seq.]
(Mandatory for contract executed on or after 1 July 1993)

<u>Applies to</u>: all non-exempt sales, exchanges, installment sales, or leases with option to buy Virginia residential real property consisting of 1 to 4 dwelling units [55-517]. Exempt transfers are those pursuant to court order (estates, foreclosures, bankruptcies, etc.); among families or co-owners; tax sales; new homes (have special requirements) [55-518]. Consult a lawyer if you need to know whether the law applies in your case.

1. **OWNER'S (SELLERS') RIGHTS AND OBLIGATIONS:**
    a. Must furnish either a disclaimer or a disclosure statement to a purchaser. [55-519.1-2]
    b. Must use a form developed by the Virginia Real Estate Board. [55-519.1-2]
    c. Must furnish the statement prior to final ratification of the sales contract, or else be subject to the purchaser's exercise of rights to cancel the contract [55-520] or to sue later for damages. [55-524B.1]
    d. If <u>"disclaiming"</u>--
        1) State that the real property with all its improvements is being sold "as is," with no representation or warranties as to condition, except as otherwise provided in the sales contract. [55-519.1]
        2) Under the common law doctrine of *caveat emptor* applied by the Virginia Courts, owner may not conceal any known defect to the extent that a purchaser's inspection of the property would not reasonably be expected to uncover that defect and owner may not divert the purchaser from making inquiries or inspecting the premises by knowingly giving false answers to questions.
    e. If <u>"disclosing"</u> detailed information about the property's condition -
        1) Must disclose all defects of which the owner has actual knowledge using a list of items, as well as answer a question as to " any other material defects affecting the physical condition of the property." [55-519.2 and Real Estate Board form]
        2) Are not required to have any independent inspections or investigations done, but if any experts are used, the owner may furnish their statements (in their respective fields of expertise) in lieu of any by the owner, provided these are properly labeled as such. [55-519.2, 55-521.B]
        3) Are not liable for any errors or omissions in the disclosure statement IF the owner had no "actual knowledge" about them, or if the owner "reasonably" relied upon representation by public agencies or by other experts as noted above, and if the owner was not grossly negligent in obtaining and transmitting the information. [55-521.A]
        4) Are not in violation of the law if information disclosed in accordance with it is later made or found to be inaccurate, provided that the owner discloses any such material change at or before settlement. [55-522]
        5) At settlement, must update the statement OR certify that the property condition is substantially the same as when the disclosure form was provided. [55-522]

2. **PURCHASER'S RIGHTS AND OBLIGATIONS:**
    a. May waive the right to receive the disclosure or disclaimer statement (but any waiver must be separate from the sales contract.) [55-520.B.v]
    b. If they do not receive a disclosure or a disclaimer statement before the contract is ratified, then they have the right to cancel the sales contract by sending written notice to the owner either by hand delivery or U.S. Mail (postage prepaid and properly addressed) any time before receiving the statement , or within 3 days of receipt (if delivered in person) or 5 days of postmark (if sent via U.S. Mail, postage prepaid). [55-520.B.i-ii]
    c. If they receive a <u>"disclaimer"</u> statement --
        1) Lose the right to cancel the sale on the basis of the statement if they settle or pre-occupy [55-520.B.iii-iv] or if they apply for a mortgage loan when the application states their right to cancel terminates at application. [55-520.B.vi]
    d. If they receive a <u>"disclosure"</u> statement --
        1) Acknowledge that the information it contains is the representation of the seller, and not of the broker or salesperson, if any. [55-519.2]
        2) May cancel the sales contract in the event of a misrepresentation by the seller in the disclosure statement. [55-524.B.2]
        3) Lose the right to cancel the sale on the basis of the statement if they settle or pre-occupy [55-520.B.iii-iv] or if they apply for a mortgage loan when the application states their right to cancel terminates at application. [55-520.B. vi]
        4) Within one year of receipt of the statement, can sue the seller for any actual damages sustained because of seller misrepresentation of defects which would have been disclosed had the seller complied with the law, and of which the purchaser was not aware at the time of settlement or occupancy. [55-524.B.1]
        5) Retain the right to pursue any remedies at law or equity otherwise available against an owner in the event of an owner's intentional or willful misrepresentation of the condition of the property. [55-524.C]
    e. If no statement is received, and the right to receive one was not waived --
        1) Within one year of settlement (if a sale) or occupancy (if a lease-option), can sue the seller for any actual damages sustained as a result of defects in the property which would have been disclosed had the seller complied with the terms of the law, and of which the purchaser was unaware at the time of settlement or occupancy. [55.524.B.1]
    f. If they cancel the contract in compliance with the Act, that termination is without penalty to them and any deposit shall be promptly returned to them. [55-520.B]

Initial to indicate receipt _____

_____

IF YOU DESIRE A COPY OF THE FULL TEXT OF VIRGINIA'S RESIDENTIAL PROPERTY DISCLOSURE ACT, ASK AT PUBLIC LIBRARIES, AN ATTORNEY'S OFFICE, THE NORTHERN VIRGINIA ASSOCIATION OF REALTORS, OR A REAL ESTATE BROKERAGE OFFICE.

K1021 (1/99)

Reprinted with permission from the Virginia Department of Professional and Occupational Regulation (DPOR) and Northern Virginia Association of REALTORS®, Inc. (NVAR), for educational purposes only. Any other use of these forms without the express written consent of DPOR and NVAR is strictly prohibited.

Figure 2.4   Disclaimer Statement

RESIDENTIAL PROPERTY DISCLAIMER STATEMENT

NOTICE TO SELLER AND PURCHASER

The Virginia Residential Property Disclosure Act requires the owner of certain residential real property, whenever the property is to be sold or leased with an option to buy, to furnish to the purchaser either (a) a RESIDENTIAL PROPERTY DISCLAIMER STATEMENT stating that the owner makes no representations or warranties as to the condition of the property, except as otherwise provided in the purchase contract, or (b) a RESIDENTIAL PROPERTY DISCLOSURE STATEMENT disclosing defects in the condition of the property actually known by the owner. Certain transfers of residential property are excluded from this requirement (see the exemptions listed on the reverse side).

◆◆◆◆◆◆◆◆◆◆◆◆◆◆◆◆◆◆◆◆◆◆◆◆◆◆◆◆◆◆◆◆◆◆◆◆◆

RESIDENTIAL PROPERTY DISCLAIMER STATEMENT

NOTE TO OWNER(S): Sign this statement only if you elect to sell the property without representations and warranties as to its conditions, except as otherwise provided in the purchase contract; otherwise, complete and sign the RESIDENTIAL PROPERTY DISCLOSURE STATEMENT.

Property Address/
Legal Description: _____

The undersigned owner(s) of the real property described above make no representations or warranties as to the condition of the real property or any improvements thereon, and the purchaser will be receiving the property "as is", that is, with all defects which may exist, if any, except as otherwise provided in the real estate purchase contract.

The owner(s) acknowledge having carefully examined this statement and further acknowledge that they have been informed of their rights and obligations under the Virginia Residential Property Disclosure Act.

_____   _____   _____   _____
Owner   Date   Owner   Date

NOTE TO PURCHASER(S): The owner(s) make no representations with respect to any matters which may pertain to parcels adjacent to the subject parcel. You should exercise whatever due diligence you deem necessary with respect to adjacent parcels in accordance with the terms and conditions as may be contained in the real estate purchase contract, but in any event, prior to settlement. You should exercise whatever due diligence you deem necessary with respect to information on any sexual offenders registered under Chapter 23 (§19.2-387 et seq.) of Title 19.2, whether the owner proceeds under subdivision 1 or 2 of subsection A of §55-519. Such information may be obtained by contacting your local police department or the Department of State Police, Central Criminal Records Exchange, at 804-674-2000 or www.vsp.state.va.us/vsp.html.

The purchaser(s) acknowledge receipt of a copy of this disclaimer statement and further acknowledge that they have been informed of their rights and obligations under the Virginia Residential Property Disclosure Act.

_____   _____   _____   _____
Purchaser   Date   Purchaser   Date

DPOR 11/5/99

K1022 (11/99)

Reprinted with permission from the Virginia Department of Professional and Occupational Regulation (DPOR) and Northern Virginia Association of REALTORS®, Inc. (NVAR), for educational purposes only. Any other use of these forms without the express written consent of DPOR and NVAR is strictly prohibited.

Megan's Law

Disclosure and disclaimer forms must contain a notice advising purchasers that they should exercise whatever due diligence they deem necessary with respect to information on violent sexual offenders registered with the Commonwealth. The form is not required for new home sales, transfers involving trusts, foreclosures, or residential leases. However, it is advocated that new disclosure language be added to all contracts and agency agreements.

Exemptions

Certain transactions are exempt from the disclosure requirements. These include

court-ordered transfers
- to settle an estate;
- pursuant to a writ of execution;
- foreclosures;
- by a trustee in bankruptcy;
- by condemnation through the right of eminent domain; and
- by suit for specific performance,

voluntary transfers of property
- between co-owners;
- between relatives;
- under a divorce settlement;
- to or from any governmental entity or public or quasi-public housing authority or agency;
- as the result of an owner's failure pay federal, state, or local taxes; and
- involving the first sale of a new home.

Buyer's Recourse

If the buyer learns of defects that either were disclosed or were misrepresented in the disclosure statement, the buyer is entitled to seek recourse. Any action brought under this act must be commenced within one year from the date the disclosure was delivered. If no disclosure was delivered, action must be commenced within one year of settlement, or within one year of occupancy in the event of lease with option to buy.

The owner is not liable for any error, inaccuracy, or omission of information in the disclosure form if the information was provided to the owner by a *reliable third party* such as a surveyor, engineer, appraiser, home inspector, or public authority. The owner is also not liable if he or she *reasonably believed the information to be correct* and there was no gross negligence involved.

License Liability

Like the owner, a real estate licensee cannot be liable for misrepresentation if he or she relied on information provided by others. However, a licensee must disclose material adverse facts pertaining to the physical condition of the property that are actually known by the licensee. [§54.1-2131B, 18 VAC 135-20-300(2)]

FOR EXAMPLE *T*, a real estate salesperson, is hosting an open house during a rainstorm. While no one is being shown the property, *T* notices that there is a leak in the attic and water seepage in the basement. *T* must disclose that information to any prospective buyers, even if the owner knowingly falsified the disclosure statement or filed a disclaimer because he or she did not want to admit that anything was wrong. If *T* fails to inform a prospective buyer about the leaking and seepage, *T* may be found guilty of misrepresentation.

STIGMATIZED PROPERTY

Stigmatized Property refers to any property that is made undesirable by some event or circumstance that had no actual effect on its physical structure, environment, or improvements. For instance, a house in which a homicide, felony, or suicide occurred may be "tainted" by that event and be difficult to sell. Buyers may hesitate to make an offer on a property that is reputed to be haunted, or in which the current or former occupant suffered from a communicable disease.

Virginia has specifically addressed the matter of stigmatized properties in the Residential Property Disclosure Act. Disclosure of this type of information, which in Virginia has been determined to be immaterial, is *not* required. In fact, a licensee who represents a seller and discloses stigmatizing information to a buyer could be construed as having breached his or her responsibilities to the client if the buyer cancels the contract due to the disclosure. The failure to disclose this information does not subject either the owner or a licensee to disciplinary action by the courts or the REB. There is also no disciplinary action of a licensee who does disclose such information as long as the seller has approved of such disclosure. The only topic of disclosure that is specifically prohibited is any discussion of HIV-positive, or AIDS.

In Practice If information is disclosed regarding persons infected with HIV, a licensee could be in violation of fair housing laws and the federal privacy act.

Similarly, a broker who enlists an assistant in providing brokerage services to a client is not liable for that broker's misrepresentations unless he or she knew or should have known about them and failed to take reasonable corrective steps. A broker is not liable for the negligence, gross negligence, or intentional acts of an assisting broker or the assisting broker's licensee.

Both clients and licensees are fully liable for their own misrepresentations, negligence, gross negligence, or intentional acts in connection with a real estate transaction.

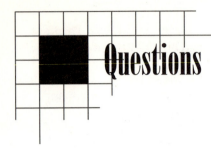

Questions

1. When a broker and seller enter into an exclusive-right-to-sell listing, which of the following is required?
   1. Net amount seller receives at closing
   2. Definite termination date
   3. Extension or protective clause
   4. Statement of the exact acreage or square footage of the parcel or lot

2. A seller offers you a listing agreement that contains the following clause: "Seller must receive the amount of $60,000 from the sale of this property. Seller agrees that the selling agent will receive, as his or her total compensation, any proceeds that remain beyond that amount after satisfaction of seller's mortgage loan and any closing costs incurred by seller." Based on these facts, you
   1. must decline this listing agreement because the clause violates REB regulations.
   2. must decline this listing agreement because it is not the standard form used in Virginia.
   3. may accept this listing agreement because the clause is standard in an open listing.
   4. may accept this listing agreement, because it specifically limits the amount of your compensation.

3. Which of the following would be the correct way to enter the termination date on a listing form?
   1. 90 days from today
   2. July 1, 2002
   3. Until property is sold
   4. Until seller decides to cancel

4. If the seller wants to be sure that the potential buyer will not cancel the contract based on the Residential Property Disclosure Statement he should
   1. state in the contract that no cancellation is possible.
   2. provide a Property Disclaimer instead of Disclosure.
   3. have Property Disclosure delivered to purchaser prior to acceptance of contract.
   4. have Property Disclosure delivered to purchaser within three days from acceptance of contract.

5. A seller's home is over 80 years old, and its plumbing and wiring systems have never been replaced, repaired, or upgraded. Which of the following statements is TRUE?
   1. The seller is required by Virginia law to disclose the property's age and the condition of its plumbing and wiring.
   2. Under the doctrine of caveat emptor, the seller is required to disclose the information to a prospective buyer at the time an offer is made.
   3. The seller may file a disclaimer instead of a disclosure, offering the property "as is," with appropriate changes made to the contract.
   4. The disclosures may be made at any time prior to closing.

6. Which of the following circumstances is expressly forbidden to be disclosed on the Residential Property Disclosure Statement form?
   1. A triple murder occurred on the property.
   2. The seller's husband committed suicide on the property.
   3. The seller recently died of AIDS.
   4. Two ghosts have frequently been seen in the attic.

7. The responsibility for obtaining information regarding released sexual offenders in a community rests with the
   1. seller.
   2. buyer.
   3. listing broker.
   4. selling broker.

8. All of the following are exempt from the Residential Property Disclosure Act **EXCEPT**
   1. a foreclosure sale.
   2. a sale by an uncle to his niece.
   3. conveyance of a primary residence from one former spouse to another under a divorce settlement agreement.
   4. a sale by a real estate licensee of a two-unit residential property.

9. A real estate broker representing the seller knows that the property has a cracked foundation and that its former owner committed suicide in the kitchen. The broker must disclose
   1. both facts.
   2. the suicide, but not the foundation.
   3. the cracked foundation, but disclosing the suicide could constitute a breach of duty to the client.
   4. neither fact.

10. Seller S has his house listed with Broker J. He has recently learned that J has been making misrepresentations about the potential value of the property. Which of the following is true?
    1. S is totally liable for any statements made by J.
    2. S needs to take reasonable steps to correct the misrepresentation.
    3. Any other broker who cooperates in the sale of the property is responsible for J's misrepresentations.
    4. S is considered to have imputed knowledge of J's actions.

3 Interests in Real Estate

EMINENT DOMAIN

In Virginia, the power of eminent domain is provided by the state constitution and statutes. Virginia law provides that easements, ingress and egress rights, flowage rights, and all similar rights and uses constitute "property." As a result, just *compensation must be paid* if they are taken or damaged by the Commonwealth through the power of eminent domain, sometimes referred to as a *taking*. This process is called *condemnation*.

Just compensation means the fair market value of the property at the time of the taking. Payment of just compensation is a prerequisite to passing of title to the property. In addition, the commonwealth must have made a genuine but ineffectual effort to purchase the property directly before beginning condemnation proceedings.

If the parties do not agree on what constitutes just compensation for the land, commissioners are appointed to hold a hearing and determine the amount. Virginia's Condemnation Act provides for a two-stage proceeding. First, the court determines the fair market value of the land taken and the damage, if any, to the remaining land. Second, if payment occurs, the court determines the rights and claims of all persons entitled to compensation.

Disclosure

Real estate licensees are required to disclose to all interested parties that a condemnation is planned for a parcel or an entire area. If a seller is aware that a governmental authority has made an offer to acquire the property and that condemnation proceedings are contemplated, prospective buyers should be made aware of this information. Because condemnation can affect the value of both the condemned property as well as neighboring properties, it is an important consideration for buyers and sellers alike.

FOR EXAMPLE *O's* property was condemned for street construction. This had an adverse impact on the value of *O's* remaining property. However, the value of adjacent parcels increased as a result of the improved access provided by the street.

ESTATES IN LAND

Virginia recognizes all the major estates in land, such as fee simple and life estates; defeasible and determinable estates; and remainders, reversions, and the possibility of reverter.

DESCENT AND DISTRIBUTION AND MARITAL ESTATES

In 1991, the Virginia legislature abolished the concepts of dower and curtesy. The Augmented Estate and Elective Share Act [§64.1-16.1] defines to whom a deceased person's property is distributed if he or she dies *intestate*, that is, without having executed a valid will. Commonly referred to as the *law of descent and distribution*, this statute is similar to the old dower and curtesy statutes because it establishes the rights of ownership to property by a surviving spouse and others.

This whole discussion of descent and distribution is a simplified overview of this complex law. See the Code of Virginia, Table of Contents, Title 64.1 Wills and Decedent's Estates on the following Web site for more detailed information.)

WWWeb.Link
http://leg1.state.va.us/000/src.htm

Intestate Distributions

The term "intestate" indicates that a person has died without executing a will. The act defines the rights of natural children, adopted children, children by previous marriages, illegitimate children, children of surrogates, and children born by in vitro fertilization. Real estate licensees are cautioned that their involvement in real estate transactions involving part of an estate can open the door to complications that may arise from claims by the heirs.

If a person dies testate, that is, having executed a valid will, but fails to specifically devise or bequeath all of his or her property, the undistributed property is treated as if the person died intestate. It is distributed to heirs in accordance with the rules of descent and distribution.

The statute defines *property* or *estate* as including

- insurance policies;
- retirement benefits (exclusive of Social Security);
- annuities;
- pension plans and deferred compensation arrangements; and
- employee benefit plans.

The surviving spouse receives one-third of this surplus. The remaining two-thirds is then distributed among the decedent's children or their descendants. If there are no children, the surviving spouse is entitled to receive the entire surplus.

FOR EXAMPLE D died without having made a valid will. D's estate, valued at $785,950, was distributed among D's surviving spouse and D's children (X, Y, and Z) as follows:
  D's surviving spouse: $261,983.33
  Children (X, Y, and Z): $174,655.55 each

If D had left a valid will disposing of $500,000 of the estate, the remaining $285,950 would be distributed to D's spouse and children as follows:
  D's surviving spouse: $95,316.67
  Children (X, Y, and Z): $63,544.44 each

Augmented Estate

Although a surviving spouse could be named in a will to receive certain property and to be further entitled to receive a share of the surplus, it is possible for the spouse to renounce the will and claim an *elective share* of the augmented estate.

An augmented estate consists of the property, both real and personal owned by the deceased at the time of death. This is *added to the* value of property transferred during the marriage to third parties without the consent of the surviving spouse, if it can be established that the deceased did not receive adequate and full consideration for the property transferred. The value of the augmented estate is the value that remains after the payment of funeral expenses, the cost of the estate administrator, and personal debts of decedent.

Other items that *could be excluded from* the augmented estate include

- property owned by the surviving spouse;
- property owned by the decedent and another, with right of survivorship;
- property conveyed during the marriage with the consent of the surviving spouse;
- property acquired by the decedent in severalty, as a gift, by will or intestate succession from someone other than the surviving spouse; and
- property transferred prior to January 1, 1991, if such transfer was irrevocable as of that date.

If a claim for an elective share is made, the surviving spouse receives one-third of the estate if there are children. If there are no children, or descendants of children, the surviving spouse is entitled to one-half of the estate. [§64.1 1-16]

A surviving spouse has the right to possess and occupy the principal family residence during the period of time that the estate matters are being settled, although the residence may be a part of the augmented estate of the deceased.

Abandonment

If a husband or wife willfully deserts or abandons his or her spouse until the death of the deserted spouse, the deserting spouse is barred from all interest of the other by intestate succession, elective share, exempt property, family allowance, and homestead allowance.

HOMESTEAD EXEMPTION

Under Virginia's homestead exemption, a householder is entitled to hold a certain amount of real or personal property exempt from unsecured debts.

The total value of the property may not exceed $5,000, plus $500 for each dependent.

Only a householder or head of a family may have the benefit of the homestead exemption. A husband and wife living together may both be deemed householders if each contributes to maintaining the household.

The exemption does not apply against

- claims for the purchase price of the homestead property;
- mechanics' liens; and
- claims for taxes.

The claim to homestead must be made by deed in the case of real property or by an inventory under oath for personal property. The owner of the homestead may sell or encumber the homestead property.

The key words in the homestead exemption are *unsecured debts*. For instance, a credit card balance is an unsecured debt. On the other hand, because a mortgage or a deed of trust is secured by real property, it has priority over the homestead exemption. The property may be sold at foreclosure to satisfy a secured debt.

In addition to the homestead estate, the householder is entitled to hold certain other items of real and personal property exempt from sale for the satisfaction of a debt, such as a family Bible, wedding and engagement rings, and a burial plot.

In certain circumstances, other items such as personal clothing, household furnishings, photographs, health aids and occupational tools also may be declared exempt.

In Practice	A real estate agent may be unaware that a homestead deed has been filed. The exemption is usually revealed in a title search conducted by an attorney or title examiner. The agent should be aware that the filing could indicate financial difficulties or even pending bankruptcy, or that judgments may be recorded.

EASEMENTS

Creating an Easement

An easement may be acquired by express grant or may be created by covenant or agreement. In Virginia, the owner of a dominant tenement may convey the land without the easement. Where the easement is not an easement by necessity, that is, not necessary for access to the property, and the appurtenance is expressly excluded by the grant, it will not convey. When a grantor conveys land by a deed that describes the property as bounded by a road or street that the grantor owns, the grantor is implying that a right-of-way exists. The grantee acquires the benefit of the easement automatically.

If the width of a right-of-way is not specified in the grant, it is limited to the width as it existed at the time of the grant. If an easement has a definite location, it may be changed with the express or implied consent of the interested parties. The change may also be implied by the parties' actions.

If the grantor reserves an easement in the property conveyed, the reservation must be expressly stated.

Easement by Prescription

An *easement by prescription* is similar to the acquisition of property by adverse possession. In an action to establish an easement by prescription in Virginia, the court must find that use of the property was

- adverse;
- under a claim of right;
- exclusive;
- continuous;
- uninterrupted; and
- with the knowledge and acquiescence of the landowner.

In Virginia, the prescriptive period is 20 years. Tacking—combining successive periods of continuous uninterrupted use by different parties—is permitted in Virginia.

When an easement is terminated, no document needs to be recorded in the clerk's office of the county where the land is located.

Questions

1. Which of the following does NOT constitute the exercise of eminent domain?
   1. A county taking a farmer's cropland for a highway
   2. The state taking from a private woodland for the construction of a roadside visitor center
   3. A county zoning ordinance change
   4. Port Authority of Hampton Roads taking riparian rights for a pier

2. For condemnation purposes, *just compensation* means
   1. fair market value at the time of the taking.
   2. fair market value at the time of purchase by the current owner.
   3. fair market value less court costs and attorneys' fees.
   4. a statutory percentage of fair market value.

3. What must happen before a condemnation suit is initiated?
   1. The owner and the government must agree.
   2. A genuine but ineffective effort to purchase must be made.
   3. The owner must have the property appraised.
   4. A statement of alternative solutions to the taking must be supplied to the owner by the condemning authority.

4. What is the status of dower and curtesy rights in Virginia?
   1. Dower and curtesy rights have been abolished.
   2. Dower is a fee simple estate; curtesy is a life estate.
   3. Dower and curtesy are identical rights in fee simple.
   4. Dower and curtesy have been combined by statute into one right.

5. *J* dies intestate. This means that she
   1. died penniless.
   2. left a will leaving everything to her dog.
   3. died without executing a will.
   4. died in a different state from her legal residence.

6. All of the following items could be *excluded* from *G*'s augmented estate **EXCEPT** a
   1. condominium owned by *G*'s wife *S*.
   2. small farm willed to *G* by his grandmother.
   3. beach property sold with *S*'s consent.
   4. 52-foot sailboat purchased during the marriage.

7. *P* is a single parent of three young children. *P*'s house is worth $75,000. What is the total maximum value of *P*'s homestead exemption?
   1. $5,000
   2. $6,500
   3. $70,000
   4. $75,000

8. Which of the following statements concerning the homestead exemption is correct?
   1. Exemption is automatic, every homeowner has one.
   2. The homeowner's filing for homestead exemption indicates financial difficulties.
   3. The homestead exemption is protection against claims for taxes, mechanics' liens and deeds of trust against the property.
   4. The $5,000 exemption includes the family Bible, a wedding ring and a burial plot.

9. All of the following are true of an easement by necessity **EXCEPT**
   1. it must be an appurtenant easement.
   2. both the dominant and the servient estates must have at some time in the past been owned by the same person.
   3. the only reasonable means of access is over the servient estate.
   4. inconvenience is a basis for the easement.

10. G has a 10-foot easement through H's forested lot for the purpose of walking to the bank of Otter River. G widens the path to 14 feet to accommodate his truck so he can launch his boat. H is furious. Which of the following is TRUE in this situation?
   1. G's original use was a right; H can do nothing.
   2. The new use is hostile, and if not stopped within 20 years, it could become an easement by prescription.
   3. The additional 4 feet is a reasonable extension of the original easement and must be granted.
   4. If G uses the extension for 15 years, the original easement is his adverse possession.

4 Forms of Real Estate Ownership

CO-OWNERSHIP

Tenancy in Common

In Virginia, *tenancy in common* may be created by

- an *express limitation* to two or more persons to hold land as tenants in common;
- a *grant* of part interest in one's land to another;
- a *devise* or *grant* of land to two or more persons to be divided between them;
- a *breakup* of estates in joint tenancy; and
- the *dissolving* of a tenancy by the entirety as a result of the divorce or mutual agreement of the parties.

A tenant in common may convey his or her undivided interest; however, a contract by one tenant in common relating to the whole estate is voidable by any cotenant who did not join in the contract.

A deceased cotenant's interest, in passing through his or her will or to his or her heirs, is subject to the statute of Wills and Decedents Estates, which protects the rights of the surviving spouse. (See "Augmented Estates" in Chapter 3.) Tenancy in common carries no right of survivorship, and the interest of the deceased does not automatically pass to a surviving cotenant.

Joint Tenancy

Virginia's joint tenancy is similar to that of most other states, insofar as the four unities of time, title, interest, and possession must be present. However, Virginia's interpretation of *unity of interest* is that one joint tenant cannot be a tenant for life and another for years. Similarly, one tenant cannot be a tenant in fee and another a tenant for life. Joint tenancy is always created by an act of the parties, never by descent or operation of law.

The doctrine of *automatic survivorship* has been abolished in Virginia. The legislature intended to place joint tenants in the same situation as tenants in common as far as augmented estates were concerned. If the deed *expressly* creates a joint tenancy with right of survivorship, as at common law, then on the death of a joint tenant the entire estate continues in the surviving tenant or tenants. The surviving spouse of the deceased joint tenant has no liability, and the deceased's creditors have no claim against the enlarged interests of the surviving tenants. Property owners who wish to have a property pass at their death to particular persons frequently create a joint tenancy as a substitute for a will.

A tenant in common or a joint tenant who commits waste may be liable to the other cotenant(s) for damages. By statute, a joint tenant or a tenant in common may demand an accounting from a cotenant who receives more than his or her fair share of rents and profits from the property. Similarly, joint tenants or tenants in common who improve a common property at their own expense are entitled to file a partition suit to divide and sell the property in order to obtain compensation for the improvements. However, if one tenant makes improvements without the consent of the other, the amount of compensation is limited to the amount by which the value of the common property has been enhanced.

Tenancy by the Entirety

Tenancy by the entirety is a special type of joint tenancy created between husband and wife. There is no right to partition or to convey a half interest. The tenancy is indestructible except by mutual agreement or divorce, in which case the tenancy by the entirety is converted into a tenancy in common.

Property held by husband and wife as tenants by the entirety is legally an asset of both parties. If one spouse contracts to convey the property, he or she cannot do so alone. The conveying spouse would be answerable to the would-be purchaser for the inability to perform.

In Practice — If a married woman has retained her maiden name, the deed should grant to, for example, "John Doe and Mary Jones, husband and wife, as tenants by the entirety," *not* to "Mary Doe, also known as Mary Jones."

Neither spouse alone may encumber the property. Any debts that could become liens on the property must be entered into jointly by both parties.

Community Property

There are no community property laws in Virginia.

LAND TRUST

Land trusts are permitted in Virginia. A *land trust* is a trust in which the assets consist of real estate. While the deed to a trustee may appear to confer full powers to deal with the real property and complete legal and equitable title to the trust property, the trustee's powers are in fact restricted by a trust agreement mentioned in the deed. The agreement typically gives the beneficiary full powers of management and control. However, even the beneficiary cannot deal with the property as if no trust existed. Land trusts generally continue for a definite term.

TENANCY IN PARTNERSHIP

A partnership may own real property, but each individual partner's interest is considered personal property. A partner is co-owner with the other partners of real property as a *tenant in partnership*.

Tenancy in partnership has the following features:

- A partner (subject to the partnership agreement) has an equal right with the other partners to possess the property for partnership purposes but may not possess it for any other purpose without the other partners' consent.
- A partner's right in a property is not assignable unless all the partners assign their rights in the same property.
- A partner's right in the property is not subject to creditors, except for a claim against the partnership itself. When partnership property is attached for a partnership debt, no rights can be claimed under homestead exemption laws by any partner or by the representative of a deceased partner.
- On the death of a partner, his or her interest in partnership property passes to the surviving partners. If the decedent was the last surviving partner, his or her right in the property vests in his or her legal representative. The surviving partners, or legal representative, have no right to possess the property for anything other than a partnership purpose.
- A partner can transfer property on behalf of all the partners if acting within the scope of the firm's business and purposes. Partners may transfer partnership property among themselves, provided all partners consent.

In Practice — Whenever a real estate licensee represents a buyer who is purchasing partnership-owned property, the licensee should have an attorney review the partnership agreement to ensure that a general partner with power to bind all other general partners executes conveyance. It is desirable to have a written resolution of the partnership authorizing the sale.

CORPORATIONS

A corporation may acquire and convey real property in its corporate name. A contract entered into by a corporation under an assumed name may be enforced by either party. If an instrument bears both a corporate seal and the signatures of the responsible corporate officers, it is presumed to be a corporate instrument, even if it lacks the required number of signatures or the corporate name.

In Practice — Anyone who purchases real estate from a corporation should require a written corporate resolution that duly authorizes the sale of property by the corporation.

COOPERATIVE OWNERSHIP

Cooperative ownership is governed by the Virginia Real Estate Cooperative Act [§55-424 through 55-506]. The Real Estate Board (REB) is charged with administrative responsibility for the Virginia Cooperative Act. A *cooperative* is "real estate owned by an association, each of the members of which is entitled, by virtue of his [or her] ownership interest in the association, to exclusive possession of a unit."

Cooperative possession is evidenced by a proprietary lease. A cooperative has common elements and *limited* common elements; it is created by a *declaration of cooperative,* filed in the clerk's office of the circuit court in the district in which the real estate is located.

When an individual purchases a cooperative unit, he or she is purchasing shares in the corporation (considered personal property) and signing a proprietary lease that allows for use of that particular unit.

The cooperative association may adopt and amend bylaws, rules, and regulations; adopt and amend budgets; hire and discharge management agents; regulate the use, maintenance, and repair of common elements; impose charges; and exercise other powers conferred by the declaration and bylaws.

Sale of a Cooperative Interest

Before the contract for the sale of a cooperative interest is executed, the purchaser must be given, among other things, a proprietary lease, a copy of the declaration and bylaws, a copy of the rules and regulations of the association, and a certificate that shows the following:

- A statement disclosing the effect of any right of first refusal or other restraint on transferability
- A statement of the amount of the monthly common expense assessment, as well as any unpaid expense currently due or payable from the sale and from the lessee
- A statement of any other fees payable by proprietary lessees
- A statement of any capital expenditures anticipated by the association for the current and next two succeeding fiscal years
- A statement of the amount of reserves for capital expenditures designated for specific projects
- The most recent regularly prepared balance sheet and income/expense statement, if any, of the association
- The current operating budget of the association and other pertinent information
- A statement of unsatisfied judgments and pending suits
- A statement of insurance coverage
- A statement of health or building code violations against the unit or common elements
- A statement of the remaining term of any leasehold estate and provisions for extensions or renewal, if any
- A statement that the public offering statement (POS), if one was prepared, is available for inspection
- A statement as to the deductibility of any real estate taxes and interest
- A statement of restrictions in the declaration that may affect the amount received by the proprietary lease holder upon sale, condemnation, or loss, to the unit or cooperative upon termination of the cooperative

- Certification that the association has filed the required reports to the REB

In the case of an initial sale of the cooperative, the purchaser must be given a POS. The POS must be provided before conveyance and not later than the date of the contract. If this does not occur, the seller has a financial liability. [§55-483]

In Practice — In the sale of a cooperative interest, it is the seller's obligation to provide a buyer with the required information. The real estate licensee, however, is often asked to obtain the information as a service to the client.

Buyer's Right to Rescind

In Virginia, purchasers of a cooperative interest have certain rights to rescind the contract. There are two types of rescission rights: initial sale rescission and resale rescission. In an *initial sale*, the first time the cooperative interest is sold after the cooperative is established, the buyer has the right to rescind within ten days following ratification of the contract or after receiving the public offering statement, whichever is later. When a cooperative unit is *resold*, that is, from an owner to a buyer, the purchaser contract is voidable by the purchaser until the certificate has been provided and for five days thereafter or until conveyance, whichever occurs first. [§55-484]

CONDOMINIUM OWNERSHIP

The REB is charged with the administrative responsibility for the Virginia Condominium Act. [§§55-79.39 through 55-79.103]

A condominium can be a multiunit structure, townhome or single-family dwelling. Even commercial properties may be condominiums. The owner of property may convert his or her property to condominium status. The owner is referred to as the *declarant* because he or she must *declare* his or her intent to have the property considered a condominium.

The declarant must provide declaration instruments to the REB that include the following:

- The name of the condominium (the name must include the word *condominium*)
- The legal description of the property
- Plats and/or plans that identify each unit
- An exact description of the horizontal and vertical boundaries of each unit
- The designation and description of common elements and limited common elements
- The exact allocation of the undivided ownership interest in the common elements
- If the property is being converted from rental property, the name of each current lessee and the date their leases expire
- Any easements that exist or that will be created
- An exact description of any proposed alterations to any existing units or common elements

In addition, the declarant must submit a copy of the *bylaws* under which the condominium will operate. The bylaws shall be specific regarding such issues as

- the form of self-governance for the unit owners;
- whether there are to be trustees, a board of directors, or other officers; their exact duties and the means by which they are to be appointed or elected;
- the extent to which the governing or executive body may delegate responsibilities to a management agent;
- the accounting and management records that will be maintained;
- a schedule of meetings of all owners and of the executive body;
- statutory requirements for meeting notices (21 days); and
- the rules and regulations that will apply to all owners.

Condominium Public Offering Statement

The declarant must also provide a public offering statement (POS). The POS includes all declaration documentation and bylaws, as well as

- the name of the declarant;
- a narrative description of the condominium, including the number of units and future plans for the addition of more units;
- copies of the bylaws and any current management contracts, including a statement of the relationship between the declarant and the contractor(s);
- a statement of the overall status of any construction or improvements;
- any encumbrances, liens, or easements that affect the title;
- the terms and conditions of any financing offered to purchasers;
- a statement of warranties, of the declarant's obligation to complete planned improvements, and a statement identifying the common elements and any user fees.

Sale of a Condominium Unit

At the *initial sale* of a condominium unit, the purchaser receives a copy of the POS along with the sales contract. The first purchaser of a condominium unit has the right to rescind a ratified contract, without penalty, within ten days, for any reason. The ten-day period begins with the date of contract ratification or on receipt of the POS, whichever is later. The right to rescind cannot be waived.

At closing, the purchaser acquires a fee simple interest in the individual unit and an *undivided percentage interest* in the common elements as a tenant in common with the other unit owners. At this time, the purchaser assumes responsibility for the individual unit purchased.

The declarant remains responsible for all unsold units and for the overall management and maintenance of the condominium development until 75 percent of the units are sold. At that point, responsibility for maintenance and management of the property shifts to the owners' association. The declarant becomes a member of the association as owner of the remaining units.

Voting Rights

Each unit owner has an assigned ownership interest and voting rights in the governance of the condominium. This interest is usually in proportion to the size of each individual unit and the amenities of the unit. The exact percentage of ownership interest is established in the declaration.

4 Forms of Real Estate Ownership

Bylaw Changes The Condominium Act states that two thirds of the total voting interest is required to change the bylaws.

Termination Once a property has been declared a condominium, its status can be changed by abandoning or dissolving it; 80 percent of the voting interest must approve the termination of a condominium's status.

Statutory Lien Rights The unit owners' association has a statutory lien on every unit for unpaid assessments levied against the unit. This lien is secondary to real estate tax liens and other liens recorded prior to the filing of the original condominium declaration.

Resale of a Condominium Unit All unit owners have the right to resell their individual units. In the event of an intended resale, the seller must obtain certain documents from the unit owners' association. These documents are collectively called the "resale certificate." The association may impose a charge of up to $100 for the preparation of the certificate. The resale certificate shall be current as of the date specified on the resale certificate. This means that the seller may obtain the certificate in advance of any purchase contract and have it immediately available for the purhcaser. The buyer's rights to receive the certificate and to cancel the contract are waived if the right is not exercised prior to settlement.

The purchaser also has a statutory right to request an update of the certificate prior to settlement. If there are one or more material changes to the certificate, the contract may be voided by the purchaser.

The certificate must be provided to the purchaser. The purchaser may cancel the contract under the following conditions:

- Within three days after the date of the contract if the certificate was provided to the purchaser on or before the date that the purchaser signs the contract.
- Within three days after receiving the certificate if hand delivered.
- Within six days of the postmark date if the certificate is mailed.

The buyer also has the right to cancel the contract if the contract does not disclose that the property is subject to the Condominium Act.

The documents required in the certificate include

- a statement of unpaid assessments against the unit;
- a statement of any assessments in addition to the regular assessment for both the current and succeeding fiscal years;
- a statement of assessments currently imposed by the association relative to the unit and common elements;
- a statement that identifies other entities for which the unit owner may be liable;
- a statement of the status of reserve and replacement funds;
- a copy of the most recent budget and financial reports of the association;
- a statement of any unpaid judgments or pending suits to which the association is a party;
- specific details of the association's insurance coverage;
- a statement that any improvements made to the individual unit or to the limited common elements comply with the condominium instruments;

- a current copy of the bylaws and rules and regulations;
- a statement of whether the condominium is located within a development subject to the Property Owner's Association Act (POA);
- a copy of the notice to the current unit owner of any current or pending rule of architectural violation;
- certification that the association has filed the appropriate reports to the REB; and
- a statement of any occupancy limitations.

In Practice — Condominium resale contracts must include wording to the effect that: (1) the offer is contingent on receipt of the condominium documents; and (2) the purchaser has three days in which to rescind the contract after receiving the documents.

TIME-SHARE OWNERSHIP

There are two types of time-share ownership recognized by the Virginia Time-Share Act [§55-360 et seq.]:

1. *Time-share estate* means a right to occupy a unit, or any of several units, during five or more separated time periods over a period of at least five years. The time-share estate includes renewal options, coupled with either a freehold interest or an estate for years, that is, a lease, in all or part of a time-share project.
2. *Time-share use* means a right to occupy a time-share unit or any of several time-share units, during five or more separated time periods over a period of at least five years, including renewal options, *not coupled with* a freehold estate or an estate for years in a time-share project. Time-share use does not mean a right subject to a first-come, first-served, space-available basis, such as exists in a country club, motel, or health spa.

The REB is charged with the administrative responsibility for the Time-Share Act.

Creation of a Time-Share

The developer of a time-share project must file and record with the REB a time-share *project instrument* that defines the project being created. This process establishes a time-share association in accordance with the Virginia Nonstock Corporations Act [§13.1-801].

A time-share association must be set up before any time-share estates may be sold. The project must be named, and the name must include the words *time-share, time-share interest, interval ownership, vacation ownership,* or other terms recognized in the industry.

Items that are to be included in the project instrument include

- the name of the time-share project;
- the complete address and legal description of the project;
- a description of the property;
- identification of the time periods;

- identification of the time-shares and the method by which additional time-shares may be created;
- the method used to allocate common expenses and voting rights assigned to each time-share;
- restrictions on use, occupancy, alteration, or alienation;
- the method by which the managing entity will provide maintenance of the time-share, if maintenance is to be provided; and
- provisions for amending the time-share instrument.

Time-Share Public Offering Statement

The POS filed for a time-share project is similar to the POS filed for a condominium. The developer may not convey any interest or advertise the property until the POS has been approved. If the time-share is being converted from another type of ownership, additional information is required regarding repairs made during the preceding three years and the physical condition of the structure. The purpose and value of reserve funds must be disclosed.

If the property to be converted is currently leased, tenants must be given 90 days' notice of the intent to convert the property to a time-share project. The tenants then have 60 days in which to contract with the developer to purchase the unit currently occupied if that unit is to be part of the overall project. Tenants on month-to-month leases must be given 120 days' notice to vacate.

Right to Rescind

The purchaser of a time-share interest at the project's *initial sale* has seven calendar days from execution of contract in which to cancel the contract without penalty. The developer is required to deliver the POS to the purchaser *prior* to the execution of the contract. The cancellation period commences on the date of contract ratification. If the seventh day falls on a Sunday or legal holiday, the right to cancel will expire on the day following the Sunday or legal holiday. The purchaser's right of cancellation cannot be waived, which must be identified in the contract.

Further, if there are material changes to the POS prior to settlement and after the initial time of contracting to purchase, the developer must provide the purchaser with the amended statement. The purchaser's right of cancellation is reinstated.

Deposits

Money received by the developer as earnest money deposits or down payments must be placed in an escrow account established by the developer and held there through the rescission period. The developer also must post a surety bond with the REB in the amount of $25,000, or the amount of the deposits received, whichever is greater. If any purchaser exercises the statutory right of rescission, the developer has 45 days in which to refund all monies paid by the purchaser.

Advertisements

Advertisements used for the marketing of time-share interests that offer gifts or prizes must clearly disclose the retail value of the gift or prize offered. The ad must also disclose the terms and conditions under which the gift is offered, the odds of actually winning a prize, and the number of gifts or prizes to be awarded. The ad must include the offer's expiration date and a statement that the offer is made for the purpose of soliciting the purchase of a time-share estate.

Transfer of Control

The developer remains in control of the project until 90 percent of the time-share estate has been sold or when all amenities and facilities have been completed, whichever is later. This is referred to as the *developer control period*. The developer control period may not exceed ten years after the sale of the first time-share interest. At the conclusion of the developer control period, the time-share owners' association assumes control and responsibility for the management and maintenance of the project. The developer must transfer control of the project to the owners' association without charging any fee. The owners' association may appoint or elect a managing agent for the project.

The owners' association has a statutory lien on every time-share estate in the project for unpaid regular and special assessments.

Beginning in the second year of owners' association management of the time-share project, the association must file an annual report with all owners. The report includes financial statements of the association, a list of officers and/or directors, and projected assessments for the coming year. The bylaws of the association may be changed by a vote of the owners. Should the owners decide to terminate the time-share project, approval by 51 percent of the voting interest of the association is required.

Resale of Time-Share

A *resale* of a time-share interest by any person other than the developer is subject to rules similar to those governing the resale of a condominium. The seller must obtain a *Certificate of Resale* from the owners' association. The certificate contains a copy of the time-share instruments; current financial statements; current bylaws; current rules and regulations of the association; fees and assessments; a disclosure of any liens that may be pending on the time-share for nonpayment of fees; and a statement of pending litigation against the developer, owners' association, or managing entity relative to the time-share project. The association may charge up to $50 for the certificate of resale.

The buyer in a time-share resale has the right to rescind the contract within five days following receipt of the certificate of resale or actual transfer, whichever occurs first. This right is without penalty and may be for any reason. Once the contract has closed, however, all rights of rescission are waived.

Statute of Limitations

Any action for misrepresentation of information in the project instruments, the POS or any contract must be initiated within two years of the date of the contract.

VIRGINIA PROPERTY OWNERS' ASSOCIATION ACT

The Virginia Property Owners' Association Act (POA Act) [§55, Chapter 26] sets forth requirements for the formation and operation of property owners' association. Each association subject to the act is governed by covenants, deed restrictions, POS, bylaws, and other restrictions designed to manage, regulate, and control the specific development, community, subdivision, or neighborhood and their common areas, if any. The specifics of the various governing documents vary among associations.

An association may be either self-managed or an independent management company may be employed to manage the affairs of the association. The act allows for a board of directors that may consist of property owners, developer representatives, and even representation from the independent management company, if used. Actions of the board, meetings, records, budgets, reports, and other asociation functions are governed by the act and the specific association documents. The board has the power to establish, adopt, and enforce rules with respect to the use of common areas and/or other areas of responsibility as established in the original declaration. A majority of votes from a quorum of the property members is usually required to repeal or amend rules and regulations. Violations of rules and regulations by the member property owner may result in the member being suspended from use of the common area facilities.

Property owners may be assessed routine fees, as allowed by the association documents, for the maintenance and upkeep of the association and common areas. Special assessments may be levied by the association. These special assessments usually require a majority vote of the property owners in accordance with the association's bylaws. Failure of a property owner to pay the authorized assessments entitles the association to place a lien on the property. [§55-516]

Exemptions

Associations with a mandatory fee of less than $150 per year for a regular annual assessment may be exempt from the Act. This exemption does not apply to developments created prior to July 1, 1991. In addition, condominiums, cooperatives, time-shares, and campgrounds are exempt from the act. However, if one of these types of ownership is located within an area that has been declared to be under the POA, the property is subject to both sets of regulations.

Disclosure Requirements

Because each association may impose certain restrictions and fees on the member property owners, potential purchasers must receive sufficient information prior to settlement about the association in order to make an informed decision to continue with the purchase. Therefore, any party who sells property subject to the act must include a statement *in the sales contract* to the effect that

- the property is located in a development that is subject to the POA;
- the act requires the seller to obtain a disclosure packet from the POA and to provide that packet to the buyer;
- the buyer may cancel the contract within three days after receiving the packet or being advised that the packet will not be provided;
- the buyer has the right to request an update of the packet; and
- the rights to cancel the contract are waived if those rights are not exercised prior to closing.

If the contract does not contain these disclosures, the sole remedy for the buyer is to rescind the contract prior to closing. [§55-51]

POA Disclosure Packet

The information in the POA disclosure packet must be current as of the date of the packet. This allows the property owner to have a packet available for the buyer at the time of contract.

The association is required to make the packet available within 14 days after an owner/member, or an owner/member's authorized agent, files a written request. The association may charge a fee reflecting the actual cost for preparation of the packet but shall not exceed ten cents per page for copying or a total of $100 for all costs incurred. [§55-512C] The associations's failure to deliver the packet in a timely manner waives any claim for delinquent assessments or fines. The maximum liability to the association for failing to provide the packet in a timely manner is actual damages, not to exceed $500. [§55-512E]

Contents of the POA Disclosure Packet

Each disclosure packet must include the name of the association plus the name and address of the registered agent, if incorporated. The packet must also include

- a statement of all assessments, fees, or charges currently imposed plus any planned expenditure that would result in additional assessment;
- a copy of the current budget plus statement of income and expenses or financial condition for the past year;
- any pending suit or unpaid judgment;
- a statement of what insurance coverage is provided for lot owners and what is expected of each individual lot owner;
- plans for any alteration of lot, or uses of common areas;
- any restrictions on the placement of For Sale signs or flags;
- a copy of the current declaration, articles of incorporation and bylaws, and all rules and regulations or architectural guidelines adopted by the association;.
- any current or pending violation of rules by the current owner; and
- certification that required reports have been filed with the REB.

An informational form prepared by the REB must accompany all POA disclosure packets. The purpose of this form is to describe the special circumstances and the relationship between lot owners and the association in order to educate the prospective purchasers and foster a better understanding between the property owners and the association.

Purchaser's Right To Request Update

The purchaser may submit a copy of the contract to the association with a request for updating of the disclosure packet. The association must respond within ten days and has the right to charge the purchaser a fee for preparation of the new packet that reflects the actual cost but not to exceed $50. [§55-512B] The purpose of this request for update of the packet is to both assure the buyer that there have been no changes and to identify the specifics of any material changes. If there have been any material changes, the buyer has no recourse for cancellation of the contract unless that right had previously been agreed upon in the purchase contract.

Purchaser's Right To Rescind

The purchaser has the right to cancel the contract

- within three days after the date of the contract, if the packet or notice that the packet is unavailable was provided before signing of the contract; or
- within three days after receiving the packet or notice that the packet is not available (if hand delivered); *or*
- within six days after the postmark date of either the packet or the notice that packet is not available was sent by U.S. mail.

The purchaser may also cancel the contract any time prior to settlement if not notified that the disclosure packet will not be available nor the packet delivered.

If the purchaser elects to rescind, the notice of rescission must be hand-delivered or sent by U.S. mail, return receipt requested, to the owner. Rescission is without penalty, and the purchaser is entitled to a full refund of any earnest money given. Any rights to rescind the contract must be exercised prior to closing.

A complete discussion of interests in real estate in Virginia may be found in the Code of Virginia, Title 55—Property and Conveyances; see the table of contents, Title 55, at the following Web address.

WWWeb.Link
http://leg1.state.va.us/000/src.htm

Questions

1. B, J and E own a parcel of property as tenants in common. E sells the entire parcel to D. Which of the following is TRUE of this situation?
   1. D is now a tenant in common with B and J.
   2. D owns the parcel in severalty.
   3. B or J can void the contract, but E is bound.
   4. The contract is void; no one is bound and nothing conveys.

2. How is a joint tenancy created in Virginia?
   1. By an act of the parties
   2. By operation of law
   3. By dissolution of a tenancy in common
   4. By all of the above

3. G and B own real property as joint tenants with right of survivorship. G dies owing money to creditors. Which of the following is correct?
   1. B owns the property in severalty and is liable to the creditors.
   2. B owns the property and is not liable to the creditors.
   3. B owns the property except for a share owned by the creditors that represents the debts' percentage of the property value.
   4. G's wife owns the property interest held by her husband and is liable for the debts incurred by her husband.

4. B and M own land as tenants by the entirety. B signs a contract to sell his share of the property to J. Based on these facts, all of the following are true **EXCEPT**
   1. B cannot sell his half-interest.
   2. While the contract appears valid, B cannot perform under the contract.
   3. J could hold B answerable for his inability to perform under the contract.
   4. M is now the sole owner of the land.

5. Which of the following is TRUE regarding Virginia's community property laws?
   1. Since 1991, the Virginia statute is patterned after California's.
   2. Virginia recognizes only some community property provisions.
   3. Augmented estates are the same as community property provisions.
   4. Virginia is not a community property state.

6. M and H are partners in a successful accounting practice. They are in the process of purchasing a small office condominium for their practice. They would NOT be able to take title as
   1. tenants by the entirety.
   2. tenants in common.
   3. joint tenants.
   4. tenants in partnership.

7. Which of the following is necessary for a corporation to convey property by deed?
   1. Corporate seal
   2. Proper signatures of all corporate officers
   3. Corporate name and required number of signatures
   4. Notarization

8. When a person wants to create a condominium, which of the following statements is correct?
   1. The structures on the property being declared a condominium must be at least two stories.
   2. A condominium regime can only be created on unimproved land.
   3. The word *condominium* must appear in the name of the property.
   4. A condominium regime can be created only for residential use.

9. Contracts for the *initial* purchase of a condominium may be rescinded without penalty how many days after the later of contract ratification or receipt of the POS?
   1. 5 days
   2. 10 days
   3. 14 days
   4. 21 days

10. If a condominium unit owner fails to pay the owners' association's assessment against his or her unit, the owners' association may
    1. place a lien against the unit.
    2. garnish the owner's wages.
    3. do nothing; as a stockholder, the unit owner has priority.
    4. revoke the unit owner's privileges and rights.

11. Some of the owners of the Riverview Condominium have decided they would like to dissolve the condominium status of the property. What vote will be necessary to do this?
    1. Majority of owners
    2. 75 percent
    3. 80 percent
    4. Cannot be done

12. *B* has a ratified contract to purchase a two-bedroom condominium unit from *T*. *B* is now suffering from "buyer remorse" and wishes to back out of the contract. She has not yet received the condominium documents. After receipt of the documents, she will have how many days to cancel the contract?
    1. 3 days
    2. 5 days
    3. 7 days
    4. 10 days

13. *H* is the owner of a time-share unit, which he bought several years ago from the developer. On March 2, *H* accepts an offer from *J* to buy the unit. On March 4, *H* hand-delivers the certificate of resale to *J*. On April 12, *H* transfers ownership of the unit to *J*. If *J* should decide to rescind the contract, what is the latest date when *J* may do so without incurring a penalty?
    1. March 7
    2. March 9
    3. March 15
    4. April 17

14. When the owner's interest in a time-share includes either a freehold interest or an estate for years, it is what type?
    1. Time-share use
    2. Time-share estate
    3. Time-share fee
    4. Time-share demise

15. *H* recently visited a brand-new time-share project on the Eastern Shore. If she decides to make an offer on the property, how long will she have to cancel the contract without penalty?
    1. None; *H* is bound to the contract
    2. 3 days after ratification of contract
    3. 7 days after ratification of contract
    4. 10 days after ratification of contract

16. What is the statute of limitations on any action for misrepresentation of information as it applies to time-shares?
    1. 7 years
    2. 2 years
    3. 1 year
    4. No limitation

17. *M* has decided she no longer wishes to purchase the town house which she currently has under contract. The town house is covered by the POA. *M* can cancel her contract
    1. whenever she wishes.
    2. within 10 days after ratification of contract.
    3. within 3 days after receiving the property disclosure packet.
    4. within 14 days after receiving the property disclosure packet.

18. *S* is 6 months behind in his POA fees. The association has the right to:
    1. confiscate *S*'s property.
    2. place a lien on the property.
    3. sue *S* for punitive damages.
    4. change the locks on *S*'s house.

19. Both the Condominium Act and the Property Owner Association Act have a set limit on the amount that may be charged for preparation of the required document packet of
    1. $50.
    2. $100.
    3. actual cost of copying.
    4. any amount they choose.

20. The REB is charged with the administration of all the following **EXCEPT** the
    1. Property Owners' Association Act.
    2. Virginia Condominium Act.
    3. Virginia Time-Share Act.
    4. Virginia Residential Property Disclosure Act.

5 Legal Descriptions

DESCRIBING REAL ESTATE

The most common method of describing real estate in Virginia is a combination of metes-and-bounds and lot-and-block.

Licensees should use great care in describing property. Both the real estate plat map and county or city tax records, as well as at least one deed by which the land was conveyed in the past, may be checked to verify that the proper legal description is being used. The description should enable the parties—or a court—to determine exactly what land the parties intended to convey. *Parol evidence*, that is, evidence of facts and circumstances not included in the deed or contract, is admissible in a court proceeding if the facts were well known in the community at the time the deed was made.

METHODS OF DESCRIPTION

The description of land by any of the following methods is legally sufficient, if the county or city and state are included:

- By courses and distances with an identifiable starting point (metes-and-bounds method)
- As bounded by natural or artificial objects or by the land of named persons (monuments method)
- By reference to a recorded map, plat, survey, deed, or other writing (lot-and-block method)
- By number or code on a recorded subdivision (subdivision method)
- By geodetic survey of townships, ranges, meridians, and so forth (rectangular government survey method)
- By house number and named street, where there is an established system of numbering (in many cases, this is not considered to be an adequate legal description because house numbers and even street names are frequently subject to change)
- By any name by which the land is generally known and identifiable
- As occupied or acquired by a named person at a definite time
- As being all the land of the grantor in a designated way or acquired in a specific way

FOR EXAMPLE This is a common property description:

All those certain lots, pieces, or parcels of land, situated in the city of Norfolk, Virginia, known, numbered and designated on the Plat of Estabrook Corporation, made by S.W. Armistead, C.E., February 1920, and recorded in the clerk's office of the Circuit Court of the City of Chesapeake, Virginia, in Map Book 17, page 4, as Lots No. 35 and 36, located on the North side of Amherst Street in Block "E" in said Subdivision known as Estabrook, and appurtenances thereunto belonging said lots being 25 x 100 feet each.

A shortened form is frequently used in listing agreements and sales contracts:

Lots 35 and 36, Block E, Plat of Estabrook, Norfolk, Virginia 23513, also known and described as 36 Amherst Street.

The following would also be an acceptable description:

All that land known as Warrens Crossing, as purchased by Nicholas Lilly on June 17, 1984, and bounded on the north by Richmond Hwy., on the south by Muddy Run, on the east by the farm belonging to John Evans, and on the south by the Redly Estate owned by Elizabeth Davies.

False Descriptions

A false description does not invalidate the deed if, after rejecting the false description, enough information remains to permit reliable identification of the land to be conveyed. A complete description can be found in the deed that conveyed the property to the seller. The identical description should be used to convey the land to the buyer.

Settlement of Disputes

Disputed boundaries between two adjoining lands may be settled by express agreement. Virginia law provides for a court proceeding to establish boundaries.

In conflicts concerning true boundaries, Virginia law gives preference to methods of description in the following order:

1. Natural monuments or landmarks
2. Artificial monuments and established lines
3. Adjacent boundaries or lines of adjoining tracts
4. Calls for courses and distances
5. Designation of quantity, such as, "approximately 3.5 acres"

This preference will not be applied where it would frustrate the intent of the parties.

In disputes among purchasers of a lot shown on a plat, the metes and bounds established accurate survey and corresponding calls of courses and distances noted on the plat will supersede errors in the plat and will control dimensions and configuration of the lots.

SURVEYING AND SURVEYS

To engage in the practice of land surveying in Virginia, a person must hold a valid surveyor's license, unless exempted by the statute. Lenders are not allowed to require that a particular surveyor perform the survey in connection with making a loan to purchase real property. Surveys are recorded in the clerk's office of the circuit court where the land is located.

Four Types of Surveys

Following are four types of surveys commonly used in Virginia:

1. A *subdivision plat* is a map of each parcel of land. The plat shows subdivided lots, streets, and similar features. The plat is generally created from a tract of land to subdivide it. The subdivided lots may or may not be "staked on the ground" once the plat has been created.
2. A *boundary survey*, as opposed to a subdivision plat, shows the boundary or perimeter of the parcel as taken from and applied to the ground. Corner stakes or other physical landmarks appear.
3. A *house location survey* is a boundary survey with the location of the house shown.
4. A *physical* or *as-built survey* is a house location survey with all other physical features of the subject property shown, including water courses, utility lines, fence lines, outbuildings, and similar features.

A recently recorded survey of a subject property may reveal matters not shown in the record.

The attorney is primarily the person obligated to examine the survey. The following conditions suggest that potential problems may exist and should be brought to the attention of an attorney:

- Property boundaries that do not conform with the recorded plat
- Structural encroachments by the property onto neighboring properties, or by neighboring structures onto the subject property
- Fences that are not on the boundary line
- Party walls
- Riparian rights of others in streams, lakes, and other bodies of water
- Utilities that service other properties
- Old roadways
- Cemeteries
- Violation of setback, side or rear building lines
- Property that may be landlocked

Any defect shown on the survey should be reported and corrective action taken where necessary.

Plat Maps

In areas of Virginia where recorded plat maps are used in lieu of individual surveys, the appropriate lot must be identified and lot dimensions must be legibly shown. Necessary endorsements to the title insurance policy must be issued pertaining to easements, deed restrictions, and property identification. The closing lawyer is responsible for obtaining the endorsements.

Subdivision Plat

In Virginia, a subdivision plat must contain all the necessary approvals of county or city officials. In addition, the dedications or consents of all owners, trustees, and other similar parties must be properly recorded. The law provides that the mere recordation of a plat transfers the streets, alleys, and other areas set aside for public use to the county or municipality in fee simple.

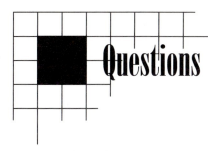

Questions

1. All of the following are satisfactory legal descriptions in Viriginia, **EXCEPT**
   1. Lot 7, Block D, Plat of Red Valley, Martin County, Virginia.
   2. the entire 77.5 Acres purchased by Edna Kelly on June 20, 1981, and known as Seaside Neck, Roanoke.
   3. 727 Olean Drive, Fletcherton, Virginia.
   4. proceeding 120 feet due west of the intersection of the east line of J Street and the north line of 11th street to a point; thence north 10 degrees 31 minutes west 100 feet.

2. A deed contains the following description: *Lots 7 and 8, Block F, Section 3, Plat of Greydon, otherwise known as 14 Havers Drive, Venus, Virginia.*
   In fact, Block F has only 6 lots, and the street address is Lot 5. Is this deed valid?
   1. No; a false element in a description invalidates the deed.
   2. No; because the lot description is faulty, a new deed is needed.
   3. Yes, if the buyer knows which property is meant.
   4. Yes; enough correct information remains to permit identification.

3. *J* and *B* bought neighboring lots in a subdivision. The representation of the lots on the plat shows that *B's* land reaches to a creek and *J's* land falls just short of the creek. At the closing, a survey of the lots shows *J* with access to the creek and leaves *B* without access. Who prevails regarding access to the creek?
   1. *B*, because the original plat representation governs.
   2. *B*, because otherwise the developer is guilty of misrepresentation.
   3. *J*, because the survey supersedes errors in the plat.
   4. A new survey must be drawn giving both buyers creek access.

4. A lender wishes to use the services of only licensed surveyors and says he will not accept other surveyors' surveys. Is this practice legal?
   1. Yes; provided the lender pays for the survey.
   2. Yes; as long as the surveyor holds a valid license.
   3. No; surveyors are selected by the clerk's office.
   4. No; the lender cannot require that a particular surveyor conduct the survey.

5. The survey for 1234 Grand Avenue shows the location of the house, the garage, the fence, utility lines, and the children's playhouse in the backyard. This is most likely which type of survey?
   1. Subdivision plat
   2. Boundary survey
   3. House location survey
   4. As-built survey

6 Real Estate Taxes and Other Liens

TAX LIENS

Uniform Taxation

In Virginia, real estate taxes are levied according to the proportion designated by tax laws. The Virginia Constitution requires that taxation be uniform. Uniform taxation requires that both the tax rate and the mode of assessing the taxable value must be uniformly applied to similar properties, that is, all property of the same class must be taxed alike.

However, the principle of uniformity does not prevent differences in taxation or the classification for taxation purposes of properties according to use in a business, trade, or occupation.

Exemptions From Taxation

Burial grounds and cemetery lots owned by a cemetery company or by lot owners and used exclusively for burial purposes are exempt from taxation.

The Virginia Constitution exempts property owned and exclusively occupied or used by religious organizations for worship purposes or ministerial residences. The exemption applies to both real and personal property.

Property owned by public libraries or nonprofit educational institutions is exempt, as long as it is primarily used for literary, scientific, or educational purposes.

In addition, property used by its owner for religious, charitable, patriotic, historical, benevolent, cultural, or public park and playground purposes is also exempt.

The controlling factor in determining whether private property is exempt from taxation is the use of the property. Public property, however, may be exempted from taxation without regard to its use.

Assessment

Taxes run with the land. The buyer of a property is responsible for paying real estate taxes for the current tax year from the date of purchase until the end of the year. In Virginia, the buyer is said to own the property on the date of closing or settlement. Taxes should be prorated between the vendee and vendor as of the date of the sale. Any delinquent taxes should be paid by the vendor at closing. Penalties and interest on delinquent taxes are established by statute.

6 Real Estate Taxes and Other Liens

In Practice   Unpaid taxes are a lien on real property. The settlement agent must verify that prior years' taxes have been paid and ascertain the status of the current year's taxes. Any other information should be obtained from city or county tax offices.

Taxes are generally not payable in advance of the due date. However, each city and county has its own particular manner of assessing taxes and setting the due date. Real estate licensees should be aware of four phases of taxes:

1. Past-due taxes
2. Taxes currently due and payable
3. Taxes not yet due
4. Prepaid taxes

The taxes for the first two phases will be collected from the seller's proceeds and paid to the proper authority by the settlement attorney. In the third and fourth phases, there are no taxes to be paid at the time a sale is closed. The closer will prorate the taxes between buyer and seller.

In phase three, the seller will be charged with the portion of the taxes that represents the number of days he or she occupied the property. The buyer will be credited with the same amount.

In phase four, where the taxes have been prepaid, the seller will receive a credit for the amount of taxes already paid for the period of time that he or she will not be occupying the property. The buyer will be charged with the same amount.

Estimating Taxes   Sometimes, past-year taxes cannot be used to estimate current taxes. It is up to the real estate licensee to use whatever information is available to reasonably estimate the current year's taxes.

New Construction   In the case of new construction, the taxes on the land are prorated based on taxes for the past year. Taxes on the new improvements are estimated using the purchase price multiplied by the county or city assessment rate. Taxes are estimated from the date the certificate of occupancy is issued, or a partial assessment may be levied against new construction not yet completed. If the closing is significantly later than the date of the certificate of occupancy or the closing date in the sales contract, the licensee should check to see if the property has been reassessed with the improvements.

Leases   As a general rule, the landlord under any ordinary lease is responsible for the taxes on the property; however, this does not apply to a perpetual leaseholder who is, in effect, the owner of the property and is entitled to its use forever. In such a case, the burden of taxation is placed on the lessee. In the case of net leases, the tenant is usually responsible for payment of the taxes.

Tax Liens   Delinquent real property taxes are both a personal debt and a lien against the property. A tax lien on real property has priority over all other liens except court costs. Thus, a tax lien overrides a vendor's lien, even though the vendor's lien may have been first. A tax lien is also prior to the landlord's lien for rent.

The Virginia statutes give real estate taxes priority over a deed of trust in the distribution of proceeds under a foreclosure sale. The foreclosing trustee must satisfy all outstanding deficiencies before distributing the remaining proceeds to other creditors. If the statute's requirements are not complied with, delinquent taxes remain a debt against the purchaser at the sale.

A lien in favor of the United States for unpaid taxes, interest, and penalties may arise against all real and personal property belonging to a taxpayer. The lien is perfected under Virginia law by filing a notice of tax lien in the circuit court for the jurisdiction in which the taxpayer resides. The tax lien remains in effect until the taxes are paid.

When taxes on real estate in a county, city, or town are delinquent on December 31 following the third anniversary of the date on which the taxes became due, the real estate may be sold to collect the tax.

FOR EXAMPLE *G's property tax was due on June 10, 1999. G failed to pay. If the tax is still delinquent on December 31, 2002, G's property may be sold for taxes on January 1, 2003.*

At least 30 days before taking any action to sell the property, the tax-collecting officer must send a notice to the last known address of the property owner. Notice of the sale must be published in a newspaper of general circulation in the area 30 to 60 days prior to the commencement of the sale proceedings.

The sale proceedings are initiated by filing a suit in the circuit court of the county or city where the real estate is located. The owner of the real estate, or their heirs, successors, and assigns, have the right to redeem the real estate *prior to the sale date* by paying all taxes, penalties, and interest due, plus costs, including the cost of publication and a reasonable attorney's fee set by the court. The former owner of any real estate sold for delinquent real estate taxes is entitled to any receipts from the sale in excess of the taxes, penalties, interest, and costs.

Special Assessments

There is a distinction between special assessments and general tax levies for purposes of funding government services and operations. *Special assessments* are taxes levied against specific benefited properties to pay for limited local improvements. They are founded on the theory of benefits brought about by improvements to adjacent properties. This public improvement enhances the value of a specific property—a sidewalk, for instance, or a repaved alley. A special assessment is distinguished from an improvement that benefits the entire community, such as a park.

The statute specifically provides that notice must be given to abutting landowners of the contemplated improvements before the ordinance authorizing the improvements is put into effect. This gives the landowner an opportunity to be heard concerning the adoption or rejection of such an ordinance. The statute provides for special assessments relating to sewers, street paving, and other local public improvements.

The only properties subject to special assessments are those of abutting landowners.

Local improvements may be ordered by a town or city council (with costs to be defrayed by special assessment) following receipt of a petition from not less than three-fourths of the landowners who will be affected by the assessment. However, the council may issue such an improvement order without a petition.

The amount of special assessment for a local improvement constitutes a lien on the property benefited by the improvement, enforceable by a suit in court. Property owners have the right to appear before the municipal authorities and protest both the authorization of the improvements and the assessments. For a complete discussion of real estate taxes, see Code of Virginia, Table of Contents, Title 58.1—Taxation, at the following website:

WWWeb.Link
http://leg1.state.va.us/000/src.htm

LIENS OTHER THAN TAXES

Mechanics' Liens

Anyone who performs labor or furnishes material with a value of $50 or more for the construction, removal, repair, or improvement of any structure has a right of lien on both the land and the building. The object of the law is to give laborers and materialmen the security of a lien on the property to the extent that they have added to its value.

The Virginia Mechanics' Lien Disclosure Act, Code of Virginia, Title 43, Chapter 1, requires that the seller of property disclose in the sales contract a warning that an effective mechanic's lien may be filed against the real property even after settlement.

The act's purpose is to protect contractors, brokers, purchasers, title agents and insurers from builders or owners who contracted for improvements, sold the property and never paid the contractor. The act requires that each residential sales contract include the following:

> **NOTICE** Virginia law §43.1 et seq. permits persons who have performed labor or furnished materials for the construction, removal, repair, or improvement of any building or structure to file a lien against the property. This lien may be filed at any time after the work is commenced or the material is furnished, but not later than the earlier of (1) 90 days from the last day of the month in which the lienor last performed work or furnished materials, or (2) 90 days from the time the construction, removal, repair, or improvement is terminated.
>
> An effective lien for work performed, prior to the date of settlement, may be filed after settlement. Legal counsel should be consulted.

While inclusion of the statement is mandatory, failure to include it will not void the contract.

A general contractor or a subcontractor may perfect a mechanic's lien by filing a memorandum of mechanic's lien and an affidavit with the clerk of court in the jurisdiction in which the property or structure is located. The filing must be within 90 days of the last day of the month in which the contractor last performed labor or furnished materials. However, under no circumstances may filing occur later than 90 days from the time the building is completed or the work otherwise terminated.

Written notice must be given to the owner of the property. The notice memorandum generally contains

- the name of the owner of the property;
- the name of the claimant;
- the amount of the claim;
- the time when the amount is due and/or, payable; and
- a brief description of the property.

A mechanic's lien is enforced by a suit, filed within six months of recording the memorandum of lien or 60 days from the completion or termination of work on the structure, whichever is later. If the person who ordered the work owns less than the fee simple estate in the land, only his or her actual interest is subject to the lien.

When a buyer constructs a building or structure, or undertakes repairs to an existing building or structure before the transaction has closed, the owner's interest will be subject to any mechanic's lien if the owner knows about the activity.

When a lien, such as a deed of trust, is created on land before work is begun or materials furnished, the deed of trust is a first lien on the land and a second lien on the building or structure. A deed of trust that is recorded before the work began is entitled to priority to the extent of the estimated value of the property *without improvements for which the lien is claimed.*

Typically, the seller must execute an affidavit at closing that declares no work has been performed or any materials furnished within 120 days before the date of closing. This declaration ensures that no mechanic can file a lien on the property after closing for labor performed or materials furnished prior to closing. Nonetheless, a buyer should be advised to obtain additional assurances that no mechanic's lien can be filed.

Closing agents are charged with the responsibility to advise buyers of possible mechanic's lien filings and must inform buyers about title insurance protection.

A lien waiver should be demanded for new construction stating that all amounts have been paid for labor performed and materials furnished in connection with the construction. The waiver should be executed by the general contractor and all subcontractors. However, no waiver is required if affirmative mechanic's lien coverage is provided by a title insurance company.

Judgments

Every money judgment rendered in Virginia by any court, or by confession of judgment, constitutes a lien on any real estate the judgment debtor owns or may own in the future. The lien is effective from the date the judgment is docketed, that is, indexed by the clerk of court. It is prudent to docket the judgment in the city or county in which the debtor's property is located. If the debtor currently has no property, it is wise to docket the judgment wherever property is located that may become the debtor's in the future (for instance, property owned by family members).

A writ of execution may be issued and the judgment enforced within 20 years from the date the judgment was rendered. A judgment may be extended beyond its 20-year life by a motion made in the circuit court, following notice to the judgment debtor and redocketing of the judgment.

If the real estate is conveyed to a grantee for value subject to a judgment lien, the judgment creditor must bring the suit to enforce the judgment lien within ten years from the date the grantee's deed was recorded.

If the judgment is for recovery of specific real property, a *writ of possession* is needed. If the judgment debtor owns real estate outside Virginia, the debtor may be required to convey it to a sheriff.

Within 30 days of the satisfaction, that is, payment of a judgment, a judgment creditor must release the judgment wherever it is docketed. Failure to do so within ten days of demand by the judgment debtor makes the creditor subject to a fine.

Estate and Inheritance Tax Liens

A lien arises on all property, real and personal, of every decedent who has a taxable estate located in the Commonwealth of Virginia if the decedent's estate fails to pay the tax imposed by the Virginia Estate Tax Act.

In the case of a nonresident decedent who has a taxable estate in Virginia, the lien arises automatically at the time of the nonresident's death. In the case of a resident decedent, the liens attach to the real estate only when a memorandum is filed by the department of taxation in the clerk's office of the county or city where such real estate is located. Once it attaches, the lien is enforceable for ten years from the date of the decedent's death.

In Virginia, the tax imposed is a *succession tax* rather than an estate tax: It is a tax on the right to succeed to the property or an interest in it, not the right to transmit it. The tax is not levied on the property of which an estate is composed but on the shifting of economic benefits and the privilege of receiving such benefits.

Attachments

The mere issuance of an attachment creates no lien on the real estate. To create a lien, it is necessary for the officer to show that levy (actual attachment or seizure) was made.

Lis Pendens

A *lis pendens*, or pending suit, does not bind or affect a subsequent purchaser of real estate unless a memorandum is properly recorded giving notice of the suit. The memorandum of notice states the title of the suit, its general object, and the court in which it is pending. The notice declares the amount of the claim, describes the property, and names the person whose estate is intended to be affected.

If the lis pendens is not docketed as provided by the statutes, a purchaser without notice of the pending suit takes good title, with no lien on the land by virtue of the pending suit.

Vendor's Lien

In Virginia, if any person conveys any real estate and the purchase money remains unpaid at the time of the conveyance, the vendor will not have a lien for the unpaid purchase money unless the lien is expressly reserved on the face of the deed. The object of this statute is to make the lien a matter of record, putting all persons who deal with the property on notice of all liens and encumbrances. The extent of the vendor's lien does not depend on the extent of the vendor's interest in the land conveyed but on the contract of the parties as gathered from the deed itself.

Landlord's Lien

The Virginia statutes give a landlord a right of lien. It exists independently of the right to hold property for payment of rent. When the landlord's lien for rent is obtained, it relates back to the very beginning of the tenancy and takes precedence over any lien that any other person has obtained or created against goods (personal property) on the leased premises since the tenancy began. A lien legally attaches to all property on the premises when it is asserted or on the premises within 30 days prior to attachment of lien. The landlord can seize the tenant's goods only to the extent necessary to satisfy the rent justly believed to be due.

Commercial Broker's Lien

A commercial real estate broker has a lien on the rent paid by the tenant in the amount of the compensation (commission) agreed on by the owner and the broker.

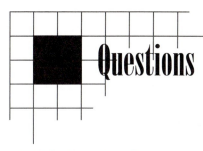

Questions

1. Which of the following is TRUE of uniform real estate taxation in Virginia?
   1. Tax rates and assessments must be uniformly applied to similar properties.
   2. All properties pay the same amount of tax.
   3. Only the tax rate needs to be uniform.
   4. Uniformity is a common law principle.

2. B's house is near the end of a block; right beside her house on the corner lot is Tasty Bakery. How must these properties be treated for real estate tax purposes?
   1. There can be no difference between them.
   2. They will be classified differently, according to use.
   3. A sliding value scale may be applied to businesses but not to residences, which are strictly ad valorem.
   4. Because the bakery abuts a residential zone, it must be treated as a residence.

3. All of the following types of real property are exempt from real property taxation EXCEPT
   1. burial grounds.
   2. government-owned land.
   3. land owned by nonprofit educational institutions.
   4. land owned by handicapped persons.

4. Which of the following statements is TRUE regarding taxes on new construction?
   1. Taxes are estimated using the purchase price multiplied by the state assessment rate.
   2. Taxes are estimated from the date of the certificate of occupancy.
   3. Improvements are not assessed as part of the previously existing property.
   4. The statutory appreciation rate is applied to new construction to estimate the current year's fair market value.

5. In Virginia, who owns a property (for real estate tax purposes) on the date of sale?
   1. The buyer owns it.
   2. The seller owns it.
   3. It is divided evenly, with each party paying half of the tax for that day.
   4. This item must be negotiated.

6. Which of the following liens would have FIRST priority?
   1. Deed of trust
   2. Mechanic's lien
   3. Property tax lien
   4. Landlord's lien for rent

7. J is relieved to learn that her home will soon be served by a city sewer line. How will this improvement most likely be paid for?
   1. General real estate tax
   2. Municipal bonds
   3. Special assessment
   4. State road-use tax

8. How long after the work was done may a mechanic wait before filing a mechanic's lien?
   1. No more than 30 days
   2. No more than 60 days
   3. No more than 90 days
   4. No more than 6 months

9. How soon after filing the lien must the mechanic enforce it by filing suit?
   1. Within 3 months
   2. Within 6 months
   3. Within 9 months
   4. Within 1 year

10. Within what period of time must a creditor on a judgment enforce the judgment once it is rendered?
    1. Within 6 months
    2. Within 1 year
    3. Within 5 years
    4. Within 20 years

7 Real Estate Contracts

THE CONTRACT

The Code of Virginia allows real estate licensees—brokers and salespersons—to prepare written contracts for the sale, purchase, option, exchange, or rental of real estate as long as the contract is incidental to a specific real estate transaction and that there is no additional charge for preparing the contract. [§54.1-2101.1] In some states, brokers and salespersons are not authorized to prepare contracts. In Virginia, the operative word is "incidental." For example: While a licensee assists a buyer in a variety of functions, such as locating property, arranging financing, selecting a settlement agent, etc., the preparation of the sales contract is incidental to the variety of services provided. In the situation of a seller who hires the licensee, the licensee performs a variety of services such as marketing the property, advertising, and showing the property to buyers, etc. As in the case of the buyer example, the preparation of the sales contract is incidental to the transaction. In a situation where either a buyer or seller contacts a licensee to merely prepare a sales contract for a fee, the licensee may be guilty of practicing law without a license because the preparation of the contract was not incidental to the transaction.

The actual contract used for the purchase and sale of real property may take any form. The only requirement is that it be in enough detail to clearly state the agreement between the parties.

Local real estate associations often have standard forms to be used by their members. For an examples of regional sales contract and its addendums, see Figure 7.1.

It is customary for real estate licensees to assist buyers and sellers with the preparation of the contract by filling in the blanks on the form. *As with all legal matters, real estate brokers and salespersons should refrain from trying to explain the legal technicalities.* Improper or misunderstood explanations could subject the licensee to legal action later.

In Practice — As with the listing agreement form, all blanks should be filled in. If the item does not apply, the notation N/A, not applicable, should be inserted.

STATUTE OF FRAUDS

The English law passed in 1667 known as the Statute of Frauds requires that the transfer of real estate be in writing. Virginia contract law prevents the enforcement of an oral contract or promise. [§11. 1] The statute does not invalidate oral contracts; rather, it addresses the contract's enforceability. The statute bars any action concerning a contract for the sale of real estate or for a lease on real property for *more than one* year unless the document is in writing. Although an oral lease for a term of more than one year is unenforceable and the parties cannot be compelled to perform, they are nonetheless free to make and comply with such an agreement. Further discussion of the Statement of Frauds may be found in the Code of Virginia, Title 8.2A-201 (Commercial Code).

CONTRACT PROCEDURES

Use of a standard form does not excuse the licensee from pointing out to both parties that the contract is a legally binding document and that legal advice should be sought if either party has legal questions. The parties may make the agreement contingent on review and approval by an attorney.

Power of Attorney — Sometimes, a party cannot be present at the closing and must be represented by an attorney-in-fact. In Virginia, the power of attorney must specify the transaction and the parties involved: a general power of attorney will not suffice. The power of attorney must be notarized and recorded with the deed.

In Practice — Many military notaries are from outside Virginia and may not comply with the requirements of the Virginia Code.

Spousal Consent — If property is owned in severalty *and the owner is married*, the seller's spouse should join in the contract so that no claims can be made later. If one or both spouses do not sign, the courts will not order specific performance on the contract unless the buyer is willing to accept a deed that remains subject to the spousal interest. The buyer may still sue the seller for breach of contract because the seller could not convey the property with a clear title.

The capacity in which each signer executes the contract should be clearly stated. The contract should indicate whether the signer is an individual, a married couple, a partnership, a corporation, a limited liability company, or any other legal entity.

Title — The buyer under a real estate sales contract expects to receive marketable title to the property from the seller. "Marketable title" and "insurable title" are not necessarily the same because a title insurance policy may list exceptions against which it does not insure.

Figure 7.1 Regional Sales Contract

REGIONAL SALES CONTRACT

This SALES CONTRACT ("Contract") is made on _____, ____, ("Contract Date") between _____ ("Purchaser") and _____ ("Seller") who hereby confirm and acknowledge by their initials and signatures below the prior disclosure that in this real estate transaction _____ ("Listing Company") represents the Seller, and _____ ("Selling Company") represents ☐ the Purchaser OR ☐ the Seller. The Listing Company and Selling Company are collectively referred to as ("Broker"). (If the brokerage firm is acting as a dual representative for both the Seller and the Purchaser, then the appropriate disclosure form is attached to and made a part of this Contract.)

1. **REAL PROPERTY.** The Purchaser will buy and the Seller will sell for the sales price ("Sales Price"), the Seller's entire interest in the land (with all improvements, rights and appurtenances) described as follows: TAX Map/ID # _____.
Legal Description: Lot(s) _____, Block/Square _____, Section _____,
Subdivision or Condominium _____, Unit # _____, Parking Space(s) # _____,
County/City _____, Deed Book/Liber _____, Page/Folio # _____,
Street Address: _____, State _____ Zip Code _____ ("Property").

2. **PERSONAL PROPERTY, FIXTURES AND UTILITIES.** The Sales Price includes the following personal property and fixtures: A. Any existing built-in heating and central air conditioning equipment, plumbing and lighting fixtures, sump pump, attic fans, storm windows, storm doors, screens, installed wall-to-wall carpeting, window shades, blinds, smoke and heat detectors, tv antennas, exterior trees and shrubs and, B. The items marked YES below as currently installed or offered.

YES	NO		YES	NO		YES	NO		YES	NO	
☐	☐	Stove or Range	☐	☐	Disposer	☐	☐	Ceiling Fan(s) # ____	☐	☐	Alarm System
☐	☐	Cooktop	☐	☐	Freezer	☐	☐	Washer	☐	☐	Intercom
☐	☐	Wall Oven(s) # ____	☐	☐	Window Fan(s) # ____	☐	☐	Dryer	☐	☐	Storage Shed(s) # ____
☐	☐	Refrigerator(s) # ____	☐	☐	Window A/C Unit(s) #	☐	☐	Furnace Humidifier	☐	☐	Garage Opener(s) # ____
☐	☐	w/ Ice maker(s) # ____	☐	☐	Pool, Equip. & Cover	☐	☐	Electronic Air Filter	☐	☐	w/ remote(s) # ____
☐	☐	Dishwasher	☐	☐	Hot Tub, Equip. & Cover	☐	☐	Central Vacuum	☐	☐	Playground Equipment
☐	☐	Built-in Microwave	☐	☐	Satellite Dish and Equip.	☐	☐	Water Treatment System	☐	☐	Wood Stove
☐	☐	Trash Compactor	☐	☐	Window Treatments	☐	☐	Exhaust Fan(s)	☐	☐	Fireplace Screen/ Doors

Other: _____
_____
_____

WATER, SEWAGE, HEATING AND CENTRAL AIR CONDITIONING: (Check all that apply)
Water Supply: ☐ Public ☐ Well _____ Hot Water: ☐ Oil ☐ Gas ☐ Elec. ☐ Other _____
Sewage Disposal: ☐ Public ☐ Septic # BR _____ Air Conditioning: ☐ Oil ☐ Gas ☐ Elec. ☐ Heat Pump ☐ Other _____
Heating: ☐ Oil ☐ Gas ☐ Elec. ☐ Heat Pump ☐ Other _____

3. **EQUIPMENT, MAINTENANCE AND CONDITION.** The Purchaser accepts the Property in the condition as of the Contract Date except as otherwise provided herein. The Seller warrants that the existing appliances, heating, cooling, plumbing, electrical systems and equipment, and smoke and heat detectors (as required), will be in normal working order as of the possession date. The Seller will deliver the Property in substantially the same condition as on the Contract Date and broom clean with all trash and debris removed. The Purchaser and the Seller will not hold the Broker liable for any breach of this paragraph.

4. **PRICE AND FINANCING**
   A. Down Payment $ _____
   B. Financing   1. First Trust $ _____
                 2. Second Trust $ _____
                 3. Seller Held Trust - addendum attached $ _____
             TOTAL FINANCING $ _____
             SALES PRICE $ _____

Regional Sales Contract - 9/99   K1261   Page 1 of 5   Please initial: Purchaser ____/____ Seller ____/____

Figure 7.1   **Regional Sales Contract (Continued)**

5. DEPOSIT. A. The Purchaser has made a deposit ("Deposit") with _____ ("Escrow Agent") of ☐ $_____ by check and/or ☐ $_____ by note due and payable on _____, _____, receipt of which is hereby acknowledged. B. The Deposit will be placed in an escrow account of the Escrow Agent after Date of Ratification to conform with the laws and regulations of the appropriate jurisdiction and/or, if VA financing applies, as required by Title 38 of the U.S. Code. This account may be interest bearing and all parties waive any claim to interest resulting from the Deposit. The Deposit will be held in escrow until: (i) Credited toward the Sales Price at Settlement; (ii) All parties have agreed in writing as to its disposition; (iii) A court of competent jurisdiction orders disbursement and all appeal periods have expired; or, (iv) Disposed of in any other manner authorized by the laws and regulations of the appropriate jurisdiction.

6. DOWN PAYMENT. The balance of the down payment will be paid at Settlement by certified or cashier's check or by bank wired funds.

7. DEED(S) OF TRUST.
  A. FIRST DEED OF TRUST. The Purchaser will ☐ OBTAIN **OR** ☐ ASSUME: a ☐ Conventional ☐ FHA ☐ VA ☐ Other _____ First Deed of Trust loan amortized over _____ years at a ☐ FIXED **OR** an ☐ ADJUSTABLE rate bearing (initial) interest of ____% per year or market rate available. Special Terms (if any): _____
  _____

  B. SECOND DEED OF TRUST. The Purchaser will ☐ OBTAIN, **OR** ☐ ASSUME a Second Deed of Trust loan amortized over _____ years at a ☐ FIXED **OR** an ☐ ADJUSTABLE rate bearing (initial) interest of ____% per year or market rate available. Special Terms (if any):_____
  _____

  C. ASSUMPTION ONLY: Assumption fee, if any, and all charges related to the assumption will be paid by the Purchaser. If the Purchaser assumes the Seller's loan; (i) The Purchaser and the Seller ☐ will, **OR** ☐ will not obtain a release of the Seller's liability to the U.S. Government for the repayment of the loan by Settlement. (ii) The Purchaser and Seller ☐ will, **OR** ☐ will not obtain substitution of the Seller's VA entitlement by Settlement. (iii) Balances of any assumed loans, secondary financing and cash down payments are approximate.

8. ADDITIONAL FINANCING TERMS.
  A. ☐ CONVENTIONAL FINANCING. Based on the financing terms specified in this Contract, the Seller will pay $_____ toward the Purchaser's charges, (including but not limited to loan origination fees, discount fees, buy down or subsidy fees, prepaids or other charges as allowed by the lender). The Purchaser will pay all remaining Purchaser's charges. If applicable, the Purchaser will pay at Settlement, or finance any initial private mortgage insurance.
  If the lender's appraisal is not equal to or greater than the Sales Price, the Purchaser will have the privilege and option of proceeding with consummation of this Contract without regard to the amount of the appraised valuation. The Purchaser's election to proceed with consummation of this Contract without regard to the amount of the appraised valuation will be made within 3 Days after the notification to the Purchaser of the appraised value. If the Purchaser does not make this election, it will be the Seller's option to lower the Sales Price to the appraised value and this Contract will remain in full force and effect at the lower Sales Price. If the Seller does not make this election, the parties may agree to mutually acceptable terms. Each election must be made by Notice within 3 Days after Notice from the other party. The parties will immediately sign any appropriate amendments. If the parties fail to agree, this Contract will become void.

  B. ☐ VA **OR** ☐ FHA FINANCING
  The Purchaser will ☐ pay at Settlement, **OR** ☐ finance any VA Funding Fee or FHA initial Mortgage Insurance Premium. Based on the financing specified in this Contract, the Seller will pay _____ toward the Purchaser's charges (including but not limited to loan origination fees, discount fees, buydown or subsidy fees, prepaids or other charges as allowed by the lender) except that the total amount of any lender charges which cannot by law or regulation be charged to the Purchaser will be paid by the Seller. These charges, if any, will first be deducted from any Seller credit, and the remaining balance, if any, will then be applied to the Purchaser's other charges. The Purchaser will pay all remaining Purchaser's charges. If VA or FHA financing applies, it is expressly agreed that, notwithstanding any other provisions of this Contract, the Purchaser will not be obligated to complete the purchase of the Property described herein or to incur any penalty by forfeiture of earnest money deposits or otherwise unless the Purchaser has been given in accordance with HUD/FHA or VA requirements a written statement by the Federal Housing Commissioner or Direct Endorsement Lender/Department of Veterans Affairs or the Lender Approval Processing Program (LAPP) underwriter setting forth the appraised value of the Property (excluding closing costs) of not less than $ _____. The Purchaser will have the privilege and option of proceeding with consummation of this Contract without regard to the amount of the appraised valuation. THE APPRAISED VALUATION IS ARRIVED AT TO DETERMINE THE MAXIMUM MORTGAGE THE DEPARTMENT OF HOUSING AND URBAN DEVELOPMENT /DEPARTMENT OF VETERANS AFFAIRS WILL INSURE/GUARANTEE. HUD/DEPARTMENT OF VETERANS AFFAIRS AND THE MORTGAGEE DOES NOT WARRANT THE VALUE NOR THE CONDITION OF THE PROPERTY. THE PURCHASER SHOULD SATISFY HIMSELF/HERSELF THAT THE PRICE AND CONDITION OF THE PROPERTY ARE ACCEPTABLE.
  If VA Financing applies, the Purchaser agrees that should the Purchaser elect to complete the purchase at an amount in excess of the reasonable value established by the Department of Veterans Affairs, the Purchaser shall pay such excess amount in cash from a source which the Purchaser agrees to disclose to the Department of Veterans Affairs, and which the Purchaser represents will not be borrowed funds except as approved by the Department of Veterans Affairs. The Purchaser's exercise of the option shall be made in writing within 3 Days of the notification to the Purchaser of the appraised value, or this Contract shall become void.
  If FHA financing applies, the Purchaser's exercise of the option of proceeding with consummation of this Contract without regard to the amount of the appraised valuation shall be made in writing within 3 Days of the notification to the Purchaser of the appraised value, or this Contract shall become void. The FHA loan amount may be approximate because the financed acquisition costs cannot be determined until the Settlement.

9. LOAN APPLICATION AND APPROVAL.
  A. FINANCING APPLICATION. The Purchaser will make written application for the financing or assumption called for in this Contract ("Specified Financing") within 7 days after Date of Ratification. The Purchaser grants permission for the Selling Company and the lender to disclose to the Listing Company and the Seller general information available about the progress of the loan application and loan approval process.
  B. LENDER'S APPROVAL CONTINGENCY. This Contract is contingent until 9 p.m. _____ Days after Date of Ratification ("Deadline") upon the Purchaser Delivering to the Seller a letter from the lender stating that the Purchaser is approved for the Specified Financing ("Lender's Letter"). Upon Seller's receipt of the Lender's Letter, this Contract is no longer contingent on the Purchaser being approved for the Specified Financing and this Contract will remain in full force and effect. TIME IS OF THE ESSENCE.
    (i) If the Purchaser does not Deliver the Lender's Letter by the Deadline, the lender's approval contingency will continue, unless the Seller at Seller's option gives Notice to Purchaser that this Contract will become void. If the Seller Delivers such Notice this Contract will become void at 9 p.m. on the third day following Delivery of Seller's Notice unless prior to that date and time:
      a. Purchaser Delivers to Seller the Lender's Letter; **OR**
      b. Purchaser removes this LENDER'S APPROVAL CONTINGENCY and provides Seller with evidence of sufficient funds available to complete Settlement without obtaining financing.
    (ii) The Purchaser may substitute alternative financing for Specified Financing provided:
      a. There is no additional expense to the Seller; and
      b. The Settlement Date is not delayed.
    (iii) If prior to satisfaction or removal of the LENDER'S APPROVAL CONTINGENCY the Purchaser receives a written rejection for the Specified Financing and Delivers a copy of the written rejection to the Seller, this Contract will become void.

Regional Sales Contract - 9/99 K1262   Page 2 of 5   Please initial: Purchaser ____/____ Seller ____/____

Figure 7.1   Regional Sales Contract (Continued)

C. DEFAULT. The Purchaser will be in default if Settlement does not occur on the Settlement Date because the Purchaser:
  (i) Fails to lock-in the interest rate(s) as specified above and the rate(s) increase so that the Purchaser no longer qualifies for such financing; **OR**
  (ii) Applies for, and fails to obtain, alternative financing instead of the Specified Financing, unless the Seller consents in writing to the alternative financing terms, in which case the alternative financing becomes the Specified Financing; **OR**
  (iii) Fails to comply with the lender's reasonable requirements in a timely manner; **OR**
  (iv) Fails to immediately give Notice to the Seller or the Broker of any material adverse changes in the Purchaser's assets, liabilities, or income; **OR**
  (v) Does not have the down payment, closing fees and any other funds to settle as provided in this Contract; **OR**
  (vi) Does or fails to do any act following the Date of Ratification that prevents the Purchaser from obtaining the financing; **OR**
  (vii) Makes any deliberate misrepresentations, material omissions or inaccuracies in financial information that results in the Purchaser's inability to secure the financing.

10. **PURCHASER'S REPRESENTATIONS.** The Purchaser ☐ will, **OR** ☐ will not occupy the Property as the Purchaser's principal residence. Unless specified in a written contingency, neither this Contract nor the financing is dependent or contingent on the sale and settlement or lease of other real property. The Selling Company ☐ is, **OR** ☐ is not authorized to disclose to the Listing Company and Seller the appropriate financial or credit information statement provided to the Selling Company by the Purchaser. The Purchaser acknowledges that the Seller is relying upon all of the Purchaser's representations including without limitation the accuracy of financial or credit information given to the Seller, Broker or the lender by the Purchaser.

11. **ACCESS TO PROPERTY.** The Seller will provide the Broker, the Purchaser, inspectors representing the Purchaser and representatives of lending institutions for appraisal purposes, reasonable access to the Property to comply with this Contract. The Purchaser and/or the Purchaser's representative will have the right to make an inspection prior to Settlement and/or occupancy, at which time the Seller will have all utilities in service.

12. **WELL AND SEPTIC.** If the Property is on well and/or septic systems, the ☐ Purchaser, at Purchaser's expense **OR** ☐ Seller, at Seller's expense, will furnish the Purchaser on or before Settlement with a certificate dated not more than 30 days prior to Settlement from the ☐ appropriate local government authority, or ☐ a private company, indicating that: A. The well water contains no more than the acceptable level of coliform bacteria and; B. The septic system appears to be functioning satisfactorily, and if known by public records, was installed pursuant to a valid health department permit. If either system is found defective or substandard according to the certificate, the Seller will take appropriate remedial action at the Seller's expense.

13. **TERMITE INSPECTION.** The ☐ Purchaser at the Purchaser's expense **OR** the ☐ Seller at the Seller's expense, will furnish a written report from a pest control firm dated not more than ☐ 30 **OR** ☐ 60 days prior to Settlement showing that all dwelling(s) and/or garage(s) within the Property (excluding fences or shrubs not abutting garage(s) or dwelling(s)) are free of visible evidence of active termites and other wood-destroying insects, and free from visible structural insect damage. Any extermination and structural repairs identified in the inspection report will be at the Seller's expense.

14. **REPAIRS.** If, as a condition of providing financing under this Contract, the lender requires repairs to be made to the Property, then the Purchaser will give Notice to the Seller of the lender's required repairs. Within 5 Days after Notice, the Seller will give Notice to the Purchaser whether the Seller will make the repairs. If the Seller will not make the repairs, the Purchaser will give Notice to the Seller within 5 Days after the Seller's Notice whether the Purchaser will make the repairs. If neither the Seller nor the Purchaser will make the repairs, then this Contract will become void. This clause will not release the Seller from any responsibilities set forth in the paragraphs titled PERSONAL PROPERTY, FIXTURES AND UTILITIES; EQUIPMENT, MAINTENANCE AND CONDITION; WELL AND SEPTIC; TERMITE INSPECTION; or OTHER TERMS, or any terms specifically set forth in this Contract and any addenda.

15. **DAMAGE OR LOSS.** The risk of damage or loss to the Property by fire, act of God, or other casualty remains with the Seller until the execution and delivery of the deed of conveyance.

16. **TITLE.** The title report and survey, if required, will be ordered promptly and, if not available on the Settlement Date, then Settlement may be delayed for up to 10 business days to obtain the title report and survey after which this Contract, at the option of the Seller, may be terminated and the Deposit will be refunded in full to the Purchaser according to the terms of the DEPOSIT paragraph. Fee simple title to the Property, and everything that conveys with it, will be sold free of liens except for any loans assumed by the Purchaser. The Seller will pay any special assessments and will comply with all orders, requirements, or notices of violations of any county or local authority, condominium unit owners' association, homeowners' or property owners' association or actions in any court on account thereof, against or affecting the Property on the Settlement Date. Title is to be good and marketable, and insurable by a licensed title insurance company with no additional risk premium. Title may be subject to commonly acceptable easements, covenants, conditions and restrictions of record, if any; otherwise, the Purchaser may declare this Contract void, unless the defects are of such character that they may be remedied within 30 Days beyond the Settlement Date. In case action is required to perfect the title, such action must be taken promptly by the Seller at the Seller's expense. The Broker is hereby expressly released from all liability for damages by reason of any defect in the title. The Seller will convey the Property by general warranty deed with English covenants of title (Virginia); general warranty deed (West Virginia); special warranty deed (D.C. and Maryland). The Seller will sign such affidavits, lien waivers, tax certifications, and other documents as may be required by the lender, title insurance company, Settlement Agent, or government authority, and authorizes the Settlement Agent to obtain pay-off or assumption information from any existing lenders.

17. **POSSESSION DATE.** Unless otherwise agreed to in writing between the Seller and the Purchaser, the Seller will give possession of the Property at the Settlement. If the Seller fails to do so and occupies the Property beyond the Settlement, the Seller will be a tenant by sufferance of the Purchaser and hereby expressly waives all notice to quit as required by law. The Purchaser will have the right to proceed by any legal means available to obtain possession of the Property. The Seller will pay any damages and costs incurred by the Purchaser including reasonable attorney fees.

18. **SETTLEMENT.** The Seller and the Purchaser will make full settlement in accordance with the terms of this Contract ("Settlement") on, or with mutual consent before, _____, ("Settlement Date") except as otherwise provided in this Contract.

19. **SETTLEMENT AGENT.** (Not for use in Virginia; see the Virginia Jurisdictional Addendum) The Purchaser selects _____ _____ ("Settlement Agent") to conduct the Settlement. Either party may retain their own counsel. The Purchaser agrees to contact the Settlement Agent within 10 Days after the Date of Ratification to schedule Settlement. The Settlement Agent will order the title exam and survey if required.

Regional Sales Contract - 9/99 K1263   Page 3 of 5   Please Initial: Purchaser ____ / ____ Seller ____ / ____

Figure 7.1 Regional Sales Contract (Continued)

20. FEES. Fees for the preparation of the Deed, that portion of the Settlement Agent's fee billed to the Seller, costs of releasing existing encumbrances, appropriate legal fees and any other proper charges assessed to the Seller will be paid by the Seller. Fees for the title exam (except as otherwise provided) survey, recording (including those for any purchase money trusts) and that portion of the Settlement Agent's fee billed to the Purchaser, appropriate legal fees and any other proper charges assessed to the Purchaser will be paid by the Purchaser. Fees to be charged will be reasonable and customary for the jurisdiction in which the Property is located. (Recording, Transfer and Grantor's Taxes are covered in the appropriate jurisdictional addenda).

21. BROKER'S FEE. The Seller irrevocably instructs the Settlement Agent to pay the Broker compensation ("Broker's Fee") as set forth in the listing agreement and to disburse the compensation offered by the Listing Company to the Selling Company in writing as of the Contract Date, and the remaining amount of Broker's compensation to the Listing Company.

22. ADJUSTMENTS. Rents, taxes, water and sewer charges, front foot benefit and house connection charges, condominium unit owners' association, homeowners' and/or property owners' association regular periodic assessments (if any) and any other operating charges, are to be adjusted to the day of Settlement. Any heating or cooking fuels remaining in supply tank(s) at Settlement will become the property of the Purchaser. Taxes, general and special, are to be adjusted according to the certificate of taxes issued by the collector of taxes, if any, except that recorded assessments for improvements completed prior to Settlement, whether assessments have been levied or not, will be paid by the Seller or allowance made at Settlement. If a Deed of Trust is assumed, interest will be adjusted to the Settlement Date and the Purchaser will reimburse the Seller for existing escrow accounts, if any.

23. ATTORNEY'S FEES. In any action or proceeding involving a dispute between the Purchaser and the Seller arising out of this Contract, the prevailing party will be entitled to receive from the other party reasonable attorney's fees to be determined by the court or arbitrator(s). In the event a dispute arises resulting in the Broker being made a party to any litigation or if the Broker is required to bring litigation to collect the Broker's Fee, the Purchaser and Seller agree to indemnify the Broker, its employees, and/or licensees for all attorney fees and costs of litigation, unless the litigation results in a judgment against the Broker, its employees and/or licensees.

24. PERFORMANCE. Delivery of the required funds and executed documents to the Settlement Agent will constitute sufficient tender of performance. Funds from this transaction at Settlement may be used to pay off any existing liens and encumbrances, including interest, as required by lender(s) or lienholders.

25. DEFAULT. If the Purchaser fails to complete Settlement, at the option of the Seller, the Deposit may be forfeited as liquidated damages and not as a penalty, in which event the Purchaser will be relieved from further liability to the Seller. If the Seller does not elect to accept the Deposit as liquidated damages, the Deposit may not be the limit of the Purchaser's liability in the event of a default. If the Deposit is forfeited, or if there is an award of damages by a court or a compromise agreement between the Seller and Purchaser, the Broker may accept and the Seller agrees to pay the Broker one-half of the Deposit in lieu of the Broker's Fee, (provided Broker's share of any forfeited Deposit will not exceed the amount due under the listing agreement). If the Seller fails to complete Settlement, the Purchaser will have all legal or equitable remedies, including specific performance and/or damages. If either the Seller or Purchaser refuses to execute a release of Deposit when requested to do so in writing and a court finds that they should have executed the agreement, the party who so refused to execute a release of Deposit will pay the expenses, including, without limitation, reasonable attorney's fees, incurred by the other party in the litigation. The Seller and Purchaser agree that no Escrow Agent will have any liability to any party on account of disbursement of the Deposit or on account of failure to disburse the Deposit, except only in the event of the Escrow Agent's gross negligence or willful misconduct. The parties further agree that the Escrow Agent will not be liable for the failure of any depository in which the Deposit is placed and that the Seller and Purchaser each will indemnify, defend and save harmless the Escrow Agent from any loss or expense arising out of the holding, disbursement or failure to disburse the Deposit, except in the case of the Escrow Agent's gross negligence or willful misconduct. If either the Purchaser or the Seller is in default, then in addition to all other damages, the defaulting party will immediately pay the costs incurred for the title examination, appraisal, survey and the Broker's Fee in full.

26. OTHER DISCLOSURES. The Purchaser and Seller are advised to seek professional advice concerning the condition of the Property or other legal and tax matters. The following subparagraphs disclose some matters which the parties may investigate further. These disclosures are not intended to create a contingency. Any contingency must be specified by adding appropriate terms to this Contract. The parties acknowledge the following disclosures:

A. PROPERTY CONDITION. See EQUIPMENT, MAINTENANCE AND CONDITION Paragraph. Various Inspection services and home warranty insurance programs are available. The Broker is not advising the parties as to certain other issues, including without limitation: water, sewer or septic; soil condition; flood hazard areas; possible restrictions of the use of the Property due to restrictive covenants, zoning, subdivision, or environmental laws, easements or other documents; airport or aircraft noise; planned land use, roads or highways; and construction materials and/or hazardous materials, including without limitation flame retardant treated plywood (FRT), radon, urea formaldehyde foam insulation (UFFI), polybutylene pipes, synthetic stucco (EIFS), underground storage tanks, asbestos and lead-based paint. Information relating to these issues may be available from appropriate government authorities.

B. LEGAL REQUIREMENTS. All contracts for the sale of real property must be in writing to be enforceable. Upon ratification and Delivery, this Contract becomes a legally binding agreement. Any changes must be made in writing.

C. FINANCING. Mortgage rates and associated charges vary with financial institutions and the marketplace. The Purchaser has the opportunity to select the lender and the right to negotiate terms and conditions of the financing subject to the terms of this Contract. The financing may require substantial lump sum (balloon) payments on the due dates. The Purchaser has not relied upon any representations regarding the future availability of mortgage money or interest rates for the refinancing of any such lump sum payments.

D. BROKER. The Broker may from time to time engage in the general insurance, title insurance, mortgage loan, real estate settlement, home warranty and other real estate-related businesses and services. Therefore, in addition to the Broker's Fee specified herein, the Broker may receive compensation related to other services provided in the course of this transaction. The Purchaser and Seller acknowledge that the Broker is being retained solely as a real estate agent and not as an attorney, tax advisor, lender, appraiser, surveyor, structural engineer, home inspector or other professional service provider.

27. ASSIGNABILITY. This Contract may not be assigned without the written consent of the Purchaser and the Seller. If the Purchaser and the Seller agree in writing to an assignment of this Contract, the original parties to this Contract remain obligated hereunder until Settlement.

28. DEFINITIONS. "Days" means calendar days unless otherwise specified. For the purpose of computing time periods, the first Day will be the Day following Delivery and the time period will end at 9 p.m. on the Day specified. If the Settlement Date falls on a Saturday, Sunday, or legal holiday, then the Settlement will be on the prior business day. "Date of Ratification" means the date of final acceptance in writing of all the terms of this Contract (not the date of expiration or removal of any contingencies). "Delivery" means hand-carried, sent by overnight delivery service, by facsimile transmission as provided for in the NOTICES Paragraph, or when receipt is acknowledged in writing. In the event of overnight delivery service, Delivery will be deemed to have been made on the Day following the sending. The masculine includes the feminine and the singular includes the plural.

Figure 7.1   Regional Sales Contract (Continued)

29. **NOTICES.** All notices ("Notice") required to be given by this Contract will be in writing and will be effective as of the date on which such Notice is Delivered:
    A. Addressed to the Seller at: _____ **OR**
    transmitted by facsimile to (____) _____;
    B. Addressed to the Purchaser at: _____ **OR**
    transmitted by facsimile to (____) _____.

30. **MISCELLANEOUS.** This Contract may be signed in one or more counterparts, each of which is deemed to be an original, and all of which together constitute one and the same instrument. Documents obtained via facsimile machines will also be considered as originals. Typewritten or handwritten provisions included in this Contract will control all pre-printed provisions that are in conflict.

31. **VOID CONTRACT.** If this Contract becomes void, both parties will immediately execute a release directing that the Deposit be refunded in full to the Purchaser according to the terms of the DEPOSIT paragraph.

32. **ADDITIONS.** The appropriate JURISDICTIONAL ADDENDUM and LEAD BASED PAINT ADDENDA (if applicable) must be attached and made a part of this Contract. The following are made a part of this Contract:
    ☐ Yes   STATE JURISDICTIONAL ADDENDUM ☐ DC ☐ VA ☐ MD ☐ WVA ☐ Other_____
    ☐ Yes ☐ No   HOME INSPECTION CONTINGENCY   ☐ Yes ☐ No   LEAD - BASED PAINT DISCLOSURE FORM
    ☐ Yes ☐ No   RADON TESTING CONTINGENCY   ☐ Yes ☐ No   LEAD - BASED PAINT INSPECTION CONTINGENCY
    ☐ Yes ☐ No   SALE OF HOME CONTINGENCY   ☐ Yes ☐ No   FHA HOME INSPECTION NOTICE
    ☐ Yes ☐ No   CONDO/COOP ADDENDUM (DC and MD)
    ☐ Yes ☐ No   HOME WARRANTY POLICY paid for by: ☐ Purchaser or ☐ Seller.
              Cost not to exceed $_____. Warranty provider to be_____.
    ☐ Yes ☐ No   OTHER (specify): _____

33. **OTHER TERMS.** _____
_____
_____
_____
_____
_____
_____

34. **ENTIRE AGREEMENT.** This Contract will be binding upon the parties, and each of their respective heirs, executors, administrators, successors and permitted assigns. The provisions hereof will survive the delivery of the deed and will not be merged therein. This Contract, unless amended in writing, contains the final and entire agreement of the parties and the parties will not be bound by any terms, conditions, oral statements, warranties or representations not herein contained. The interpretation of this Contract will be governed by the laws of the appropriate jurisdiction.

SELLER: **PURCHASER:**

_____/_____(SEAL)   _____/_____(SEAL)
Date   Signature   Date   Signature

_____/_____(SEAL)   _____/_____(SEAL)
Date   Signature   Date   Signature

Date of Ratification (see DEFINITIONS PARAGRAPH) _____, _____
****
For information purposes only:

Listing Company's Name and Address: Selling Company's Name and Address:
_____   _____
_____   _____
_____   _____

Office # _____ FAX # _____   Office # _____ FAX # _____
MRIS Broker Code: _____ MRIS Office ID# _____   MRIS Broker Code: _____ MRIS Office ID# _____
Agent Name _____   Agent Name _____
Agent MRIS ID# _____   Agent MRIS ID# _____
Agent Email Address _____   Agent Email Address _____

©This is a suggested form owned by certain REALTOR® Associations ("Associations"). This form has been created and printed exclusively for the use of REALTORS® and members of the Associations, who may copy or otherwise reproduce this form in identical form with the addition of their company logo and with any other changes being set forth in a clearly marked separate addendum. Any other use of this form by REALTORS® or members of Associations, or any use of this form whatsoever by non-members of Associations, is prohibited without prior written authorized consent of the Associations.

Regional Sales Contract - 9/99 K1265   Page 5 of 5

Figure 7.1   Regional Sales Contract (Continued)

VIRGINIA JURISDICTIONAL ADDENDUM

This Addendum is made on _____, _____, to a Sales Contract ("Contract") dated
_____ between _____ ("Purchaser")
and _____ ("Seller")
for the purchase and sale of the Property: _____.

    1. **SELLER FINANCING.** The Seller shall provide a ☐ First ☐ Second ☐ Third Deed of Trust loan for $_____ secured by the Property, payable at approximately $_____ per month or more including _____ % interest per year, the payment to be applied first to interest with the remainder applied to principal and with the balance due _____ years from the date of settlement. If the Property or any interest therein is transferred, sold or conveyed, the note shall be due and payable in full unless the transfer, sale or conveyance is consented to in writing by the then current noteholder. The note may be paid in full or in part at any time without penalty. Any default or failure to pay any other lien or encumbrance on the Property shall be a default of the trust unless cured within 10 Days after written notice from the noteholder. A late charge of 5% shall be due on monthly payments received more than 10 Days late. The trust will require that the Purchaser provide immediate written proof to the noteholder of payment for taxes and insurance when due. The trust will contain a provision assigning rents to the noteholder in the event of default. The Purchaser shall furnish the Seller within 5 business days after the date of Contract Acceptance with a financial statement and credit report from a credit reporting agency at the Purchaser's expense, and promptly comply with additional reasonable requests of the Seller. The Seller grants loan approval under the terms of this paragraph unless the Seller notifies the Purchaser otherwise in writing within 3 business days after receipt of all the Purchaser's financial data. Approval shall not be unreasonably withheld. This Contract is contingent, ☐Yes ☐No, for _____ business days after the date of Contract Acceptance on the Seller obtaining a written commitment for the sale of the note at settlement at a discount not to exceed _____%, or this Contract shall be voidable at the option of the Seller.

    2. **VIRGINIA PROPERTY OWNERS' ASSOCIATION ACT.** The Seller represents that the Property ☐ is, **OR** ☐ is not located within a development which is subject to the Virginia Property Owners' Association Act ("POA Act"). If the Property is within such a development, the POA Act requires the Seller to obtain from the property owners' association an Association Disclosure Packet and provide it to the Purchaser. The information contained in the Association Disclosure Packet shall be current as of a date-specified on the Association Disclosure Packet.
    The Purchaser may cancel this Contract: (1) within 3 Days after the date of Contract Acceptance, if on or before the date of Contract Acceptance, the Purchaser receives the Association Disclosure Packet or Notice that the Association Disclosure Packet is not available; (2) within 3 Days after hand-delivered receipt of the Association Disclosure Packet or Notice that the Association Disclosure Packet is not available; or (3) within 6 Days after the postmark date if the Association Disclosure Packet or Notice that the Association Disclosure Packet is not available is mailed to the Purchaser. The Purchaser may also cancel this Contract at any time prior to settlement if the Purchaser has not been notified that the Association Disclosure Packet will not be available and the Association Disclosure Packet is not delivered to the Purchaser. Written notice of cancellation shall be hand-delivered or mailed, return receipt requested, within the cancellation period to the Seller. Such cancellation shall be without penalty; this Contract shall become void, both parties will promptly execute a release and the Deposit shall be refunded in full to the Purchaser.
    The Purchaser, at the Purchaser's expense, may submit a copy of the Contract to the association along with a request for assurance from the association that the information submitted in the Association Disclosure Packet remains materially unchanged, or if there have been material changes, a statement specifying such changes.
    The right to receive the association disclosure packet and to cancel this Contract terminates at settlement.

    3. **VIRGINIA CONDOMINIUM ACT.** The Seller represents that the Property ☐ is, **OR** ☐ is not a condominium unit. If the Property is a condominium unit, this Contract is subject to the Virginia Condominium Act which requires the Seller to obtain from the Unit Owners' Association certain financial and other disclosures ("Resale Certificate") and provide it to the Purchaser. If the required disclosures are not available on the Date of Ratification, the Seller shall promptly request them from the Unit Owners' Association and provide them to the Purchaser who shall acknowledge receipt in writing upon Delivery. The information contained in the Resale Certificate shall be current as of a date-specified on the Resale Certificate.
    The Purchaser may cancel this Contract: (1) within 3 Days after the Contract Date, if the Purchaser receives the Resale Certificate on or before the date that the Purchaser signs the contract; (2) within 3 Days after receiving the Resale Certificate if the Resale Certificate is hand delivered; or (3) within 6 Days after the postmark date if the Resale Certificate is sent to the Purchaser by United States mail, return receipt requested. Written Notice of cancellation shall be hand-delivered or mailed, return receipt requested, within the cancellation period to the unit owner selling the unit. Such cancellation shall be without penalty; this Contract shall become void, both parties will promptly execute a release and the Deposit shall be refunded in full to the Purchaser.
    Within three days of receiving the Resale Certificate from the Seller, the Purchaser, at the Purchaser's expense, may submit a copy of the Contract to the Unit Owner's Association along with a request for assurance from the association that the information submitted in the Resale Certificate remains materially unchanged, or if there have been material changes, a statement specifying such changes. If the Purchaser fails to submit a proper request and any required fees to the Unit Owners' Association within this three day period the Purchaser thereby waives the right to cancel the Contract based on material changes to the disclosures contained in the Resale Certificate or based on the Unit Owners' Association's failure to provide the required statement. The right to receive the Resale Certificate and to cancel this Contract terminates at settlement.
    If the Purchaser submits a timely request for a statement of assurance together with any required payments to the Unit Owner's Association, the Purchaser may cancel the Contract within three days of (1) receipt of a statement that there have been one or more material changes to the Resale Certificate, or (2) the date upon which the Unit Owners' Association was required to have furnished such statement, but only if the Unit Owners' Association fails to provide the required statement within the time permitted by law.
    Notice of cancellation shall be in writing and sent in accord with the Notice provisions of the Contract. Purchaser's failure to send Notice of cancellation within the allotted time frames shall extinguish Purchaser's rights to cancel the contract under the Virginia Condominium Owners' Association Act. Such cancellation shall be without penalty; this Contract shall become void, both parties shall promptly execute a release and the Deposit shall be refunded in full to the Purchaser.

NVAR - Virginia Jurisdictional Addendum - 5/01 - K1277   Page 1 of 2   Please Initial: Purchaser ____/____ Seller ____/____

Figure 7.1 Regional Sales Contract (Continued)

4. **TARGET LEAD-BASED PAINT HOUSING.** The Seller represents that any residential dwellings at the Property ☐ were **OR** ☐ were not constructed before 1978. If the dwellings were constructed before 1978, then, unless exempt under 42 U.S.C. 4852d, this Contract is **not complete** and **not ratified** unless it includes, and the Seller and the Purchaser both accept, the following **two** amendatory forms: A. "Sale: Disclosure and Acknowledgment of Information on Lead-Based Paint and/or Lead-Based Paint Hazards", **AND** B. "Sales Contract Addendum for Lead-Based Paint Testing".

5. **VIRGINIA RESIDENTIAL PROPERTY DISCLOSURE ACT.** The Virginia Residential Property Disclosure Act requires the Seller to deliver a disclaimer or disclosure statement prior to the acceptance of this Contract unless the transfer of the Property is exempt. The law allows the Seller, on a disclaimer or disclosure statement provided by the Real Estate Board, either to: (1) make no representations or warranties to the condition of the Property and sell the Property "as is", except as otherwise provided in this Contract; **OR** (2) make a written disclosure concerning the Property, based on the Seller's knowledge of its condition. If the Seller furnishes a disclosure statement, then the Seller is required at settlement to disclose any material change in the physical condition of the Property or to certify to the Purchaser that the condition of the Property is substantially the same. If the disclaimer or disclosure required by law is delivered to the Purchaser after the acceptance of this Contract, the Purchaser may terminate this Contract by giving written notice to the Seller either by hand delivery or by United States mail, postage prepaid, at or prior to the earliest of (1) 3 Days after delivery of the disclosure or disclaimer in person, (2) 5 Days after the postmark if the disclosure or disclaimer is properly mailed, (3) settlement on the Property, (4) occupancy of the Property by the Purchaser, (5) written waiver by the Purchaser in a separate document, or (6) the Purchaser's application for a mortgage loan where such application contains a disclosure that the right to terminate ends upon applying for the mortgage loan.

6. **POSSIBLE FILING OF MECHANICS' LIEN.**   **NOTICE**
Virginia law (Section 43-1 et seq.) permits persons who have performed labor or furnished materials for the construction, removal, repair or improvement of any building or structure to file a lien against the property. This lien may be filed at any time after the work is commenced or the material is furnished, but not later than the earlier of (i) 90 Days from the last day of the month in which the lienor last performed work or furnished materials or (ii) 90 Days from the time the construction, removal, repair or improvement is terminated. AN EFFECTIVE LIEN FOR WORK PERFORMED PRIOR TO THE DATE OF SETTLEMENT MAY BE FILED AFTER SETTLEMENT. LEGAL COUNSEL SHOULD BE CONSULTED.

7. **CONSUMER REAL ESTATE SETTLEMENT PROTECTION ACT.**
Choice of Settlement Agent: You have the right to select a settlement agent to handle the closing of this transaction. The settlement agent's role in closing your transaction involves the coordination of numerous administrative and clerical functions relating to the collection of documents and the collection and disbursement of funds required to carry out the terms of the contract between the parties. If part of the purchase price is financed, your lender will instruct the settlement agent as to the signing and recording of loan documents and the disbursement of loan proceeds. No settlement agent can provide legal advice to any party to the transaction except a settlement agent who is engaged in the private practice of law in Virginia and who has been retained or engaged by a party to the transaction for the purpose of providing legal services to that party.

Escrow, closing and settlement service guidelines: The Virginia State Bar issues guidelines to help settlement agents avoid and prevent the unauthorized practice of law in connection with furnishing escrow, settlement or closing services. As a party to a real estate transaction, you are entitled to receive a copy of these guidelines from your settlement agent, upon request, in accordance with the provisions of the Consumer Real Estate Settlement Protection Act.

This section supersedes the SETTLEMENT AGENT section of the Contract. ☐ Purchaser ☐ Seller wishes to employ _____ _____ ("Settlement Agent") to represent the Contract. The Purchaser agrees to contact the Settlement Agent within 10 Days of Contract Acceptance to schedule settlement, which Settlement Agent shall order the title exam and survey if required.

8. **ADDITIONAL FEES.** Grantors tax shall be paid by the Seller. The Purchaser shall pay recording charges for the Deed and any purchase money trusts.

9. **TIME IS OF THE ESSENCE AS TO ALL TERMS OF THIS CONTRACT.**

SELLER: **PURCHASER:**

_____/_____(SEAL)   _____/_____(SEAL)
Date   Signature   Date   Signature

_____/_____(SEAL)   _____/_____(SEAL)
Date   Signature   Date   Signature

© 2001 Northern Virginia Association of REALTORS, Inc.
This is a suggested form of the Northern Virginia Association of REALTORS®, Inc. ("NVAR"). This form has been exclusively printed for the use of REALTOR® and Non-Resident members of NVAR, who may copy or otherwise reproduce this form in identical form with the addition of their company logo. Any other use of this form by REALTOR® and Non-Resident members of NVAR, or any use of this form whatsoever by non-members of NVAR is prohibited without the prior written consent of NVAR. Notwithstanding the above, no REALTOR® or Non-Resident member of NVAR, or any other person, may copy or otherwise reproduce this form for purposes of resale.

NVAR - Virginia Jurisdictional Addendum - 5/01 - K1277   Page 2 of 2

Figure 7.1   Regional Sales Contract (Continued)

NVAR CONTINGENCIES/CLAUSES ADDENDUM TO SALES CONTRACT

This Addendum is made on _____, _____, to a Sales Contract ("Contract") dated
_____, _____ between _____("Purchaser") and
_____("Seller")
for the purchase and sale of the Property: _____.
The following provisions if initialed by the parties are incorporated into and made a part of this Contract:

1. CONTINGENCIES. This Contract is contingent upon the satisfaction of the contingencies set forth below ("Contingencies") until the expiration of the time periods for such Contingencies set forth below ("Deadlines"). **This Contract will become void unless each Contingency has been removed in writing by the Deadline, or satisfied, or terminated.** If this Contract is voided, the parties will sign an agreement releasing each other party from the terms of this Contract, the Deposit will then be refunded to the Purchaser, and the parties will have no further liability under this Contract.

    A. HOME INSPECTION. This Contract is contingent until 9 p.m. _____ Days after the Date of Ratification ("Deadline") upon inspection of the Property by a professional home inspector and/or other professional inspector(s) at the Purchaser's discretion and expense. The Seller will have all utilities in service at the time of the inspection(s). The Contingency will terminate at the Deadline unless by the Deadline the Purchaser has Delivered to the Seller a copy of the inspection report(s) and

        (i) a written addendum listing the specific existing deficiencies. The Seller may, at the Seller's option, within _____ Days after Delivery of the addendum, elect in writing to remedy the deficiencies prior to settlement. If the Seller does not elect to make the repairs, or makes a counter-offer, or does not respond, the Purchaser will have _____ Days after Delivery of Seller's counter-offer or the expiration of the period in which Seller had to respond, to respond or remove this Contingency and take the Property in its present physical condition or this contract will become void. Any counter-offer of Purchaser, and any subsequent counter-offer by either party, shall be responded to by the other party within _____ Days of Delivery of such counter-offer. The failure of one party to respond to such counter-offer within the required response period shall result in the Contract becoming void at the expiration of that response period.

        Unless otherwise agreed to in writing between the parties, this clause does not release the Seller from any responsibilities set forth in the Contract paragraphs titled: PERSONAL PROPERTY, FIXTURES AND UTILITIES; EQUIPMENT, MAINTENANCE AND CONDITION; WELL AND SEPTIC; TERMITE INSPECTION; OTHER TERMS, any other property condition paragraph, or any items specifically set forth in this Contract and any addendum, amendment, or Notice.

-OR-

        (ii) Notice voiding this Contract.

    B. RADON TESTING. This Contract is contingent until 9 p.m. _____ Days after the Date of Ratification ("Deadline") upon the Purchaser, at the Purchaser's discretion and expense, having the Property inspected for the presence of radon by a testing firm ("Testing Firm") listed with the National Radon Safety Board ("NRSB"), or The National Environmental Health Association ("NEHA") using an U.S. Environmental Protection Agency ("EPA") approved testing method. **Testing device to be placed and retrieved by an NRSB or NEHA listed technician.** This contingency will terminate at the Deadline unless by the Deadline the Purchaser has Delivered to the Seller a copy of the radon testing report which confirms the presence of radon that equals or exceeds the action level established by the EPA together with either:

        (i) A written addendum requiring the Seller at Seller's expense prior to Settlement to address the radon condition by contracting with an **NRSB or NEHA listed remediation firm** to reduce the presence of radon below the action level established by the EPA and by providing the Purchaser with written re-test results performed by a **Testing Firm** confirming such reduction of radon. The Seller may, at the Seller's option, within _____ Days after Delivery of the addendum, elect in writing to remedy the condition prior to settlement.

    If the Seller does not elect to perform in accordance with the addendum, or makes a counter-offer, or does not respond, the Purchaser will have _____ Days after Delivery of Seller's counter-offer or the expiration of the period in which Seller had to respond, to respond or remove this Contingency and take the Property in its present physical condition or this contract will become void. Any counter-offer of Purchaser, and any subsequent counter-offer by either party, shall be responded to by the other party within _____ Days of Delivery of such counter-offer. The failure of one party to respond to such counter-offer within the required response period shall result in the Contract becoming void at the expiration of that response period.

-OR-

        (ii) Notice voiding this Contract.

    C. SALE OF THE PURCHASER'S PROPERTY AND KICK-OUT. This Contract is contingent until 9 p.m. _____ Days after the Date of Ratification ("Deadline") upon the sale of the Purchaser's property located at _____
_____("Purchaser's Property"). If the Purchaser does not satisfy or remove this contingency by the Deadline pursuant to paragraph C(iii) below, this Contract will become void.

      (i) The Seller may continue to offer the Property for sale and accept bona fide back-up offers to this Contract until this contingency is satisfied or removed. If a back-up offer is accepted, the Seller will Deliver Notice to the Purchaser requiring that this contingency be satisfied or removed pursuant to paragraph C(iii) below not later than 9 p.m. _____ days after Delivery of the Notice, or this Contract will become void.

      (ii) The Purchaser's Property will be listed exclusively and actively marketed by a licensed real estate broker and entered into a multiple listing service within 3 Days after the Date of Ratification at a price not to exceed $ _____.

      (iii) The Purchaser may:

NVAR - 1226 10/2000   Page 1 of 3

Figure 7.1   **Regional Sales Contract (Continued)**

(a) satisfy this contingency by Delivering to the Seller by this contingency Deadline a copy of the ratified contract for the sale of the Purchaser's Property with evidence that all contingencies, other than financing, have been removed or waived, along with a prequalification letter as described in the QUALIFICATION LETTER CONTINGENCY paragraph of this addendum for the purchaser of the Purchaser's Property.

-OR-

(b) remove this contingency by Delivering to the Seller (1) the Lender's Letter stating that the financing is not contingent in any manner upon the sale and settlement of any real estate or obtaining a lease of any real estate and that the Purchaser has sufficient funds available for the down payment and closing costs necessary to complete Settlement; OR (2) Evidence of sufficient funds available to complete Settlement without obtaining financing.

(iv) If the Purchaser satisfies the requirements of paragraph C(i) above, this Contract will remain contingent upon the settlement of the sale of the Purchaser's Property. This paragraph will survive the satisfaction of the contingency for the sale of the Purchaser's Property. Settlement (under this Contract) may not be delayed more than _____ Days after the Settlement Date (specified in this Contract) without the parties' written consent. If a further delay is required to obtain coinciding settlements and the parties do not agree, then this Contract will become void. If at any time after the Date of Ratification the contract for the sale of the Purchaser's Property becomes void, the Purchaser will immediately Deliver Notice to the Seller together with evidence of such voiding, at which time either the Seller or the Purchaser may declare this Contract void by Delivering Notice to the other party.

D. QUALIFICATION LETTER CONTINGENCY. This Contract is contingent until 9 p.m. _____ Days after the Date of Ratification ("Deadline") upon the Purchaser Delivering to the Seller a prequalification letter from an institutional lender stating that the financing described in this Contract is available to the Purchaser and, based upon a preliminary credit report and the information provided by the Purchaser, the financing should be committed subject to appropriate verification, approval and commitment. At anytime after the Deadline but prior to Delivery to the Seller of the prequalification letter, the Seller may with Notice to the Purchaser declare this Contract void.

E. CONTINGENT ON THE SELLER PURCHASING ANOTHER HOME. This Contract is contingent until 9 p.m., _____ Days after the Date of Ratification upon the Seller Delivering a notice to the Purchaser that: (1) the Seller has entered into a ratified contract to purchase another home; OR (2) the Seller removes this Contingency.

F. GIFT LETTER. This Contract is contingent until 9 p.m., _____ Days after the Date of Ratification ("Deadline") upon the Purchaser providing a gift letter and necessary documentation satisfactory to the lender in the amount of $_____ from _____. At anytime after the Deadline but prior to Delivery to the Seller of the gift letter, the Seller may with Notice to the Purchaser declare this Contract void. Once the gift letter has been Delivered, if the Purchaser does not have the gift funds to settle as provided in this Contract, the Purchaser will be in default.

G. THIRD PARTY APPROVAL. This Contract is contingent upon the approval of _____ by 9 p.m. ___ Days after the Date of Ratification ("Deadline"). If Notice of disapproval is not Delivered to the other party by the Deadline, this contingency will terminate and this Contract will remain in full force and effect. No Notice of approval is required. If Notice of disapproval is Delivered by the Deadline, this Contract will become void.

H. GENERAL. This Contract is contingent until 9 p.m. _____ Days after the Date of Ratification("Deadline") upon:

_____
_____
_____
_____
_____
_____
_____
_____
_____
_____

2. **CLAUSES.**

Figure 7.1 Regional Sales Contract (Continued)

A. BACK-UP CONTRACT OR OFFER. This Contract is first back-up to another contract or offer dated _____ _____, _____ between the Seller and _____ as the purchaser. This Contract becomes the primary contract immediately upon Notice from the Seller that the other contract or offer is void. The Purchaser may void this back up Contract at any time by Delivering Notice to the Seller prior to Delivery of Notice from the Seller that this Contract has become the primary Contract. If the other contract settles, this Contract will become void. The rights and obligations of the parties under the primary contract are superior to the rights and obligations of the parties to this back-up Contract.

B. "COINCIDING" SETTLEMENTS. Settlement of this Contract is contingent upon the settlement of the contract for the sale of the Purchaser's property located at _____ ("Purchaser's Property"). Settlement (under this Contract) may not be delayed more than _____ Days after the Settlement Date (specified in this Contract) without the parties' written consent. If a further delay is required to obtain coinciding settlements and the parties do not agree, then this Contract will become void. If at any time after the Date of Ratification the contract for the sale of the Purchaser's Property becomes void, the Purchaser will immediately Deliver Notice to the Seller together with evidence of such voiding, at which time either the Seller or the Purchaser may declare this Contract void by Delivering Notice to the other party.

C. "AS IS" PROPERTY CONDITION. The Property is sold in its "As Is" physical condition, to be determined as of the ☐ Contract Date, ☐ the date of the home inspection **OR** ☐ other _____. The Seller makes no representation or warranty, express or implied, as to the condition of the Property or any equipment or system contained therein. All clauses in this Contract pertaining to Property condition, termites or compliance with city, state or county regulations are hereby deleted from this Contract. The Seller will have no obligation to make repairs to the electrical, plumbing, heating air conditioning, or any other mechanical system, equipment or fixture. Smoke detectors will be installed as required by the laws or regulations of the appropriate jurisdiction.

D. REAL ESTATE LICENSED PARTIES. The parties acknowledge that ☐ the Seller **OR** ☐ the Purchaser is a real estate licensee in ☐ DC ☐ MD ☐ VA ☐ WV ☐ Other _____.

E. PRE- OR POST-SETTLEMENT OCCUPANCY AGREEMENT. The parties adopt the attached occupancy agreement as part of this Contract.

Copies of any addenda, amendments, and Notices required by the Contract will be provided to the Brokers at the Brokers' addresses provided in the Contract. The parties agree that any such copies sent to the Broker will NOT constitute Delivery and will be for informational purposes only.

Except as modified by this Addendum, all of the terms and provisions of this Contract are hereby expressly ratified and confirmed and will remain in full force and effect.

WITNESS OUR SIGNATURES AND SEALS:

SELLER: **PURCHASER:**

_____/_____(SEAL)   _____/_____(SEAL)
Date   Signature   Date   Signature

_____/_____(SEAL)   _____/_____(SEAL)
Date   Signature   Date   Signature

© 2000 Northern Virginia Association of REALTORS®, Inc.

This is a suggested form of the Northern Virginia Association of REALTORS®, Inc. ("NVAR"). This form has been created and printed exclusively for the use of REALTORS® and Non-Resident members of NVAR, who may copy or otherwise reproduce this form in identical form with the addition of their company logo. Any other use of this form by REALTORS® and Non-Resident members of NVAR, or any use of this form whatsoever by non-members of NVAR, is prohibited without the prior written consent of NVAR. Notwithstanding the above, no REALTOR® or Non-Resident member of NVAR, or any other person, may copy or otherwise reproduce this form for purposes of resale.

NVAR - 1226 10/2000   Page 3 of 3

Equitable Title

When the buyer and seller have ratified, that is, signed, the sales contract, the buyer's interest is called *equitable title*. A buyer's equitable title gives the buyer an insurable interest in the property. While Virginia law places the risk of damage to the property during this period on the buyer, most sales contracts in Virginia provide that the seller bears the risk of loss. Licensees should ensure that this point is addressed in the contract.

WARRANTIES

As discussed in previous Chapters, the principle of *caveat emptor*, "let the buyer beware," is still the law in Virginia regarding previously owned homes.

Existing Homes

In most areas, the seller will warrant that the heating, plumbing, electrical, and air-conditioning systems are in normal working order at the time of settlement. The buyer usually has the opportunity for a walkthrough inspection prior to settlement to verify that no material changes have occurred since the signing of the sales contract (such as storm damage, vandalism, or the removal of fixtures). If there have been any changes, the seller is required to inform the buyer of them, regardless of whether a walkthrough is to be performed. It is a buyer's responsibility to determine what conditions beyond the property's boundaries may affect its value.

New Construction

For new homes, the builder normally supplies a detailed warranty, primarily to limit his or her liability, which includes either a five-year or ten-year warranty against foundation defects. At the time of closing, there is an implied warranty that the dwelling and its fixtures (to the seller's best actual knowledge) are free from structural defects and constructed in a professional manner. A *structural defect* is a flaw that reduces the stability or safety of the structure below accepted standards or that restricts the normal use of the structure. The implied warranties continue for one year after the date of transfer of title or the buyer's taking possession, whichever occurs first.

Questions

1. The buyer and seller agree to the sale of Blackacre for $100,000. No written contract is signed, but the seller accepts payment in full from the buyer and delivers the deed. Which of the following statements is TRUE?
   1. The sale is without legal effect; the seller continues to own Blackacre.
   2. The sale violates the Statute of Frauds' maximum amount for oral contracts.
   3. The sale is enforceable in a court of law under the Statute of Frauds, due to the parties' compliance.
   4. The sale is unenforceable under the Statute of Frauds, but the parties are free to comply with its terms.

2. Which of the following statements with regard to a power of attorney is NOT TRUE?
   1. A general power of attorney may be used in a real estate transaction.
   2. A party that cannot attend the closing on a property may designate an attorney-in-fact.
   3. A power of attorney must be notarized.
   4. A power of attorney must be recorded with the deed.

3. Two weeks after a buyer and seller signed a sales contract on a house, the house burned to the ground. If the contract is silent on the issue, which party is liable?
   1. The buyer only, under his or her equitable title interest.
   2. The buyer and seller share the risk of loss equally.
   3. The seller, because he or she continues to possess title to the property.
   4. The seller, under the implied condition of good faith.

4. *D* built a house with the intention of selling it. During construction, the foundation cracked and *D* was forced to build the bearing walls of a lighter material to keep the entire structure from collapsing. *D's* engineer told him that a strong wind would probably blow the house down. Nonetheless, the cracked foundation and structural shortcuts were easily covered over, and *D* sold the house to a first-time homebuyer without mentioning the defects. Two weeks after closing, the house collapsed in a thunderstorm. Is *D* liable?
   1. No, under *caveat emptor*.
   2. No, because the buyer never asked about specific defects.
   3. Yes; due to the implied warranty against structural defects.
   4. Yes, due to the failure to have the property inspected.

5. *P* owns a vacation cabin in the Blue Ridge Mountains. *K* stops by *P's* house and asks to rent the cabin from February through December for $550 per month. *P* agrees. If *K* fails to make the rent payments, is the contract enforceable?
   1. No; an oral contract for the sale or lease of real estate is not enforceable.
   2. No; contracts for more than $5,000 must be in writing to be enforceable.
   3. Yes; the Statute of Frauds applies only to the sale of real property.
   4. Yes; an oral lease for a term of less than one year is enforceable.

8 Transfer of Title

REQUIREMENTS FOR A VALID CONVEYANCE

In Virginia, the requirements for a valid deed are as follows:

- Grantor who has the legal capacity to execute the deed
- Grantee
- Consideration
- Granting clause
- Accurate legal description of the property
- Any relevant exceptions or reservations
- Signature of the grantor, sometimes with acknowledgment
- Delivery and acceptance of the deed

Grantor

In Virginia, the same person may be the grantor and grantee in a deed. For example: *G* can convey the deed to his farm to himself and his grandson *M*.

Grantee

The grantee named to receive a deed to real property should be legally competent to receive the property. The grantee's full name should be used in preparing the deed. A deed to a nonexistent person is a valid conveyance to the intended but misnamed grantee if the intended grantee exists and the intention of the parties can be determined.

Competence

The grantor is presumed to have been competent at the time a deed was executed. The test of legal capacity is the party's mental ability to understand the nature and consequences of the transaction at the time it is entered into. The burden of proving incompetence is on the party who attacks the validity of the deed.

In Virginia, a conveyance of land by a minor is a valid transfer of title, unless it is repudiated by the minor after he or she attains majority. Repudiation may occur even though the grantee has already conveyed the property to another purchaser without notice that a minor was the grantor in the previous transaction.

Habendum Clause

The *habendum clause*, "to have and to hold," is rarely used in Virginia.

8   TRANSFER OF TITLE

Power of Attorney

If a seller or buyer is unable to attend the closing, there are two options:

1. Prepare all papers to be signed in advance of the closing or
2. Use a power of attorney

A power of attorney must be signed by the seller with the same formalities as a deed. Although a power of attorney can be general or specific, *a specific power of attorney is required to convey real property in Virginia.* In reviewing a power of attorney, the licensee should have a lawyer verify that it specifically authorizes performance of all necessary acts, and that the attorney-in-fact performs in accordance with the authority granted in the power of attorney.

Affidavits and other sworn statements cannot be signed by the attorney-in-fact. These must be signed by the principal prior to the closing. The deed or other instrument to be signed must indicate that it is being signed by an attorney-in-fact. Normally, this is accomplished by a recital in the body of the instrument or under the signature line.

If an institutional lender is making a new loan, the lender's permission should be obtained for a borrower to execute a power of attorney. The lender may not allow the use of an attorney-in-fact, especially if the loan is subject to truth-in-lending requirements.

A power of attorney must be recorded, and the recording fees are charged to the party using the attorney-in-fact. If the power of attorney is not recorded, it is as though the deed were unsigned by the party being represented by the attorney-in-fact.

TRANSFER TAXES AND FEES

Recordation Tax

With certain exceptions, all deeds are subject to state and city or county recording tax. The state tax is currently $.15 per $100 (or fraction of $100) of the consideration paid or the value of the property, whichever is greater. The county or city tax is one-third of that amount, or $.05 per $100 (or fraction of $100).

These taxes are usually paid by the buyer and collected at closing. Payment of these taxes is a prerequisite to having the deed recorded.

> **In Practice**   Recording fees are subject to change. Licensees should always be aware of the most current tax rates and fees.

Grantor Tax

In addition to the recordation taxes, all deeds are subject to a grantor's tax of $.50 per $500 (or a fraction of $500) of the purchase price or the value of the grantor's equity in the property being transferred, in the case of assumption. (In many areas of Virginia, the rate is quoted as $1.00 per $1,000.) The grantor's tax is paid by the seller and is collected at closing and paid to the clerk of the county where the deed is recorded.

Calculating Virginia Transfer Taxes
B purchases S's home for $175,600

1. STATE AND CITY RECORDATION TAX

$175,600 ÷ 100 = 1,756 "recordation tax units"

B will pay $263.40 in state recordation taxes (1,756 × $.15 = $263.40) and $87.80 in county or city recordation tax (1,756 × $.05 = $87.80)

2. GRANTOR TAX

$175,600 ÷ 500 = 351.2 "grantor tax units"

Round up to 352 "grantor tax units"

Sue's grantor tax is 352 "grantor tax units" × $.50 = $176

Tax on Deeds of Trust and Mortgages

Unless exempted, deeds of trust and mortgages are taxed on a sliding scale, according to the amount of the obligation (that is, the debt) that the instrument secures. If the amount is not ascertainable, the tax is based on the fair market value of the property, including the value of any improvements as of the date of the deed. Deeds of trust are also subject to city or county recordation taxes, clerk's fees, and any plat recordation fees.

Deeds of trust that secure both construction loans and permanent loans are normally subject to tax on deeds of trust.

Transfer and Clerk Fees

For each document admitted to record, the clerk of court collects a transfer fee that is generally paid by the buyer. In addition to the transfer fee, the clerk of court collects a clerk fee for recording plats, powers of attorney, certificates of satisfaction, and release of judgments. The amount of the fee is usually based on the number of pages that must be recorded.

The buyer generally pays the fees to record the "new" items, and the seller pays for the release of the "old" items. The payment of fees is usually negotiable.

ADVERSE POSSESSION

To establish title to land by adverse possession in Virginia, it is necessary to show actual, hostile, exclusive, visible, and continuous possession of property for the statutory period of 15 years. The possession by the defendant must be actual and continuous: More than just a sporadic taking of timber or occasional camping is required. The adverse possession must be exclusive to constitute an ouster of the true owner.

When several persons enter upon land in succession, these possessions cannot be "tacked" to preserve the essential continuity unless there is a "privity of estate" between them. In other words, the intent to establish a continuous succession of adverse possessors must be proven.

Adverse possession cannot be claimed if the possession has been abandoned by the claimant during the required time period. The occupancy necessary to support a claim of title of adverse possession must be hostile and without the true owner's permission.

TRANSFER OF A DECEASED PERSON'S PROPERTY

When any person with title to real estate that may be inherited dies testate, that is, having executed a legal will, the real estate will pass according to the terms of the instrument.

In Virginia, circuit courts serve as probate courts. Normally there is a probate section in the clerk's office where wills, lists of heirs, affidavits, and other documents related to probate are located. As with other documents, a "will index" is located in the circuit courts.

> **In Practice** When a licensee lists a property that is part of a decedent's estate, he or she should establish that the rate of commission to be paid has been approved by the court handling the probate.

Until probate, the will is only the legal declaration of a person's intended disposition. A will may be revoked at any time after execution, while a deed cannot be revoked after it has been delivered to the grantee. The rule of construction in determining whether an instrument is a will or a contract is that if it passes a *present interest*, it is a deed or contract; but if its rights or interests do not convey until the death of the maker, it is a testamentary paper, or will.

Validity

A testator can only have one last will and testament. A will may be set aside for fraud, undue influence, force, or coercion.

No person of unsound mind or under the age of 18 years is capable of making a valid will. Virginia law only requires testamentary capacity at the time the will is made; the testator's subsequent capacity is not relevant.

Neither the testator's poor health or impaired intellect is sufficient, standing alone, to render a will invalid.

No will is valid unless it is in writing. A valid will must be signed by the testator or by some other person in the testator's presence and by his or her direction in such a way as to make it clear that the name is intended as his or her signature. A will is also valid that is wholly in the testator's handwriting (a *holographic will*) if the testator signs the will and acknowledges it in the presence of at least two competent witnesses who are both present at the same time. These witnesses also must sign the will in the presence of the testator. The testamentary intent must appear on the face of the paper itself. Virginia law is silent on the subject of oral (unwritten) or deathbed (nuncupative) wills.

In Practice When representing the purchaser of property from a decedent's estate, or in taking a listing of estate property, it is wise for a real estate licensee to request a certified copy of the will and determine whether the executor under the will has the power of sale. Where the executor does not have the power of sale, or in dealing with an intestate's property, all the heirs and their spouses must execute a deed as grantors conveying the property to the grantee.

Questions

1. Which of the following would most likely invalidate a deed?
   1. Grantee's name misspelled
   2. Property description consisting of street address, city, and state
   3. Failure of all grantors to sign
   4. Failure of all grantees to sign

2. An heir was to have inherited real property under his uncle's will. However, the uncle sold the property shortly before he died. The heir now wants to have the sale rescinded on grounds of the uncle's incompetence. Will the heir win?
   1. Yes; any such pleading by a close relative will prevail in court.
   2. Yes; the grantor would have had to prove competence in court during his or her lifetime.
   3. No; a deed can be invalidated due to incompetence only during the grantor's lifetime.
   4. No; a person is presumed competent unless a court has ruled otherwise.

3. K, a minor, inherited the Blackacre estate and immediately sold it to W, who believed that K was 23 years old. W then sold the property to X. Two years later, K repudiated the sale of Blackacre. Which of the following is TRUE?
   1. K's repudiation is without effect because W no longer owns the property.
   2. K's original sale of Blackacre was voidable by K, and K may recover the property from X.
   3. Because W believed that K was not a minor, the sale cannot be invalidated.
   4. A minor cannot repudiate the sale of real property in Virginia.

4. Which of the following statements is TRUE with regard to using a power of attorney for a real estate transaction?
   1. Either a general or a specific power of attorney may be used.
   2. Both the seller and the purchaser must sign the power of attorney.
   3. Affidavits and other sworn statements may be signed by the attorney-in-fact.
   4. The lender's permission should be obtained for a borrower to execute a power of attorney.

5. The seller in a transaction was called out of town on business the day before the closing. Any affidavits or sworn statements the seller is required to deliver at the closing must be signed by the
   1. seller.
   2. seller's attorney-in-fact.
   3. buyer's attorney-in-fact.
   4. seller's real estate agent.

6. A property sold for $192,745. Which of the following is a correct statement of the recordation and grantor taxes to be paid?
   1. Seller will pay $385.60; Buyer will pay $192.74.
   2. Buyer will pay $385.60; Seller will pay $193.
   3. Buyer will pay $385.55; Seller will pay $192.75.
   4. Seller will pay $386; Buyer will pay $193.

7. The seller would be expected to pay which of the following?
   1. Recordation tax for recording of the deed
   2. Recordation tax for recording of the deed of trust
   3. Grantor tax of $.50 per $500 of purchase price
   4. Transfer fee for each document admitted to record

8. All of the following are entitled to prevail on a claim of title by adverse possession, **EXCEPT** a person who
   1. has been in possession of the property for 19 years.
   2. held the property for five years after "inheriting" it from a parent, who was in adverse possession for ten years.
   3. has been entering an orchard and taking apples every October since 1972.
   4. has been parking his or her car on a neighbor's property for 20 years without permission.

9. M's great-aunt S has died and left M her lakeside cabin in her will. M will receive title to the property:
   1. as soon as the will is read.
   2. after the will has gone through probate.
   3. as soon as she arranges for a closing.
   4. exactly one year from the day Aunt S died.

10. Because K was very ill, and she wrote a will in her own handwriting, leaving all her property to L. Three witnesses heard K say, "This is my will." The witnesses watched K's friend sign K's name to the document, because K was too exhausted to do it herself. "That's as good as my signature," K said weakly. The witnesses signed the will. What is the status of this document?
    1. The will is invalid because Virginia does not recognize holographic wills.
    2. The will is valid.
    3. The will is invalid, because K did not sign it herself.
    4. The will is valid, but cannot be enforced because it is a nuncupative will.

9 Title Records

SETTLEMENT AGENT

Either as part of the purchase agreement or immediately subsequent to ratification, a settlement agent is selected by either the buyer or the seller. The Consumer Real Estate Settlement Protection Act (CRESPA) [§6.1-2.19 et seq.] provides specific language that is to be included in all contracts for the purchase of real estate containing not more than four residential dwelling units. The *settlement agent* will usually be either an attorney or a title company, must be registered with the Virginia State Bar, carry errors and omissions or malpractice insurance, and maintain a surety bond of not less than $100,000. No interest may be earned on funds deposited in connection with any escrow, settlement, or closing. The settlement agent is provided a copy of the purchase agreement by either the buyer or seller. See the Code of Virginia, Title 6.1-2.19, at the following web address:

WWWeb.Link
http://leg1.state.va.us/000/src.htm

The escrow, closing, or settlement services include placing orders for title insurance, receiving and issuing receipts for money received from the parties, ordering loan checks and payoffs, ordering surveys and inspections, preparing settlement statements, determining that all closing documents conform to the parties' contract requirements, setting the closing appointment, following up with the parties to ensure that the transaction progresses to closing, ascertaining that the lenders instructions have been satisfied, conducting a closing conference at which the documents are executed, receiving and disbursing funds, completing form documents and instruments selected by and in accordance with instructions of the parties to the transaction, handling or arranging for the recording of documents, sending recorded documents to the lender, sending the recorded deed and the title policy to the buyer, and reporting federal income tax information for the real estate sale to the Internal Revenue Service. [§6.1-2.20] For further information about the Internal Revenue Service, see the following:

WWWeb.Link
www.irs.gov

TITLE EXAMINATION

An important function of the settlement agent is to obtain a title examination. The seller should be asked to provide the settlement agent with any information specific to the title condition of the property, such as any unrealized deeds, existing title insurance policies, any known unrecorded deed, lien, or encumbrance information, etc. The seller is required to have marketable title at the time of settlement and must be given a reasonable time to correct any title defects found before settlement. If title defects are found, the seller should be formally notified and then take whatever actions are necessary to correct the defects.

The real estate licensee is not specifically involved with the title examination but can facilitate communication between the settlement agent and the seller or buyer.

Procedure

In a title examination, the prospective seller's chain of title is developed by searching through the grantee index backward in time to some predetermined point to establish the source of title for each owner in the chain. Then, for each grantor in the chain of title, the examiner searches the grantor's index from the date the grantor acquired title to the date it was transferred to the next grantor in the chain. This process, called *adversing the title,* is done to determine whether any person not in the seller's direct chain of title might have some adverse claim or interest recorded against the property to be conveyed.

Finally, the examiner will search other indexes to determine whether there are any unrecorded claims against the property, such as judgment liens, mechanics' liens, or tax liens. While real estate licensees do not perform a title search in the normal course of taking a listing, they should alert the parties' attorneys in the event of even the slightest hint of title issues.

Title examinations may be classified as full or limited searches. In a *full search*, the seller's title must be established for at least 60 years. A *limited search* is a title examination that goes back fewer than 60 years. Limited searches are appropriate for some loan assumptions and second mortgage closings, unless the second mortgagee requires lender's title insurance.

A chain of title consists of consecutive terms of ownership; a gap in the chain could be caused by an unrecorded deed, a name change, an unadministered estate, a foreign divorce decree, or some other circumstance. Unless the missing link can be reconstructed from reliable sources, the defect could destroy the closing.

Errors such as an erroneous legal description, a misspelled name, or an improper execution in a prior recorded deed in the seller's chain of title must be corrected before the closing can proceed. Where possible, these problems can be cured by a correction deed from the same grantor to the same grantee; the correction deed must be recorded. A correction deed may not be used to change a greater estate to a lesser estate, nor can it be used to change the identity of the grantor altogether. It is the responsibility of the seller to locate the parties, then to correct the deed.

Title Report

At a minimum, the title report should reveal

- title holder of record;
- legal description of property;
- existing lenders;
- other lienholders (such as mechanics' lienors, judgment lienors, and tax lienors);
- status of taxes;
- easements, covenants, and other restrictions;
- objections to marketability;
- other matters affecting title; and
- requirements for vesting marketable title in the purchaser.

TITLE INSURANCE

Settlement agents are required by Virginia law to advise purchasers and borrowers of the availability of owner title insurance, and of the benefits of acquiring it. It is to the benefit of the purchaser to have title insurance because the premium paid is nominal compared with the potential cost an owner could incur in connection with a suit to quiet title or other litigation regarding a defect in title.

If the purchaser is obtaining a loan secured by a deed of trust on the property, the lender will require that a lender's title insurance policy be provided. This policy only protects the lender's interest and will diminish in protection as the loan is paid down.

The additional charge to obtain an owner's policy that protects the owner for the full value of the property is minimal compared to the amount of protection provided.

TITLE ISSUES

Judgment Liens

Judgments constitute liens against all real property that the defendant owns or subsequently acquires. If the seller denies being named in the judgment, and it is not certain that the judgment is against the seller, an affidavit to this effect may be sufficient to protect the purchaser.

Judgments against prior owners of property may remain as valid liens against the property despite the fact that the property has been subsequently conveyed. The purchaser should require the seller to satisfy all judgments against the property because they remain as liens against the property for 20 years and are subject to execution.

Deed of Trust

A real estate licensee should be aware that it is not unusual for a title examiner to discover an unreleased deed of trust on the property. Most often, this is due to the failure of the lender or closer to have a certificate of satisfaction or deed of release signed by the beneficiary and recorded in a timely manner. Unreleased deeds of trust often go unnoticed until the seller attempts to sell the property. When the lender was a bank or mortgage company and the lien was in fact paid off, it is relatively easy to have a certificate of satisfaction executed and recorded prior to closing. However, if an individual or private lender was involved, these situations can cause delays in the closing, primarily owing to the problems associated with locating the individual.

Mechanics' Liens

Reported mechanics' or materialmen's liens must be treated as adverse claims against the property. The purchaser should require that these liens be paid and satisfied of record or discharged by the filing of a proper bond at or prior to closing. Unreported liens are also of concern to the purchaser, who will take the property "subject to" all mechanics' and materialmen's liens for work or materials furnished within the last 90 days. For this reason, the purchaser should require that the seller provide an affidavit that there have been no improvements performed or materials supplied within the 90 days prior to the date of closing. This affidavit, commonly known as a "90-day letter," is required by all lenders and title insurance companies.

Mechanics' liens are generally not covered by standard title insurance. However, insurance carriers will provide this coverage for an additional premium.

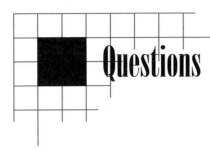

Questions

1. When is the seller of real property required to have marketable title?
   1. At the time the listing is taken
   2. When a sales contract is signed
   3. By the time the buyer's loan is approved
   4. At closing

2. B is purchasing property from S. Prior to closing, certain defects are found in S's title. What is the status of the sales contract between these parties?
   1. It is automatically rescinded.
   2. Because the seller has a reasonable time to correct defects, the contract is still in effect.
   3. The buyer may, at his or her option, cancel the contract and recover the earnest money.
   4. The contract is in force, and the buyer must close the transaction and accept the transfer as long as the defects are curable.

3. According to the Consumer Real Estate Consumer Protection Act, the selection of a settlement agent is made by the
   1. seller.
   2. buyer.
   3. either the buyer or the seller.
   4. either the buyer or the seller's agent.

4. At the time of taking a listing, the listing agent will find it helpful to ask to see all documents concerning the property that the seller has available in order to do all of the following **EXCEPT**
   1. find out about unrecorded deeds.
   2. verify deed of trust loan numbers and payment status.
   3. learn of any liens that may not be recorded.
   4. determine whether a seller has marketable title at the time a property is held out for sale.

5. A full title search goes back how many years?
   1. 20
   2. 40
   3. 60
   4. 80

6. Which of the following changes may not be accomplished by using a correction deed?
   1. A change from a fee simple to a life estate
   2. Correction of an erroneous legal description
   3. Respelling of a misspelled name
   4. Correcting the signature on an improperly executed deed

7. In cases where title must be cleared by having correction deeds signed, who is responsible for locating the parties who must sign?
   1. The buyer
   2. The seller
   3. The settlement attorney
   4. The real estate licensee who represents the owner

8. T has recently purchased a property from J. T has reason to believe that there is an outstanding judgment lien against J. Which of the following is TRUE?
   1. No need to worry because the property has been conveyed.
   2. No need to worry because T was not named in the judgment.
   3. T should be worried because judgment liens remain against the property.
   4. T should be worried because J has really bad credit.

9. In preparing for the settlement on S's sale of property to J, it was discovered that an unreleased deed of trust is still shown on the county records. This MOST LIKELY occurred because:
   1. S never paid off the deed of trust.
   2. S's lender neglected to have a deed of release signed and recorded.
   3. S's original settlement attorney absconded with the funds.
   4. S still owes for county property taxes.

10. All of the following are protections offered to an owner insured by a standard title insurance policy, **EXCEPT**
    1. losses suffered because of defects in the record title.
    2. hidden defects not disclosed by the public record.
    3. the cost of defending the title against adverse claims.
    4. mechanics' and materialmen's liens.

10 Virginia's Real Estate License Law

VIRGINIA REAL ESTATE LICENSE LAW

The Code of Virginia 54.1, Chapter 21, is the section of the statute that governs the practice of real estate professionals. The purpose of the law is to protect the public interest against fraud, misrepresentation, dishonesty, and incompetence in real estate transactions.

The law designates the Real Estate Board (REB) as the authority with the power to enforce, amend, and promulgate rules and regulations for implementing the law.

Definitions [§54.1-2100 et seq. and 18 VAC 135-20-10]

Certain words and phrases are used throughout both the License Law and the Rules and Regulations of the REB. These words and phrases have specific, statutory meanings separate and apart from any definition they might have outside the real estate profession. Several of these definitions have been addressed in Chapter 1 and are repeated here for emphasis.

Actively Engaged—Employment by, or affiliation as, an independent contractor with a licensed real estate firm or sole proprietor in performing acts of real estate brokerage for an average of 40 hours per week.

Associate Broker—An individual, licensed by the REB as a broker, other than one who has been designated as the principal broker. An associate broker is required to meet the same educational, experience, and testing requirement as a principal broker. An associate broker, because of his or her affiliation with a firm or sole proprietorship, is subject to the same restriction of brokerage activity as a salesperson.

Client—An individual who has entered into a brokerage relationship with a licensee.

Firm—Any sole proprietorship (non-broker owned) partnership, association, limited liability company (LLC), or corporation, other than a sole proprietorship (principal broker owned), that is required by regulation to obtain a separate brokerage firm license.

Inactive Status—Any broker or salesperson who is not under the supervision of a principal broker or supervising broker, who is not affiliated with a firm or sole proprietorship, or who is not performing any real estate activities.

Independent Contractor—A licensee who acts for or represents a client other than as a standard agent and whose duties and obligations are governed by a written contract between licensee and the client.

Licensee—Any person, partnership, association, corporation, or LLC that holds a license issued by the REB to act as a real estate broker or real estate salesperson.

Principal Broker—The individual broker designated by each firm to assure compliance with Chapter 21 of Title 54.1 of the Code of Virginia and to receive all communications and notices from the REB that may affect the firm and/or its licensees. In the case of a sole proprietorship, the licensed broker who is the sole proprietor has the responsibilities of the principal broker. The principal broker shall have responsibility for the activities of the firm and all of its licensees.

Principal to a Transaction—Any party to a real estate transaction in the capacity of a seller, buyer, lessee, or lessor.

Real Estate—As defined in the Virginia law, real estate includes condominiums, leaseholds, time-sharing, and any other interest in real property. Ownership of a cooperative apartment is also considered real estate ownership, even though the shares held by members of the co-op are construed as personal property.

Sole Proprietor—Any individual, not a corporation, who is trading under his or her own name or under a fictitious or assumed name, as provided by the regulations. A licensed broker who is a sole proprietor shall have the same responsibilities as a principal broker. A sole proprietor who is not licensed must designate a licensed broker to perform the duties of a principal broker.

Standard Agent—A licensee who acts for or represents a client in an agency relationship. A standard agent shall have the obligations as provided in Article 3 of Title 54.1 of the Code of Virginia that covers the law of agency as it relates to real estate and who is obligated to adhere to the Virginia Real Estate License Law.

Supervising Broker—The individual broker designated by the firm to supervise the activities of any one of the branch offices.

THE REAL ESTATE BOARD (REB) [§54.1-2104, 2105]

The REB is composed of nine members. Seven members may be either brokers or salespersons with at least five consecutive years' experience immediately prior to appointment, and two are citizen (consumer) members. Appointments are made by the governor for a term of four years. Sitting members may be reappointed for one additional four-year term. Members of the REB select the chairperson.

Authority

The REB, by statute, may do all things necessary and convenient for carrying into effect the provisions of the law. REB's authority includes

- issuing and renewing real estate licenses;
- enforcing the license law;
- taking disciplinary action for violations of license law or rules and regulations by
  - suspending or revoking a license,
  - levying fines, or
  - denying license renewal;
- establishing requirements for real estate licensing;
- approving schools for teaching authorized courses for real estate brokers and salespersons;
- determining license fees; and
- waiving all or part of the prelicense requirements if an applicant for licensure is currently licensed in another state or the District of Columbia.

In addition to administering the real estate license law, the REB has the responsibility of administering

- the Virginia Fair Housing Act;
- the Virginia Condominium Act;
- the Virginia Time-Share Act;
- the Virginia Real Estate Transaction Recovery Fund; and
- the Virginia Cooperative Act.

There are some aspects of real estate practice with which the REB does *not* become involved. For example, the REB does not

- arbitrate disputes between salespersons and brokers;
- become involved in disputes between brokers;
- establish commission rates or commission splits;
- standardize listing agreements, sales contacts, or many other forms used in the industry, although from time to time the REB may be charged with development of specific forms such as the disclosure forms required by the Virginia Residential Property Disclosure Act.

The REB could become involved in any of these matters in case of a violation of the license law or the rules and regulations.

WHO MUST HAVE A LICENSE? [§54.1-2106.1; 18 VAC 135-20-20]

Any person, firm, partnership, association, LLC, corporation, or sole proprietorship (broker or nonbroker owned) who, for a fee, commission, or other valuable consideration, performs an act of real estate brokerage for others, is required by Virginia law to be a licensed real estate broker or salesperson. The phrase "act of real estate brokerage" includes: selling or offering real estate for sale; buying or offering to buy real estate; negotiating the purchase or exchange of real estate; and renting, leasing, or negotiating a lease for real estate. Licensees may incorporate or form an LLC; however, no partnership, association, LLC, or corporation may be granted a license unless every member or officer (or manager of an LLC) who actively participates in brokerage activities holds a broker's license. A single performance of any one of these acts requires a real estate license.

Operating Without a License

If the REB is aware of someone who is engaging in acts of real estate brokerage without a license, it will investigate the matter. If the suspicion is true, the REB may refer the matter to the commonwealth attorney for action. Any penalty for such activities against the individual or firm will be determined by the court. Operating without a license is considered to be a Class 1 misdemeanor with a penalty of up to $1,000 per violation. A third or subsequent violation within a single three-year period constitutes a Class 6 felony. The civil penalties against one person or business entity cannot exceed $10,000 per year. The Department of Professional and Occupational Regulation (DPOR) also has the authority to investigate unlicensed activity and to enforce licensure and regulatory provisions of Title 54.1 by instituting proceedings in general district or circuit courts.

REQUIREMENTS FOR LICENSURE
[18 VAC 135-20-30 through 135-20-60]

The following general requirements apply for any person seeking licensure either as a salesperson or broker, or for licensure by reciprocity. The applicant must

- be at least 18 years old;
- if licensed in another jurisdiction, be in good standing in every jurisdiction where licensed;
- have a good reputation for honesty, truthfulness, and fair dealing, and be competent to transact real estate business in such a manner as to safeguard the public interest;
- not have been found guilty of violating the fair housing laws of Virginia or any other jurisdiction;
- meet the current educational requirements by achieving a passing grade in all required courses before sitting for the licensing exam and applying for licensure;
- pass a written license examination approved by the REB within 12 months prior to applying for a license and follow all rules established by the REB or the testing service regarding the conduct of license applicants, including any written or verbal instructions communicated prior to the examination date or at the test site;
- be in good standing, and not have had a real estate license suspended, revoked, or surrendered in connection with a disciplinary action, or been the subject of disciplinary action in any jurisdiction;
- not have been convicted, in any jurisdiction, for a misdemeanor involving moral turpitude, sexual offense, drug distribution, physical injury or any felony (a plea of *nolo contendere* "no contest," is considered a conviction);
- follow all rules established by the REB with regard to conduct at the examination.

An applicant for a broker's license must meet additional educational requirements and must have been actively engaged as a real estate salesperson for 36 of the previous 48 months. Note that the definition of "actively engaged" means an average of 40 hours per week. The specific licensing requirements for a broker, salesperson, and reciprocal licenses are discussed later in this Chapter.

If a license applicant has had a real estate license suspended, revoked, or surrendered in connection with a disciplinary action or has been subject to disciplinary action in any jurisdiction, the applicant must include a detailed explanation of the circumstances that caused the action, along with his or her application for licensure.

If an applicant has been convicted of a misdemeanor involving moral turpitude, sexual offense, drug distribution, or physical injury, or any other felony, the following must be submitted with the license application:

- An official FBI record, the original state police criminal record, and certified copies of court papers relative to the conviction.
- A written account of the part that he or she played in the offense, and the current status or resolution of the final conviction. If a prospective licensee is concerned about becoming licensed due to a past criminal conviction, the applicant must first meet the educational and testing requirements for licensure. The documentation is submitted with the license application.

Real Estate Examination

All initial applications for licensure must be made within 12 months of the examination date. Failure to apply within this time period will require retaking the exam.

Real Estate Salesperson

An applicant for licensure as a real estate salesperson must, in addition to the general requirements discussed above, have successfully completed a "Principles of Real Estate" or similar course approved by the REB. The course must contain 4 semester credit hours or a minimum of 60 classroom, correspondence, or other distance learning instruction hours prior to making application for the examination.

Real Estate Broker

Applicants for a real estate broker's license must meet the following requirements in addition to meeting the salesperson licensing requirements. An applicant must

- have been actively engaged as a real estate salesperson for 36 of the 48 months immediately preceding the date of application for licensure as a real estate broker, and
- have successfully completed 12 classroom or correspondence semester credit hours (four 45-hour courses, or 180 classroom hours) of study approved by the REB in such subjects as brokerage, real estate law, real estate investments, real estate finance, and real estate appraisal, or related approved subjects prior to the licensing examination. All applicants are required to complete the 45-hour brokerage course.

Applicants may ask the REB to determine the acceptability of related courses (other than brokerage).

Concurrent Licenses

Brokers who are active in more than one legal entity, that is, who work for more than one brokerage firm, may apply for concurrent licenses. Concurrent licenses will be issued to brokers who provide written affidavits stating that written notice of the applicant's concurrent status has been provided to the principal broker of each firm with which the applicant is or will be associated.

Concurrent licensure does not refer to persons holding licenses in multiple states.

Branch Office Licenses

A successful real estate broker often has offices in several different markets. When a broker maintains multiple offices within Virginia, a *branch office license* must be issued for each branch office. The application form must include the name of the firm, the location of the branch office, and the name of the branch office's supervising broker. The branch office license is maintained at the branch office. In addition, a roster of every salesperson and broker assigned to the branch shall be posted in the office.

Active and Inactive Licenses

An *active license* means that the licensee is affiliated with or employed by a broker. The licensee's broker must certify his or her license application and agrees to be responsible for the licensee's brokerage activities. When the REB has approved the application, the license will be issued and sent to the broker. The licensee is now considered to have *active* status: He or she is licensed to engage in real estate activities and receives a "pocket card" as evidence of his or her status as a broker or salesperson. The principal broker is responsible to maintain the licenses of every salesperson and broker (affiliated with or employed by the brokerage entity) at the main place of business.

Alternatively, an individual may satisfy all the licensing requirements and pass the license examination but choose to apply for *inactive* license status. Although the person has an inactive license, he or she is not affiliated with or employed by a broker and *may not* engage in acts of brokerage or earn compensation, including referral fees. The license of an inactive licensee is maintained by the REB.

Active to Inactive Status. Any licensee may request that his or her license be placed on inactive status, which means that the licensee is no longer affiliated with or employed by any broker.

If a licensee changes from active to inactive status, it is the responsibility of the individual licensee to make application for the change and to request that the broker return the actual license. The REB, on receipt of the change of status application, notifies the former broker of the change request. If the broker has not yet returned the license of the individual involved in the change, the broker must do so by certified mail so that it is received by the REB within ten days of the date of notification.

No licensees shall engage in acts of real estate brokerage or earn compensation while their licenses are on inactive status.

Inactive to Active Status. When an inactive licensee wishes to activate his or her license and affiliate with a broker, proper application must be made to have the license activated. This is accomplished by filling out an application form, having the broker certify the application and mail the form with the proper fees to the REB. If a licensee has been on inactive status for 3 years or more, the licensee must meet educational requirements in effect at that time to be reinstated to active status. If the licensee was engaged in a real estate related field while he or she was inactive and can demonstrate to the REB that the knowledge of real estate has been retained, the REB may waive the education requirements. If the licensee was on inactive status at the time the license was renewed, the licensee must submit evidence that he or she did successfully complete the required 8 hours of continuing education during the 24 months preceding reactivation.

Referral Agents

A referral agent is a real estate licensee who does not engage in real estate activities such as listing and selling property. As the title implies, a referral agent refers prospective buyers or sellers to the broker with whom the agent is affiliated. If a sale results from the referral, the broker may pay the licensee a fee for the referral. The referral agent's license is displayed either in the referral office or the main office of the broker with whom he or she is affiliated. The REB considers a person acting in the capacity of a referral agent to be active, not inactive. A referral agent will be required to complete the mandatory 8 hours of continuing education within each 2-year licensing cycle.

LICENSURE BY RECIPROCITY [18 VAC 135-20-60]

A person who holds a real estate license issued by another state may apply to the REB for a license by reciprocity. Applicants may obtain a Virginia real estate license by reciprocity if they

- are at least 18 years old;
- have received the salesperson's or broker's license by passing a licensing examination that is substantially equivalent to Virginia's examination;
- within 12 months prior to applying for a Virginia real estate license, have passed a written examination covering Virginia real estate license law and the regulations of the REB and have followed all rules regarding conduct at the examination;
- are in good standing as a licensed broker or salesperson in their state and have not have been subject to suspension, revocation, or surrender of their license in connection with a disciplinary proceeding;
- (for a salesperson's license) have been actively engaged in real estate practice for 12 of the preceding 36 months, or have met educational requirements substantially equivalent to Virginia's;
- (for a broker's license) have been licensed as a real estate broker and actively engaged as a broker or salesperson for 36 of the 48 months immediately prior to application; and
- satisfy the reputation and criminal record requirements demanded of licensees in Virginia.

Consent to Suits

One additional requirement for nonresidents is that they file an irrevocable *consent to suits and services*. A *consent to suits and services* is a binding legal agreement that allows the Director of Professional and Occupational Regulation to accept *service* of any legal process or pleading on the nonresident licensee's behalf.

The service of legal documents on the director is as valid and binding on the licensee as if service had been made on the licensee in person. [§54.1-2111]

FOR EXAMPLE J is licensed in Maryland and wishes to also be licensed in Virginia. In case J's actions result in potential harm to a member of the public, it will be necessary for the aggrieved party to be able to file a suit against J. The consent to suits and services form authorizes the Director of the DPOR to accept notice of the suit in J's behalf. Otherwise, J might be able to legally avoid having court action taken against him.

LICENSURE OF BUSINESS ENTITIES [18 VAC 135-20-45]

A partnership, association, LLC, or corporation engaged in real estate brokerage must obtain a real estate license prior to transacting real estate business. The license application must disclose the name under which the licensee intends to do business and by which it will be known to the public. The entity's license is issued in that name. This license is separate and distinct from any license issued to any member of the firm.

Every individual member, partner, trustee, manager, or officer of the organization who is actively engaged in the brokerage business must be licensed as a salesperson or associate broker. Every employee who renders professional services in the name of the firm must have a real estate license. Every office, including branch offices, must be managed by the broker or an associate broker.

A business entity may obtain a salesperson's or associate broker's license operating under the name of the business entity. This was added in response to the current practice of several salespersons forming a "team." The "team" and all the participants must be licensed by name, and must still operate under the supervision of a principal broker.

Partnerships and Associations

A partnership or association acting as a real estate broker must file a certificate that discloses:

- the name, business address, and home address of each person in the partnership or association;
- the name and style of the partnership or association;
- the address of the partnership's or association's Virginia office; and
- the length of time for which it is to continue.

Any change in the partnership or association must be filed with the REB within 30 days of the effective date of the change.

Corporations

Any corporation acting as a real estate broker must be authorized to do business in Virginia. The corporation must file a certificate with the REB that discloses

- the name, business and home addresses of each officer;
- the corporation's name and style; and
- the corporation's Virginia address and its place of business.

Every change in officers must be disclosed to the REB within 30 days of the effective date of the change.

Limited Liability Companies

Any limited liability company (LLC) acting as a real estate broker must be authorized to do business in Virginia. The LLC must file a certificate with the REB that discloses

- the name, business address, and home address of each licensed manager or member of the company;
- the name and style of the LLC; and
- the address of the Virginia office of the LLC company.

Every change in officers must be disclosed to the REB within 30 days of the effective date of the change.

RENEWAL OF LICENSES [18 VAC 135-20-90 through 135-20-130]

The real estate licenses of salespersons, brokers, and firms expire every two years, on the last day of the month in which the license was issued. For a licensee to continue his or her professional real estate activities, the license must be renewed. Renewal requirements apply to active and inactive licensees alike.

The REB reserves the right to deny the renewal or reinstatement of any license for the same reasons that it would deny initial licensure or discipline a current licensee.

The Renewal Process

The REB mails renewal notices, usually 45 days to 60 days prior to expiration, to each licensee at the last known home address of that individual. Renewal notices for firms are mailed to the last known business address. *Failure to receive a notice of renewal does not relieve the licensee of the responsibility to renew.*

The applicant for renewal completes the application form and returns it to the REB, along with the required fee and any other documentation that may be required. The application form and fees must be *received* by the REB prior to the expiration date that appears on the license.

If the licensee does not renew his or her license prior to expiration, the licensee must apply to have the license reinstated.

The regulations allow for reinstatement of a license up to one year following expiration. If the application to reinstate is received within 30 days of expiration, there is no monetary penalty. However, from the 31st day up to one year, application for reinstatement is subject to the current reinstatement fee. The reinstatement fee is a flat fee and is *not* in addition to the normal renewal fees.

After 12 months, reinstatement is not possible under any circumstances, and the licensee must meet all educational and examination requirements in effect at that time and apply for licensure as a new applicant.

Once the license has expired, the licensee may *not* engage in any acts of real estate brokerage or receive compensation until the license has been reinstated. Licensees who engage in acts of real estate brokerage after their licenses have expired are legally subject to the penalties associated with operating without a license. This applies even during the reinstatement period. On the date a license expires, the licensee is out of business until the license is reinstated.

Continuing Education [18 VAC 135-20-100]

As a condition of renewing their licenses, all active real estate brokers and salespersons, whether or not they are Virginia residents, must complete one or more continuing education courses, totaling at least eight hours, during each licensing term. Licensees who are called to active duty in the United States Armed Forces must complete the continuing education requirement within six months of their release.

The course or courses must be provided by an accredited university, college, community college, or other accredited institution of higher learning, or by an approved proprietary school, that is, a privately-owned school, real estate educational institution, or a program sponsored by a real estate association. The courses may be taken by correspondence or by other distance learning instruction.

Four of the eight hours must cover the subjects of fair housing laws, state real estate laws and regulations, and ethics and standards of conduct. The remaining four hours may cover any approved subject. Nonresident licensees may substitute continuing education completed in their jurisdiction for the remaining four hours. The approved subjects include the following:

- Property rights
- Contracts
- Deeds
- Mortgages and deeds of trust
- Types of mortgages
- Leases
- Liens
- Real property and title insurance
- Investment
- Taxes in real estate
- Real estate financing
- Brokerage and agency contract responsibilities
- Real property management
- Search, examination and registration of title
- Title closing
- Appraisal of real property
- Planning subdivision developments and condominiums
- Regulatory statutes
- Housing legislation
- Fair housing
- REB regulations
- Land use
- Business law
- Real estate economics
- Real estate investments
- Federal real estate law
- Commercial real estate
- Americans with Disabilities Act
- Environmental issues impacting real estate
- Building codes and design
- Local laws and zoning ordinances
- Escrow requirements
- Ethics and standards of conduct

The REB may approve other subjects as well.

Licensees are responsible for retaining proof of completed continuing education for three years. A certificate of course completion issued by the school and containing the hours of credit completed is adequate proof of course completion. Failure by the licensee to provide course completion certification as directed by the REB will result in the license not being renewed and, possibly, disciplinary action.

The REB requires each school to establish and maintain a record of continuing education for each student for a minimum of five years.

Any person who is *active* at the time of license renewal must complete the required course or courses as a condition of renewal. The courses *must* be completed prior to the date the license expires. An active licensee who does not complete the continuing education requirement prior to license expiration may complete the courses during the period of time allowed for license reinstatement (one year) but cannot reinstate the license until the continuing education courses are completed.

Any person who is *inactive* at the time of license renewal may renew his or her inactive license and is *not* required to complete the courses as a condition of renewal. However, when that licensee chooses to activate the license, he or she must document that the required continuing education courses have been completed within the past 24 months.

Referral agents are considered active and therefore must complete the courses as a condition of renewal.

EXEMPTIONS FROM LICENSURE [§54.1-2103]

The law recognizes that under certain circumstances, individuals or business operations engaging in what could be considered an act of real estate brokerage may be entitled to exemption from the requirements of licensure. Those conditions include, but are not limited to, the following:

- Owners, lessors, and their employees dealing with their own property
- Persons acting as attorneys-in-fact under a power of attorney for final consummation of contracts for sale, lease, or exchange of real estate
- Attorneys-at-law in the performance of duties as an attorney-at-law, to include the sale of real estate, condemnation proceedings, and so forth
- Receivers, trustees in bankruptcy, administrators, executors, or other persons acting under court order
- Trustees under trust agreements, deeds of trust, or wills, or their employees
- Corporations managing rental housing when officers, directors, and members in the ownership corporation and the management corporation are the same persons and the management corporation manages no property for others
- Any existing tenant of a residential dwelling who refers a prospective tenant to the owner of the unit or to the owner's agent or employee and receives, or is offered, a referral fee from the owner, agent, or employee

- Auctioneers when selling real estate at public auction when employed by the owner (an auctioneer cannot advertise that he or she is authorized to sell real estate)
- Salaried residential property managers
- Appraisers, mortgage bankers, and loan officers in the normal practice of their profession

All real estate licensees are always required to comply with the REB regulations, even though they also may be in one of the exempt categories.

Rental Location Agents

Rental location agents provide a service to the real estate industry but are not required to maintain a real estate license. Rental location agents are no longer regulated.

License, Renewal, and Registration Fees

The statute allows for the collection of fees associated with the issuance and renewal of licenses. The REB has the authority to set these charges. The purpose of these fees is to help defray the cost of administering the license law and to fund services provided by the REB to the real estate community throughout Virginia. The current fee structure is shown in Table 10.1

Table 10.1 Current Licensing Fees [18 VAC 135-20-80; 135-20-120]

REAL ESTATE LICENSING FEES

Applications:

Salesperson by education and examination	$ 95.00*
Salesperson by reciprocity	$ 84.00*
Business Entity	$ 95.00*
Broker by education and examination	$105.00*
Broker by reciprocity	$105.00*
Broker concurrent	$ 65.00
Firm	$145.00*
Branch Office	$ 65.00
Transfer	$ 35.00
Activate	$ 35.00

(Fees marked with (*) include $20.00 *original* licensure assessment for the Transaction Recovery Fund.)

Renewal:

Salesperson	$ 39.00
Broker	$ 42.00
Business Entity	$ 39.00
Firm	$ 65.00
Branch Office	$ 38.00

Reinstatement:

Salespersons and Brokers	$ 85.00
All others	$ 85.00

Note: These fees are subject to change at any time. From time to time additional assessments to the Transaction Recovery Fund may be assessed to all licensees.

OBTAINING A LICENSE

Once a license applicant has successfully completed the educational requirements, the applicant's next step is to take and pass an examination administered by the REB or a designated testing service. In Virginia, real estate licensing examinations are prepared by the PSI Real Estate Licensing Examination Service.

An examination application is provided by the educational provider, who certifies that the applicant has successfully met the educational requirements prescribed by the REB. The applicant makes an appointment to take the examination, which is offered each weekday.

The examination is administered by computer, and applicants will know the results as soon as they have completed the exam. If the applicant passes, successful notification appears on the computer screen. License application forms for submittal to the REB will be available at the test center. If the applicant does not pass, unsuccessful notification appears on the screen. Registration forms for submittal to PSI to retake the examination will be available at the test center. There is no prescibed waiting period. All candidates also receive an official score report in writing at the test center. If the applicant fails one portion of the exam (state or national) that portion must be retaken and passed. All license applications must be received by the Department of Professional and Occupational Regulation (DPOR) within one year of passing the exam. Exam results are confidential and are only reported to the applicant and to the Department of Professional and Occupational Regulation.

More information and test application forms may be found on the following website:

WWWeb.Link
www.psiexams.com (click on Virginia)

BROKERAGES [18 VAC 135-20-160 through 135-20-170]

There may be only *one* principal broker for each firm, regardless of the number of agents affiliated with that firm or the number of offices the firm operates.

Name of Business A brokerage business may be known by any name that identifies the owner or owners, or it may use an assumed or fictitious name. If the firm chooses to operate under an assumed or fictitious name, the application for licensure of the firm must be accompanied by a certificate of ownership that has been filed with the clerk of the court in the jurisdiction in which the business operates. This fictitious or assumed name is the name by which the business will be known to the public.

Place of Business Every licensed broker who is a resident of Virginia must maintain a place of business within the commonwealth. A *place of business* is defined as one where the business of real estate brokerage is normally transacted and where business calls can be directed and received. A place of business may be located in a private residence only if the business area is separate and distinct from the living quarters and is accessible to the public.

Office Supervision

If a broker operates more than one office in Virginia, the broker shall designate one location to be the main office and all other locations will be designated as branch offices.

Each place of business, including branch offices, must be supervised and personally managed by an on-premises broker who is in the office or easily accessible during normal business hours. Only the principal broker or an associate broker may be designated to manage an office, and the designated person may manage only one office.

Signage

The broker may display a sign at his or her office(s). Any sign must state the name by which the brokerage is known to the public, that is, the name that appears on the license issued by the REB, and the words *Real Estate*, *Realty*, or the name of a generally recognized organization of real estate professionals. The signs must indicate clearly that the business being conducted is real estate brokerage.

Change of Location, Name, or Ownership

In the event the broker's main office changes location, or the name of the brokerage changes, it is the principal broker's responsibility to advise the REB of the change within ten days. The REB will issue new licenses for the remainder of the license period. This is necessary because the broker's name and business address appear on individual licenses.

If the location of a branch office changes, only the branch office license needs to be returned.

Salespersons and individual brokers are responsible for keeping the REB informed of their current home addresses and of any changes in their name or address within 30 days of the change.

Transfer and Termination of Affiliation

If the licensee transfers from one broker to another, it is the responsibility of the licensee, along with the new broker, to make proper application to the REB to effect the transfer and have a new license issued.

Upon receipt of an application to transfer or change of status request, the REB notifies the former broker of the request. If the old license has not been previously returned, the former broker must return it by certified mail so that it is received within ten days of the notification.

All licenses are the property of the REB. All licenses must be returned to the REB upon termination of the licensee, termination of the business entity, death of a licensee, status change, or change of name and address.

Disclosure by Licensee [18 VAC 135-20-210]

A licensee must disclose, in writing, his or her position and license status when acquiring or disposing of any interest in real property for any of the following:

- Himself or herself
- Immediate family members

- Members of his or her firm
- Any entity in which he or she has an ownership interest

This disclosure applies to all licensees, regardless of whether the licensee's status is active or inactive.

BROKER ESCROW ACCOUNTS
[§54.1-2108; 18 VAC 135-20-180]

Any broker who holds money belonging to others pending consummation or termination of a real estate transaction must maintain an escrow account solely for those funds. There is, however, no requirement that a broker hold a buyer's earnest money deposit, for instance, prior to closing. The money may be held by a settlement agent, an attorney, or even the seller. Who holds the earnest money deposit is a matter to be negotiated in the sales contract. Other funds that require an escrow account include down payments, rental payments, and security deposits. If a fund is to be deposited in an escrow account, it must be deposited by the fifth business banking day following ratification (sale) or receipt (lease), unless otherwise agreed in writing.

Establishing and Maintaining an Escrow Account

Each account established shall be opened and maintained in a federally insured depository in Virginia. When the account is opened, it must be made clear to the financial institution that the account is an escrow account. Each account—and all checks, deposit slips, and bank statements relating to it—must be labeled *Escrow* as part of the account name. The designation of the account as an escrow account precludes attachment of the funds by the broker's creditors. It also puts the financial institution on notice that this account contains funds that belong to people other than the broker who opened the account.

The principal broker will, and the supervising broker may, be held responsible for these accounts. Individual salespersons and associate brokers do *not* have escrow accounts.

Once deposited, no funds may be removed from the escrow account until the transaction is consummated unless agreed to, in writing, by all principals to the transaction. In the event that the transaction is not consummated, the broker or supervising broker shall hold funds in escrow until one of the following events occurs:

- All principals to the transaction agree, in writing, to the disposition;
- A court orders disbursement; or
- The broker can determine, in accordance with the specific terms of the contract, exactly who is the rightful recipient of the funds.

If the broker makes the determination of how funds will be distributed in accordance with the contract, the principal or supervising broker must advise each principal concerning the intended distribution. Notice of distribution must be given in writing and hand-delivered or must be sent by regular and certified mail to ensure that it is received. The notice advises the parties of the intended distribution and states that unless a written protest is received by the broker within 30 days, the funds will be distributed as outlined in the notice. If the principals cannot agree, the broker must petition the court to step in and decide how the money should be disbursed.

Any money in the escrow account that will ultimately belong to the broker may be left in the account and not be considered commingling, provided that these funds are clearly identified in the account records and that these funds are removed from the account at periodic intervals of not more than six months. Withdrawals from the escrow account for payment of commissions shall be paid to the firm by a check drawn on the escrow account.

If necessary, the broker may use a nominal amount of personal funds to establish or maintain the escrow account and not be guilty of commingling, provided that any funds so used are clearly identified in the account records.

Interest-Bearing Accounts

There is no legal requirement that escrow funds be held in an interest-bearing account. If the escrow account does earn interest, the broker must disclose, in writing, to all parties involved exactly how any earned interest will be disbursed. Such disclosure shall be made at the time the contract or lease is written.

Property Management

Brokers acting as property managers need to maintain escrow accounts. They will be receiving monies as security deposits that will ultimately be returned to tenants. They also receive rental money that belongs to the property owner. Brokers who manage several different properties should establish separate accounts for each property, even if the properties are owned by the same person. A broker cannot use funds from one property for another or disburse monies from an escrow or property management escrow account unless there is sufficient money on deposit in the account.

Financial Records

The broker must maintain a bookkeeping system that accurately and clearly discloses full compliance with the requirements of these regulations. The records must include the following information:

- The source of the funds
- The date the funds were received
- The date the funds were deposited
- Where the funds were deposited
- The date money was disbursed from the account
- The name of the person or persons who received the money

Escrow account records must be maintained for three years from date of consummation or termination of the transaction.

Protection of Escrow Funds

The mismanagement of escrow funds is the basis of many complaints filed with the REB. If the REB has reason to believe that a broker is unable to properly protect escrow funds, for whatever reason, it may petition the court to intercede. The court may bar the licensee from any further activity with the escrow account and may take whatever other actions are necessary to protect the funds. The court may appoint a receiver to manage the funds, pending a complete investigation by the REB. It is the court that makes the appointment, not the REB.

If, as a result of the investigation, it is determined that the licensee has been at fault or has mismanaged the escrow funds, he or she must pay the costs of the receiver. If the licensee has no funds to pay the receiver, the receiver will be paid from any monies in the escrow account that would normally be due the licensee. If no such funds are available, the REB shall determine whether the receiver will be paid from the Transaction Recovery Fund.

If the investigation determines that the licensee is not at fault, the receiver will be paid from the funds of the REB.

ADVERTISING [18 VAC 135-20-190]

The REB regulations define *advertising* to be any oral or written communication between a licensee and anyone else. Advertising includes telephone communications, insignias, business cards, telephone directory listings, listing agreements, contracts of sale, billboards, signs, letterheads, and radio, television, magazine, newspaper, and Internet advertisements.

All advertising must be under the direct supervision and control of the principal broker or supervising broker.

Any ad must indicate, affirmatively and unmistakably, that the advertising party is a real estate broker. There can be no suggestion or implication that the property being advertised is "for sale by owner." The name of the firm, as it is known to the public, must appear in every ad. The name of the brokerage must be clear and legible.

No advertisement may be published in which only a post office box, phone number, or street address appears. People responding to the ad must know they are dealing with a real estate broker.

If a licensee is selling property that he or she owns, or in which he or she has an ownership interest, all advertisements must disclose the fact that the owner is licensed, unless the property is listed with a recognized real estate entity. This disclosure cannot imply that the licensee is operating a real estate brokerage business. It must be clear in the advertisement that a real estate entity is involved in the transaction.

Institutional and Noninstitutional Advertising

Institutional advertising is an advertisement in which no specific licensee or property is identified. Rather, a logo or service mark (owned by an entity other than the licensee) is used. This type of advertising is generally associated with franchise-type brokerage organizations, but it may be used by independent firms as well. The ad must clearly state that the services offered are those of real estate brokerage.

If a broker of a franchise office uses the same type of ad, the ad also requires a statement that the office is independently owned and operated. This disclosure is required in radio, television, newspaper, telephone directory, and oral advertising. However, the disclosure is not required for noninstitutional advertising, such as

- telephone calls;
- signs located on a specific property for sale or rent;
- ads for a single, specific property containing no more than 28 lines; or
- single-line, one-column telephone directory ads.

However, in oral noninstitutional advertising, the licensee's name must be disclosed. In communications other than telephone conversations, the independent ownership and operation of the firm or sole proprietorship must be disclosed.

FOR EXAMPLE ABC Realty Franchise places an advertisement in the local newspaper. Because this is an institutional advertisement, it displays the ABC Realty logo, a photo of a single-family home, and the message, "List your home today with an ABC Realty broker!"

Marianne Smith, an ABC Realty broker, decides to use this same advertisement as a mailing to attract new business. In order to comply with the advertising regulations, Marianne must also list her name and disclose that her office is independently owned and operated.

DEATH OR DISABILITY [§54.1-2109]

If a sole proprietor or the only broker in a firm dies or becomes disabled, the REB may authorize an unlicensed individual to conclude the broker's business. The individual appointed may be an adult member of the broker's family, an employee of the broker, or some other suitable person. The person appointed may act only to conclude the business of the broker and may act in this capacity for a period of not longer than 180 days.

If the deceased was a sole proprietor or the only broker in the firm, two things happen by operation of law:

1. All listings are terminated.
2. The licenses of any licensees affiliated with the broker or firm must be returned to the REB because there is no longer a broker to be responsible for licensees, who are not allowed to operate in their own names.

If the principal broker of a large real estate firm dies, the officers of the firm designate a new principal broker and immediately file the appropriate form with REB naming the new principal broker.

THE VIRGINIA REAL ESTATE TRANSACTION RECOVERY FUND [§54.1-2112 et seq.]

Purpose of the Fund The Virginia Real Estate Transaction Recovery Fund was established for the purpose of reimbursing parties who suffer monetary loss due to a licensee's improper or dishonest conduct.

Maintenance of the Fund The establishment and maintenance of the fund is the duty of the Director of the Department of Professional and Occupational Regulation. The cost of administering the fund is paid out of interest earned on deposits. The REB may, at its discretion, use part of the interest earned by the fund for research and education for the benefit of licensees.

Each new licensee, whether salesperson or broker, must pay $20 into the fund. Monies collected must be deposited into the fund within 30 days after receipt by the director.

The fund's minimum balance is $400,000. If the balance of the fund falls below $400,000, the REB may assess each active and inactive licensee a proportionate amount to bring the balance to the statutory minimum. No licensee may be assessed more than $20 during any two-year period ending on June 30 of even-numbered years. Licensees who fail to pay the assessment within 45 days of receiving the first notice are given a second notice. Failure to pay the assessment within 30 days of the second notice results in automatic suspension of the licensee's license. The license will be suspended until such time as the director receives the amount due. The REB has the power to assess all licensees at one time or upon individual licensees' renewals.

At the close of each fiscal year, if the balance of the fund is more than $2 million, the excess amount over $2 million is transferred to the Virginia Housing Partnership Fund.

Claims Procedure

A person who files a claim for payment from the fund must first obtain a judgment against the licensee from a Virginia court of competent authority. After a licensee has been found guilty of misconduct, the injured party must take appropriate legal action against the licensee. Appropriate legal action includes

- forcing the sale of the licensee's assets to satisfy all or part of the claim;
- investigating any listings held by the licensee and determine any commissions that may be due;
- filing a claim in bankruptcy court, if the licensee has filed bankruptcy; and
- requiring the licensee to submit to interrogatories, if necessary.

If any portion of the claim remains unsatisfied, the individual may file a claim with the REB requesting payment from the fund for the unsatisfied portion of the claim within 12 months from the date of the final judgment.

The claim must be accompanied by an affidavit stating the licensee's improper conduct and the actions taken to recover damages from sources other than the fund.

A claimant must have pursued all legal means for possible recovery before a claim can be filed with the REB. On receipt of a claim, the REB will promptly consider the request and notify the claimant, in writing, of its findings.

Limitation on Recovery

No fund payment will be made to any of the following:

- Any licensee or a licensee's personal representative
- The spouse or child of any licensee against whom the judgment was awarded, or their personal representative
- Any financial or lending institution
- Any person whose business involves the construction or development of real property

The claim can be only for the difference between the original loss and any amount previously recovered through the legal process associated with the final judgment.

The amount of the claim is limited to actual monetary damages suffered in the transaction, court costs, and attorney's fees. The claim cannot include interest, punitive, or exemplary damages, even though these amounts may have been included in the judgment awarded by the court.

Funds Available

If at any time the amount of claims to be paid from the fund would deplete the fund to an amount below the statutory minimum of $400,000, the processing of all claims will be suspended. The REB will assess regulants as previously outlined. As funds become available to satisfy the pending claims, they will be paid in the order in which they were originally received.

In all cases, the REB may withhold payment of any claim for 12 months if it has reason to believe that additional claims may be filed. In the event that there are multiple claims against a licensee that exceed the maximum allowable payment from the fund, each claimant will receive a proportionate share of the total payment.

Monetary Limitations on Claims

Single Transaction. In a single transaction, the maximum payment from the fund to all injured parties is $50,000. The maximum amount any single claimant may recover from the fund based on a single transaction is $20,000, regardless of the number of claimants.

Multiple Transactions. If the same licensee is involved in multiple fraudulent transactions during any two-year period ending June 30 of even-numbered years, the maximum payment to all claimants combined is $100,000.

If a payment is made from the fund, the claimant must *subrogate* his or her rights to the REB. Subrogation permits the REB to take action against the licensee to recover the amount of claims paid due to the licensee's misconduct.

Penalty

Payment from the fund causes the licensee's license to be *immediately revoked*. The respondent may also be subject to other disciplinary action by the REB. The licensee may not apply for a new license until the fund has been repaid in full, plus interest at the judgment rate of interest from the date of payment from the fund.

Repayment to the fund does not guarantee that the license will be reissued. The REB may take disciplinary action against a licensee for a disciplinable violation regardless of whether or not he or she has reimbursed the fund.

STANDARDS OF CONDUCT

The regulations promulgated by the REB establish certain required standards of professional behavior expected of all real estate licensees in Virginia.

Disclosure of Interest [18 VAC 135-20-210]

If a licensee has any family, business, or financial relationship with any of the principals to the contract, all parties to the contract must be informed of the relationship in writing in the offer to purchase or lease. This requirement applies to any licensee who could be considered an "interested party" to the transaction.

Disclosure of Brokerage Relationships and Dual or Designated Agency [18 VAC 135-20-220]

Unless disclosure has been made previously, a licensee must disclose to an actual or prospective buyer or seller who is not the client of the licensee and who is not represented by another licensee the party he or she represents. In the case of both buyers and sellers, the disclosure must be made when "substantive discussions about specific property" take place. The disclosure must be provided "at the earliest practical time, but in no event later than the time specific real estate assistance is first provided."

The disclosure must advise prospective buyers, sellers, landlords, or tenants of the duties of real estate brokers and salespersons under Virginia law, and it must encourage them to obtain relevant information from other sources.

A licensee who is acting as a dual or designated representative must obtain the written consent of all parties "at the earliest practical time." The disclosure may be made in conjunction with other required disclosures if it is conspicuous, printed in bold lettering, all capitals, underlined, or within a separate box.

In Practice The REB's regulations do not contain a list of specific events that trigger the disclosure requirement. Common sense should tell the licensee when disclosure is required: If in doubt, disclose.

Licensees Dealing on Own Account [18 VAC 135-20-230]

Licensees may—and many do—sell or lease property that they personally own. Years of training, experience, and expertise give a licensee particular effectiveness as a FSBO (*fizz-boe* is an acronym for "For Sale By Owner"). Some licensees feel that there is no point in paying a broker's commission to someone else to do what they can do perfectly well themselves. While permissible, licensees who engage in transactions on their own are still bound by the rules and regulations of the REB in the same manner as if they were representing a client in a professional capacity.

Provision of Records to the Board [18 VAC 135-20-240]

The REB has the authority to audit a broker's transaction records. Records must be kept for three years following consummation or termination of a transaction. Licensees must respond to any inquiry from the REB within 21 days.

Unworthiness and Incompetence [18 VAC 135-20-260]

Actions that constitute unworthy and incompetent conduct include the following:

- Obtaining a license by false or fraudulent representation—for instance, providing false information in the license application or cheating on the license examination. It is also improper for a currently licensed real estate salesperson to sit for the salesperson's licensing examination, or for a currently licensed broker to sit for the broker's examination (of course, a qualified, licensed salesperson may sit for the broker's exam).
- Holding more than one license as a real estate broker or salesperson in Virginia, unless permitted to do so by law. Only brokers may hold more than one Virginia license.
- Having been finally convicted or found guilty of a misdemeanor involving moral turpitude, sexual offense, drug distribution, physical injury, or any felony. Any plea of nolo contendere is considered a conviction. Just as an individual can be denied a license because of past criminal convictions, a license can be taken away on the same basis.
- Failing to inform the board in writing within 30 days of pleading guilty

or nolo contendere or being convicted or found guilty of any felony or of a misdemeanor involving moral turpitude, sexual offense, drug distribution, or physical injury.
- Having been found guilty of violating the Virginia Fair Housing Act or any other local, state or federal fair housing laws.
- Failing to act in such a manner as to safeguard the interests of the public, or otherwise engaging in improper, fraudulent, or dishonest conduct.

Conflict of Interest [18 VAC 135-20-270]

Actions constituting a conflict of interest include the following:

- Being employed by, affiliated with, or receiving compensation from a real estate broker other than the licensee's principal broker, without the written consent of the principal broker.
- Acting for more than one party in a transaction without the written consent of all principals for whom the licensee acts. Dual agency is not illegal in Virginia, provided that the principals to the transaction know about it and agree to it in writing.
- Acting as a standard agent or independent contractor for any client in a real estate transaction outside the licensee's brokerage firm or sole proprietorship. All of a licensee's, salesperson's, or associate broker's acts of real estate brokerage must be conducted in the name of the employing broker.

Improper Brokerage Commission [18 VAC 135-20-280]

Brokers may pay commissions or fees to any licensees affiliated with their firm. Brokers also may pay commissions or fees to other brokers (or firms), regardless of where those brokers are located.

Salespersons and associate brokers may only receive compensation from the broker whose name appears on their license.

If commissions are earned but not paid during the period of employment or affiliation with a broker, the previous broker may pay the licensee directly, even though the licensee may be affiliated with another broker or no longer actively licensed.

Licensees are prohibited from receiving kickbacks from a third party who provides services or goods necessary to fulfill a contract, such as an appraiser, home inspector, or surveyor, when one of the principals to the contract is paying for the services unless full written disclosure is made to the principal. The principals must be informed, in writing, of any "finder's fees" or commissions paid to the licensee.

Similarly, a licensee may not personally pay for services required by the terms of a real estate contract without written disclosure of the payment to the principals. For instance, a buyer might be short of the cash needed to pay for a survey of the property. If the licensee agrees to pay for the survey personally, there could be accusations later that the survey was inferior or not done by a competent professional surveyor unless all of the principals agree to the arrangement. The licensee has a personal interest in the transaction being completed; offering to pay for one of the steps necessary for completion could appear to be self-serving.

Net listings are not permitted in Virginia.

Finally, no licensee may charge money or other valuable consideration *to*, or accept or receive money or valuable consideration *from*, any person or entity *other than the licensee's principal* for expenditures made on the principal's behalf without the written consent of the principal.

Improper Dealing
[18 VAC 135-20-290]

Actions that constitute improper dealing include

- entering into a brokerage relationship that does not have a specific, definite termination date. Most listing and buyer representation agreements include a blank space in which the date may be inserted.
- offering property for sale or lease without the owner's knowledge and consent, or on terms other than those authorized by the owner.
- placing *any* sign on *any* property without permission. This regulation could include the placement of directional signs on the property of someone other than the seller.
- advertising property for sale, rent, or lease in any newspaper, periodical, or sign without including in the advertisement the name of the firm or sole proprietorship.

Misrepresentations and Omissions
[18 VAC 135-20-300]

The regulations prohibit specific actions as misrepresentations or omissions. They are

- using "bait and switch" tactics by advertising or by offering real property for sale or rent with the intent not to sell or rent at the price or terms advertised, unless the advertisement or offer clearly states that the property advertised is limited in specific quantity and the licensee or registrant did in fact have at least that quantity for sale or rent;
- failing to disclose material information related to the property that is reasonably available to the licensee—a dual representative may not disclose confidential information to either client;
- failing to promptly present *every* written offer, rejection or counteroffer to the buyer and seller;
- failing to include the *complete* terms and conditions of the real estate transaction in any offer to purchase or rent, including identification of all those holding any deposits;
- knowingly making any false statement or report, or willfully misstating the value of any land, property, or security for the purpose of influencing a lender regarding applications, advance discounts, purchase agreements, repurchase agreements, commitments of loans, or to change the terms or time limits of a loan;
- making *any* misrepresentation; and
- making a false promise through agents, salespersons, advertising, or other means.

Delivery of Instruments
[18 VAC 135-20-310]

Actions constituting improper delivery of instruments include

- failing to promptly deliver complete and legible copies of any written listings, offers to lease, offers to purchase, counteroffers, addenda, and ratified agreements to each party in a transaction: Anyone who signs his or her name to a document is entitled to a copy.
- failing to provide timely, written notice of any material change in the transaction to all parties.
- failing to deliver a complete and accurate statement of money received and disbursed by the licensee, duly signed and certified by the principal or supervising broker (or his or her authorized agent), to the seller and

buyer at the time a real estate transaction is completed. However, if the transaction is closed by a settlement agent other than the licensee (or his or her broker), and if the financial disclosure is provided on the applicable settlement statement, the licensee is not required to provide a separate statement of receipts and disbursements.
- refusing or failing without just cause to surrender any document or instrument to the rightful owner upon demand.

Record Keeping and Escrow Funds [18 VAC 135-20-320]

The regulations provide for the manner in which financial and transaction records are to be kept and escrow funds maintained.

Actions that constitute improper record keeping and maintenance of escrow funds include

- failing to retain a complete and legible copy of each disclosure of a brokerage relationship, executed contract, listing or buyer agency agreement, notice, closing statement, and other material documents related to a real estate transaction in the broker's control or possession for a period of three years from the date of the closing or ratification;
- failing to maintain, for a period of three years from the date of the closing, a complete and accurate record of monies received and disbursed on behalf of others;
- failing to account for or remit, within a reasonable time, any funds coming into a licensee's possession that belong to others;
- accepting any note, non-negotiable instrument (such as a promissory note or postdated check), or anything of value not readily negotiable, as a deposit on a contract, offer to purchase, or lease, without acknowledging its acceptance in the agreement; and
- commingling any person's funds with the personal or business funds of a principal or supervising broker or his or her employees, associates, corporation, firm, or association, or failing to deposit those funds in an account designated to receive only those funds as required by Virginia law (that is, escrow accounts).

Principal and Supervising Broker's Responsibility for Licensees [18 VAC 135-20-330]

A principal or supervising broker is liable for the unlawful acts of a real estate salesperson, employee, partner, or affiliate of a principal or supervising broker only if the REB finds that the principal or supervising broker knew or should have known of the unlawful act or violation.

Effect of Disciplinary Action on Subordinate Licensees [18 VAC 315-20-340]

If a principal broker's or sole proprietor's license is revoked or suspended, or if renewal is denied, the licenses of any and all individuals affiliated with or employed by the affected firm are automatically ordered returned to the REB until such time as they are reissued upon the written request of another sole proprietor or principal broker. That is, affiliated licensees must either transfer or become inactive.

COMPLAINT PROCEDURE

The REB has the authority to investigate the activities of any licensee. The REB usually investigates as a result of a written complaint, but it does have the authority to start an investigation on its own initiative.

A complaint must be in writing and supported by documentary evidence that clearly demonstrates that the accused licensee's actions violate the law. The REB reviews the complaint first, to determine if the actions described are within its scope of authority. If not, the complaint is referred to the proper regulatory authority or returned to the complainant.

All complaints must be filed within three years of the transaction date or, in specific situations, within two years of discovery.

If it is determined that the complaint should be investigated, the named licensee and his or her principal broker is notified. The REB recognizes that a person is innocent until proven guilty and is entitled to have his or her day in court before any sanctions are imposed.

An investigator from the Enforcement Bureau of the Department of Professional and Occupational Regulation interviews the complainant, the accused licensee, and witnesses. The investigator's findings are reported to the REB without comment or recommendation. The REB then reviews the investigator's report. The case may be dismissed if the REB feels that no violation occurred.

If the REB finds that a violation has occurred, the licensee is given an opportunity to admit guilt and settle the matter through a consent order. The licensee agrees to refrain from the wrongful act, promises not to do it again, and agrees to accept whatever sanctions are imposed by the REB. A respondent who does not agree to the consent order may request an Informal Fact Finding Conference (IFFC).

The IFFC is presided over by a member of the REB, who hears testimony of the respondent, claimant and witnesses. Based on the testimony, the REB member either recommends that the case be dismissed or allows the respondent to admit guilt and enter a consent order. The final decision to accept either option requires ratification by the full REB membership.

If a consent order is not agreed to, the matter is referred to a formal hearing conducted by a hearing officer appointed by the Virginia Supreme Court. An assistant attorney general is assigned to present the facts and argue the case that a violation has been committed. The hearing officer reports to the REB and states his or her conclusions, based strictly on the law. The hearing officer does not recommend sanctions. After a review of the hearing officer's report, the REB either closes the case or cites the violations and imposes sanctions.

If the REB finds the licensee guilty, it may impose a monetary penalty of up to $2,500 for each violation. The REB may also suspend, revoke, or deny renewal of the respondent's license. The REB's decision is final, although the licensee may appeal the decision through the Court of Appeals. In all of these proceedings, the accused has the right to be represented by legal counsel.

Automatic License Suspension or Revocation

There are two instances in which disciplinary action may be taken against a licensee, and his or her license may be suspended or revoked without review or a hearing:

1. If a licensee does not pay the assessment to the Transaction Recovery Fund, his or her license will be automatically *suspended.*
2. If a payment is made from the Transaction Recovery Fund, the license of the respondent will be automatically *revoked.*

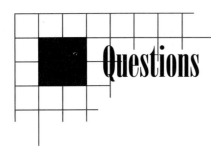

Questions

1. Which of the following is an accurate description of the Real Estate Board?
   1. 7 members; 6 licensees and 1 consumer
   2. 7 members; 5 licensees and 2 consumers
   3. 9 members; either licensed brokers or salespersons
   4. 9 members; 7 licensees and 2 consumers

2. Is it possible to become licensed in Virginia without taking the Virginia real estate license examination?
   1. No.
   2. Yes; if the person is licensed to practice law in Virginia.
   3. Yes; because any person who is currently licensed in another jurisdiction and meets all requirements for reciprocity may be licensed in Virginia.
   4. Yes; if the person is an appraiser.

3. Which of the following is a requirement to obtain a real estate salesperson's license in Virginia?
   1. Successful completion of 12 credit hours of real estate law, investments, finance, and appraisal
   2. An associate degree or certificate in real estate from an accredited college, university, or proprietary school
   3. United States and Virginia citizenship
   4. Successful completion of a course of 60 classroom, correspondence, or distance learning hours in a general principles of real estate

4. All of the following are requirements for a broker's license **EXCEPT**
   1. a college degree or certificate in business, finance, management, appraisal, or real estate.
   2. 12 semester hours of designated real estate courses.
   3. three years of experience as a salesperson.
   4. not have violated Virginia's fair housing laws, or those of any other state.

5. A broker's business is growing, and now she wants to open a branch office. Which of the following is TRUE?
   1. The office must have an escrow account.
   2. The office may be managed by a salesperson with 3 years of experience.
   3. The office must have a separate license.
   4. The branch office will display the licenses of all salespersons and associate brokers assigned to that particular office.

6. A licensed salesperson may hold a concurrent license with more than one Virginia broker under which of the following circumstances?
   1. Under no circumstances
   2. With the permission of his or her sales manager
   3. With the written consent of the brokers being represented
   4. With the permission of the REB

7. A licensee who allows his or her license to expire has how long to reinstate the license without monetary penalty?
   1. Up to 15 days
   2. Up to 30 days
   3. No more than 365 days
   4. One year from the last transaction

8. A licensee was out of town on vacation. When she returned on October 10, she found her license renewal notice and realized that her license had expired on July 31. If she wants to remain licensed, she must
   1. reapply for a new license as a new applicant.
   2. meet the current educational requirements.
   3. apply for reinstatement of her license and pay the current reinstatement fee.
   4. apply to have her license placed on inactive status.

9. How often are real estate licenses renewed in Virginia?
   1. Annually, in the month issued
   2. Every 2 years, in the month of the licensee's birthday
   3. On June 30 of each even-numbered year
   4. Biennially, in the month issued

10. All of the following statements are correct regarding an active licensed broker who has been licensed in Virginia since 1975, **EXCEPT**
    1. the broker may be licensed in more than one legal real estate entity.
    2. the broker is exempt from the continuing education requirements on the basis of having been licensed for more than 15 years.
    3. the broker may contract to be a property manager.
    4. the broker's office may be located in his or her home under certain circumstances.

11. Yore Realty opens its first office in Richmond. Which of the following is a permissible sign to place in front of the office?
    1. "Yore office"
    2. "Yore House: We Serve Richmond's Homeowners"
    3. "Yore Realty"
    4. "Yore: A Member of the Greater Richmond Chamber of Commerce"

12. A salesperson decides to retire. When the salesperson terminates his or her affiliation, what must he or she do?
    1. Give the broker an official letter of termination that he or she can send to the REB.
    2. Nothing; the broker is responsible for notifying the REB of the change.
    3. Return all customer cards to the employing broker.
    4. Return his or her license, along with a letter of termination, to the REB.

13. If a broker establishes an account to hold money belonging to others, which of the following is CORRECT?
    1. All checks, deposit slips, and bank statements must include the word "Escrow" as part of the account name.
    2. Accounts may be labeled either "Trust" or "Escrow."
    3. The account cannot be in the same bank as the broker's personal checking account.
    4. An individual account is required for each transaction.

14. If a broker is holding an earnest money deposit, how long must the funds be held if the sales contract does not close?
    1. Until the buyer requests a refund
    2. Until the broker is asked for the money by an attorney representing one of the parties
    3. Until all parties to the contract agree to the intended distribution
    4. Until the broker decides it is appropriate to do so

15. A broker manages three properties for the same owner. One property is in need of emergency repairs, but there is not enough money in the management account to cover the cost. The broker borrows money from the escrow account of one of the other properties to make the repairs. Which of the following is true?
    1. The broker has acted properly by safeguarding the client's interest.
    2. Such action is proper because all properties are owned by the same person.
    3. The broker is in violation of regulations for improperly handling escrow funds.
    4. The broker must use personal funds for repairs if there is not enough money in the management account.

16. Every Virginia real estate office is required to
    1. maintain escrow account records for 5 years.
    2. keep transaction records for 3 years.
    3. display signage at the office location.
    4. employ at least 1 salesperson.

17. What must appear on all "For Sale" signs placed on property by a broker?
    1. The broker's phone number
    2. The name of the person who listed the property
    3. The selling price of the property
    4. The name of the broker

18. Some ads placed by real estate franchise companies (noninstitutional advertising) must include specific disclosures. All of the following forms of advertising are exempt from the disclosure requirements **EXCEPT**
    1. one-column line listings in a telephone directory.
    2. "For Sale" yard signs on specific properties.
    3. a newspaper ad of less than 28 lines describing a single-family house.
    4. a newspaper ad of less than 28 lines describing a subdivision development.

19. A licensed salesperson is selling her own condominium and advertises it as follows: "For Sale By Owner: 3 bed. condo unit in high rise. Call 987-6543 for details. Owner licensed." Based on these facts, which of the following is true?
    1. Because the salesperson is acting in a private capacity, she is exempt from the advertising laws.
    2. The advertisement is proper because the owner has disclosed her licensee status as required by law.
    3. Virginia's advertising regulations do not apply to condominiums.
    4. The ad should have included her office number and broker.

20. Seller S's listing broker commits a fraudulent act in connection with the sale of a property on March 15, 1999. On March 30, the transaction closes. On November 1, S sues the broker, alleging fraud. On December 20, the jury finds in favor of S. When must S file a claim with REB to recover money from the Transaction Recovery Fund?
    1. The request must be filed within 30 days following the illegal activity: in this case, by April 15, 1999.
    2. Within 1 year after having been awarded a judgment by the courts: in this case, by December 20, 2000.
    3. Within 1 year of filing suit: in this case, by November 1, 2000.
    4. Within 2 years of the date of closing: in this case, by March 30, 2001.

21. What is the minimum balance of the Virginia Real Estate Transaction Recovery Fund?
    1. $800,000
    2. $750,000
    3. $600,000
    4. $400,000

22. After proper investigation, a payment is made from the Transaction Recovery Fund owing to the improper activities of H, a licensee. What happens when the payment is made?
    1. H's license is automatically suspended.
    2. The REB takes no further action if H repays the fund within 30 days.
    3. H's license is automatically revoked.
    4. H is subject to a fine of $2,000.

23. A licensed salesperson obtains a listing. Several days later, the salesperson meets prospective buyers at the property and tells them, "I am the listing agent for this property, and so I'm very familiar with it." Under these circumstances, the salesperson
    1. has failed to properly disclose his or her agency relationship.
    2. has properly disclosed his or her agency relationship with the seller.
    3. is in violation of REB regulations, because the listing belongs to the broker.
    4. has created a dual agency, which is a violation of REB regulations.

24. A broker is convicted on May 1 of possession and distribution of a controlled substance. Both the crime and the conviction took place in the state of Maryland. On June 15, the broker calls the REB and leaves a message informing the REB of the conviction. Based on these facts, which of the following is TRUE?
    1. The broker has properly informed the REB within 60 days after the conviction, and the broker's license may be renewed.
    2. Both the conviction and the broker's failure to notify the REB within 30 days violates REB regulations.
    3. Because the conviction did not occur in Virginia, it is not evidence of unworthy conduct.
    4. The conviction is evidence of both improper dealing and fraud.

25. When a salesperson takes an exclusive-right-to-sell listing, it is important that the listing agreement include all of the following information, **EXCEPT**
    1. the name of the employing broker.
    2. a definite date on which the listing will expire.
    3. an adequate property description.
    4. the net amount that the seller will receive from the sale.

26. Several weeks after a closing, an associate broker received a thank-you letter and a nice bonus check from the seller of the house. The associate broker cashed the check because he felt it was earned. In this situation, which of the following is TRUE?
    1. The associate broker may accept the bonus because he is licensed as an associate broker.
    2. Accepting the money is allowed if more than 30 days have elapsed since the closing.
    3. The associate broker may accept the money if his broker permits him to do so.
    4. Accepting the money is a violation of REB regulations.

27. Under the terms of a sales contract, the seller is required to provide a termite certificate. The seller requests that the salesperson order one. The salesperson does so, knowing she will receive a referral fee from the pest control company. Is this a violation of the license law?
    1. No, if the fee is less than $25.
    2. No, if the fee is disclosed in writing to the parties to the contract.
    3. Yes; a salesperson may not receive a referral fee.
    4. Yes; special fees may be paid to the salesperson only by the seller.

28. W, an airline pilot, told M, a broker, about some friends who were looking for a new home. M contacted the friends and eventually sold them a house. When may M pay W for the valuable lead?
    1. As soon as a valid sales contract is signed by the parties.
    2. Only after the sale closes.
    3. After the funds are released from escrow.
    4. M may not pay W for the lead.

29. When a sole proprietor has his or her license suspended for 2 years, what effect does this have on the associate brokers and salespeople affiliated with the proprietor?
    1. The affiliates' licenses will be revoked, subject to reinstatement after 1 year.
    2. The affiliates' licenses will be also be suspended for a 2-year period.
    3. The suspension has no effect on the affiliates.
    4. The affiliates' licenses must be returned to the REB.

30. When a salesperson is alleged to have violated the license law, possibly resulting in disciplinary action, which of the following statements is TRUE?
    1. An investigation will be conducted by the REB.
    2. The salesperson is entitled to a jury trial before any action can be taken.
    3. The salesperson's license will be temporarily suspended until the REB can schedule a formal hearing.
    4. The employing broker also is charged with the same violation.

11 Real Estate Financing: Principles And Practice

This chapter primarily discusses the financing of single-family residential real estate in Virginia. It does not address commercial or more sophisticated transactions, but many of the concepts addressed apply to such transactions.

PURCHASE CONTRACTS AND FINANCING

A licensed real estate broker or agent who has negotiated a sale may prepare a routine contract for the transaction. If a first deed of trust loan is to be obtained, the contract usually is made contingent on the purchaser's obtaining the loan. The real estate licensee must be careful in describing the loan because of the complexity of the terms for prevailing loans. The seller may add the provision that the purchaser must apply for the loan promptly and, should the purchaser not notify the seller by a certain date that loan approval has been obtained, the contingency shall be deemed waived. Typically, preprinted real estate contracts provide that the purchaser has a specified number of days from the date of the contract in which to apply for financing. The contract should specifically state what type of financing is contemplated: cash, assumption, seller financed, FHA, VA, or conventional loan obtained through an institutional lender.

The contract should provide a ceiling on the interest rate the borrower will accept. If this condition is not included, the purchaser could be bound by the contract even if the interest rate rises several percentage points between the date the contract is ratified and the date the purchaser locks in the interest rate with a lender. The lack of an interest rate cap could end up significantly increasing the cost of the home for the buyer.

If an existing loan is to remain on the property, the contract should specify whether it will be assumed or whether title will be taken subject to the existing loan.

INSTITUTIONAL FINANCING

Conventional Loans

In Virginia, deeds of trust, rather than mortgages, are the instruments primarily used in residential sales transactions. Nearly every type of financial institution makes conventional deed of trust loans. In Virginia, the note and deed of trust give the lender the right, in the event the borrower should default, to accelerate maturity and direct the trustee to hold a nonjudicial foreclosure—a foreclosure without a court hearing—to determine the propriety of the action. By signing the note and deed of trust, the borrower waives various rights, including the right to a court hearing.

It is extremely important that the borrower fully understand the nature of the note and deed of trust.

The note and deed of trust are generally prepared by the lender. Standard forms are available for specialized loans such as those insured (e.g., FHA) or guaranteed (e.g., VA) by the government. The note is not usually recorded although the deed of trust should always be promptly recorded.

The note and deed of trust should be signed in the exact manner and in the same name as the title is held. No witnesses are necessary. The deed of trust must be acknowledged, that is, notarized, to permit its recordation in the land records of the circuit court where the property is located. Further, VA and FHA notes, and notes to be sold out of state, require notarization with a seal. Good sources of information on residential financing are available on the Internet at the following web addresses:

WWWeb.Link
www.hud.gov [for FHA]
www.va.gov [for VA]
www.fanniemae.com,
www.freddiemac.com [for conventional loan products]

Late Charges

Many conventional first deed of trust loans contain a provision for a late charge if a monthly payment is not made within a certain period of time after the due date (referred to as a *grace period*). The fact that a late charge may be collected must be disclosed in the loan's truth-in-lending statement. In Virginia, late charges may not exceed 5 percent of the installment due and cannot be collected unless the payment is not made within 7 calendar days after the due date. Most lenders permit 15 days. The late charge must be specified in the contract between the lender and the borrower. Late charges in excess of the statutory amount are void only with regard to the excess amount; an inflated late charge does not affect the underlying obligation.

Other Charges

In addition to such charges as points, late charges, and escrows, Virginia law permits lenders to charge a *loan origination fee* for granting a loan.

Other allowable closing costs are the fees charged for title examination, title insurance, recording charges, taxes, hazard insurance, mortgage guarantee insurance, appraisals, credit reports, surveys, document preparation, real estate tax service fees, lender inspection, and attorney or settlement agent charges for closing the loan and settlement on the property.

The lender generally requires a house location survey. The survey must be current (within the past six months), and the survey must be done by a certified land surveyor.

CREDIT LINE DEEDS OF TRUST

A *credit line deed of trust* permits the note holder to make advances from time to time secured by the real estate described in the deed. The total amount of advances may not exceed the maximum credit line extended to the borrower. Virginia law permits credit line deeds of trust, subject to certain rules. The trust document must identify itself as a credit line deed of trust on the front page in capital letters and underscored type. The phrase THIS IS A CREDIT LINE DEED OF TRUST gives notice that the note holder named in the deed of trust and the grantors and other borrowers identified in the deed have an agreement.

From the date of the recording of a credit line deed of trust, the lien has priority over all other deeds, conveyances, and other instruments or contracts in writing that are unrecorded at that time and of which the note holder has no knowledge. The credit line deed of trust also has priority over judgment liens subsequently docketed. However, if a judgment creditor gives notice to the note holder at the address indicated on the credit line deed of trust, the deed of trust has no priority over the judgment for any advances or extensions of credit subsequently made under the deed of trust.

DUE-ON-SALE CLAUSES

Loans that contain a due-on-sale clause, also called an alienation clause, are not assumable unless the lender chooses to waive the due-on-sale clause. Due-on-sale clauses are enforceable in Virginia. When a loan containing a due-on-sale clause is made on real property comprising not more than four residential dwelling units, the deed of trust must contain the following language, either in capital letters or underlined:

> NOTICE—The debt secured hereby is subject to call in full or the terms thereof being modified in the event of sale or conveyance of the property conveyed.

PURCHASE-MONEY FINANCING

Purchase money financing occurs when a mortgage or deed of trust is given as part of the purchaser's consideration for the purchase of real property. Purchase money financing may be provided by a third party or by the seller. It commonly refers to a seller taking back a second trust in lieu of cash to make up the difference between the first trust and the selling price for the property.

FOR EXAMPLE *T* wants $100,000 for his property. The purchasers are able to secure a $70,000 loan secured by a first deed of trust. Since they only have $10,000 in cash available for a down payment, they ask *T* to accept a purchase-money deed of trust for $20,000. The rate and terms must be agreed upon between *T* and the purchasers.

A purchase-money deed of trust has priority over other claims or liens against the purchaser except for property tax or IRS tax liens.

DEFERRED PURCHASE-MONEY DEED OF TRUST

When the seller is an older person or when an installment sale tax treatment is desired, a deferred purchase-money deed of trust, held by the seller, is a useful method of financing. One advantage to sellers is that they usually receive a substantial down payment. Such an arrangement may be prohibited, however, if there is to be a first deed of trust to an outside (institutional) lender. A purchase-money deed of trust held by the seller should state that it is granted to secure *deferred purchase money*, while a purchase-money deed of trust to a third party states that it is granted to secure *purchase money*. If it is a second deed of trust, it can be for a short term with a balloon payment at the end. The first lender's guidelines must be followed. If it is subordinated, the purchase-money second deed of trust should include a provision that any default in a senior encumbrance or lien will also be considered a default on a second deed of trust.

RELEASES

Whenever the borrower pays off any note, a marginal release is made on the face of the instrument wherever the document is recorded. Alternatively, a certificate of satisfaction or a partial satisfaction form is filed in the deed books in the clerk's office in the county where the land is located.

VIRGINIA HOUSING DEVELOPMENT AUTHORITY

The Virginia Housing Development Authority (VHDA) was created in 1972 by the Virginia General Assembly. Its purpose is to make housing more affordable for those with low-income or moderate-income. Currently, VHDA is self-supporting, and funding for its programs are provided by the private sector through the sales of VHDA bonds. Federal and state tax dollars are not used to fund VHDA lending programs.

A board of commissioners composed of ten members appointed by the governor provides for oversight.

Basic VHDA services include

- Single-Family loan programs. Creative and lower interest rate loans for low-income to moderate-income homebuyers who have not had an ownership interest is his or her primary residence during the three years prior to making application for the loan.
- Multifamily loan products. Mortgage loans to developers of multifamily projects (primarily for rentals for low and moderate income tenants.)
- Administration of the federal low-income housing Tax Credit Program.
- Administration of the federal Section 8 rent subsidy programs.
- Virginia Housing Fund. Loans for multifamily housing that will serve low-income and moderate-income residents in difficult situations or locations.
- Administration of some functions of the Virginia Housing Partnership Fund.

VHDA offers a variety of different loan programs including those made in conjunction with FHA and VA. VHDA's new Flexible/Alternative program allows for 100 percent loan-to-value financing. A Homeownership Education course may be required of first-time buyers depending on their credit score.

Specific guidelines for the various VHDA loan products may be obtained from a local lender or by contacting VHDA headquarters in Richmond or online at the following web address:

WWWeb.Link
www.vhda.com.

VHDA also builds and operates residential housing, nursing care facilities, and nursing homes providing medical and related facilities for the residence and care of the elderly.

FORECLOSURE

There are three ways to foreclose a deed of trust in Virginia:

1. Decree of court (strict foreclosure)
2. Conveyance of the property by the grantors and the trustees to the beneficiary in consideration of the debt ("deed in lieu of foreclosure")
3. Sale by the trustee pursuant to a power of sale ("trustee sale")

Although an exhaustive discussion of foreclosure procedures is not necessary here, it is important for licensees to be aware that bankruptcy of the mortgagor is an automatic stay of foreclosure. If a lien is foreclosed, that is, no bankruptcy was granted, the lien and all inferior liens are wiped out. Superior liens, however—those that have priority over the foreclosed lien— are not affected. A purchaser takes the property subject to any prior liens.

VA and FHA Loans

Foreclosure of VA and FHA loans is subject to certain additional requirements. For instance, the loan must have been in default for three months prior to the commencement of foreclosure; notices must be given to both the debtor and the insuring agency; and the lender must take affirmative steps to avoid foreclosure, including personal interviews and acceptance of partial payments.

Trustee's Powers and Duties

Virginia is a *title theory* state.

Legal title to the property conveyed by the deed of trust is vested in the trustee for the benefit of the note holder. The trustee can act only in a manner authorized by statute or the express or implied terms of the trust.

The trustee is the agent for both the grantor (the homeowner) and the beneficiary (the lender) and is bound to act impartially between them. The trustee is obliged to seek every possible advantage to the trust in the course of any sale. This includes using all reasonable diligence to obtain the best price possible. The trustee may adjourn the sale from time to time to meet any unexpected occurrences, but the re-advertisement of the sale must be in the same manner as the original advertisement.

If it is clear at the sale that the property will be sold for a grossly inadequate or sacrificial price, it is the trustee's duty to adjourn the sale. In addition, if the trustee knows of facts that might keep bidding low, such as a cloud on title, he or she must adjourn the sale and remove the hindrance.

By statute, the trustee must ascertain whether there are any real estate tax liens against the property being sold. The trustee is obligated to pay the taxes out of the proceeds of sale and give the tax lien priority over the deed of trust. In addition, the purchaser is required to see that the taxes are paid. If the taxes are not paid, the trustee may be liable personally and the purchaser takes the land subject to the tax lien (though not personally liable for its payment). The trustee should also pay the prorated portion of the current year's real estate taxes.

Caveat Emptor

The rule of *caveat emptor* "let the buyer beware", applies in foreclosure sales, with regard to both the quality of title and the condition of the property.

Advertisement

The terms of the deed of trust will determine how the property is advertised. Even if the number of advertisements meets the terms, Virginia law provides that the sale may take place no earlier than the eighth day after the first advertisement and no later than 30 days after the last advertisement.

Conflict of Interest

A trustee may not purchase the property held in trust without written permission from the trustor. The trustee is bound by law to secure the highest possible price for the property, while a purchaser seeks to procure the property at the lowest possible price. The trustee's duty to the trust transcends any potential personal interest he or she may have or acquire in the property.

Auction

The sale must be held in accordance with the terms of the deed of trust, which specifies the time, manner, and place of sale. Unless the deed of trust states otherwise, the sale is held at the property itself, or near the circuit court building, or at some other place selected by the trustee in the city or county in which the property is located.

At the sale, the trustee sells the property to the highest bidder, and the successful purchaser executes a memorandum of sale. The trustee obtains the deposit from the purchaser.

Trustee's Deed

The trustee cannot convey a greater interest than the deed of trust gives authority to sell. The sale is subject to encumbrances that have priority over the deed of trust. Accordingly, the trustee's deed should contain only a special warranty of title. However, the form of the deed and the title conveyed must conform to the manner in which the property was advertised.

Disbursement of Proceeds

The trustee must apply the proceeds of sale in the following order:

1. discharge the *expenses of executing the trust,* including a commission to the trustee of 5 percent of the gross proceeds;
2. *discharge all taxes, levies, and assessments* with costs and interest, if they have priority over the deed of trust;
3. discharge, in the order of their priority, any *remaining debts and obligations* secured by the deed of trust and any liens of record inferior to the deed of trust, with interest; and
4. render the *residue of the proceeds to the grantor* (foreclosed mortgagor) or his or her assigns.

When the sale is made under any recorded deed of trust, the trustee must file a report and accounting with the commissioner of accounts within four months of the sale.

USURY

A *usurious transaction* is a contract for the loan of money at a greater rate of interest than allowed by law. Virginia law provides that loans secured by a first deed of trust on real estate may be lawfully enforced with *no limitation on the amount of interest*, if that arrangement is properly stated in the instrument or separate agreement. The contract generally is considered to be the promissory note. Most prudent lenders insert the rate in the note.

The law provides that disclosure of charges may be contained in an interest disclosure statement if such disclosure is not otherwise specified in the note. It further provides that an interest rate that varies in accordance with any exterior standard or that cannot be ascertained from the contract without reference to exterior circumstances or documents is enforceable as agreed in the signed contract. For instance, a note providing for an interest rate of 3 percent above the stated prime rate of a specific bank would be enforceable.

Allowable Interest Rates

Where the seller in a bona fide real estate transaction takes back a purchase-money deed of trust, the promissory note may provide for *any rate of interest agreed to by the parties*. Usury is not applicable to such a transaction because the interest rate is considered a time-price differential and thus part of the purchase price.

WET SETTLEMENT ACT

The Wet Settlement Act applies to transactions involving purchase-money loans secured by first deeds of trust on real estate containing not more than four residential dwelling units. The act applies only to lenders regularly engaged in making loans secured by real estate.

At or before the loan closing, the lender must disburse the loan proceeds to the settlement agent. The lender may not charge or receive interest on the loan until disbursement of the loan funds and the loan closing have occurred.

The settlement agent or attorney will have the deed, deed of trust, and any other necessary document recorded and will disburse the settlement proceeds within two business days of settlement. A settlement agent or attorney may not disburse any loan funds prior to recording the deed of trust or other security instrument perfecting the lender's security instrument. As a result, the seller will not receive his or her equity, and the real estate professional will not receive a commission check at the closing. Rather, all funds will be disbursed after the documents are recorded by the settlement agent.

Any person who suffers a loss because of the failure of a lender or settlement agent to disburse funds as required by law is entitled to recover double the amount of any interest collected in addition to actual damages, plus reasonable attorney's fees from the party that failed to disburse the funds appropriately.

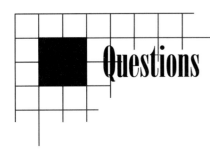

Questions

1. When borrowers sign a note and deed of trust, what have they agreed to regarding a court hearing if they default?
   1. To request the hearing within 30 days of default notice
   2. To permit the lender to set the place and time of the hearing
   3. To waive the hearing
   4. To abide by the court's ruling without appeal

2. The responsibility for preparing any promissory notes involved in a closing belongs to the
   1. seller's broker.
   2. settlement attorney.
   3. lender.
   4. buyer.

3. Which of the following statements is TRUE regarding a loan that is sold outside Virginia?
   1. The note must be acknowledged and recorded.
   2. The note must be notarized with a seal.
   3. The deed must be notarized.
   4. A loan secured by Virginia property may not be sold out of state.

4. What is the maximum late charge that may be assessed on a mortgage loan payment?
   1. No limit if the charge is stated in the loan contract
   2. 5 percent
   3. 10 percent
   4. 15 percent

5. *M* purchased a house with a conventional first deed of trust loan. *M*'s annual payment is $18,540, with monthly payments due on the tenth of each month. The loan has no provision for a grace period. If *M* makes a payment on June 18, can her lender legally impose a late charge?
   1. Yes; but no more than $154.50.
   2. Yes; but no more than $77.25.
   3. Yes; but no more than an amount equal to one month's interest.
   4. No; late fees on conventional first deeds of trust are illegal in Virginia.

6. A deed of trust that permits the borrower to receive advances from time to time up to a maximum amount secured by real property is referred to as an
   1. conventional loan.
   2. escrow credit loan.
   3. mortgage loan deed of trust.
   4. credit line deed of trust.

7. On a first deed of trust, what is the maximum interest that may be charged?
   1. No limit if the rate is stated in the loan contract
   2. 18 percent per year
   3. 20 percent per year
   4. 2 percent per month

8. What is the primary purpose of the Virginia Housing Development Authority?
   1. To encourage more housing development in Virginia
   2. To make housing more affordable for low and moderate income buyers
   3. To obtain funds from state tax dollars
   4. To replace VA and FHA funding in Virginia

9. *B* is granted a $40,000 maximum credit line deed of trust. He borrows $15,000 against it and then receives notice that a judgment for $10,000 has been docketed against him. *B* then withdraws $12,000 to pay other creditors; this amount is a new advance against his credit line deed of trust. The judgment creditor forecloses. Assuming the sale of the property brings enough money, what is the order in which the various amounts will be paid?
   1. $15,000, $10,000, $12,000
   2. $15,000, $12,000, $10,000
   3. $27,000, $10,000
   4. $10,000, $27,000

10. A sales contract on a Virginia property is signed on Monday, May 1. Closing takes place on Friday, June 10, and the deed of trust is recorded on Tuesday, June 15. The borrower's first payment is due on August 30. When is the soonest that the broker may receive his or her commission check?
    1. May 1
    2. June 10
    3. June 15
    4. August 30

12 Leasing

LEASING REAL ESTATE IN VIRGINIA: PRINCIPLES

Leases and landlord-tenant relationships are governed by Title 55, Chapter 13 [§§55-217 through 55-248] of the Code of Virginia, Table of Contents, Title 55, Chapter 13 at the following Web address:

 WWWeb.Link
http://leg1.state.va.us/000/src.htm

Sale of Rental Property

When property that is currently being rented is sold, the new owner stands in the same legal relationship to the lessee as did the previous owner. Likewise, the lessee may have like benefits of the lease as enjoyed with the previous owner "except the benefit of any warranty in deed or law." [§55-218]

Appointment of Agent by Nonresident

A nonresident of Virginia who owns real property consisting of four or more rental units (whether residential or commercial) must appoint a Virginia resident as agent for the purpose of receiving any notices, service of process, or other legal paper that would otherwise have been served on the owner. If an agent is not appointed, or if the one appointed cannot be found, the Secretary of the Commonwealth serves as agent. The secretary forwards any papers to be served on the owner to the owner's home address.

Termination of a Lease

Virginia law requires different notice periods depending on the length of the lease being terminated. The notice periods are a

- *3-month* notice to terminate a year-to-year lease,
- *30-day* notice to terminate a month-to-month lease, or
- *120-day* written notice to terminate a month-to-month lease, where the termination is due to rehabilitation of the property or a change in the property's use (such as conversion to a condominium).

If a definite termination date has been established, no notice is required.

Tenant Holdover

A tenant who, through no fault of his or her own, is unable to vacate the premises at the end of the lease term is not legally held to another full term of the lease. Rather, the tenant is liable to the lessor only for use and occupation of the premises and for any loss or damage suffered by the lessor. There may, however, be further legal issues.

Desertion

If a tenant whose rent is in arrears deserts the premises, the landlord may post a written notice in a conspicuous location on the premises requiring the tenant to pay the rent. A month-to-month tenant has ten days after the notice is posted; a yearly tenant has one month.

If the tenant fails to pay, the landlord may enter the premises, and the tenant's rights are ended. Nonetheless, the tenant still owes the rent up to the time of the landlord's reentry.

Failure to Pay Rent

For residential tenants, Virginia law specifies that failure to pay defaulted rents within five days of receiving notice results in the tenant's forfeiture of the right to possession.

Destruction of Premises

In some states, if the improvements on leased land are destroyed, the lessee is still bound by the terms of the lease and must continue paying full rent. Virginia has reversed and repealed this common-law doctrine. Tenants who are not at fault in the destruction of the improvements are entitled to a reduction in the amount of rent until the improvements are rebuilt and the tenants' previous use of the property can be restored.

A tenant's obligation to leave the property in good condition at the end of the lease terms is not an obligation that requires the tenant to rebuild in the event of destruction that was not his or her fault. Similarly, landlords are also under no positive duty to rebuild destroyed premises. Tenants are entitled to have the rent reduced in proportion to the diminished value of the leased premises. Tenants must be able to prove to the court that the destruction was not their fault and that the leased premises have been diminished in value to them.

Seizure of Tenant Property (Distress)

Goods belonging to a tenant may be seized for nonpayment of rent for up to five years after the rent is due, whether or not the lease has ended. The seizure is made by a sheriff or other officer, based on a warrant issued by a judge or magistrate. The warrant is based on a petition from the lessor. The lessor's petition must show: (1) the grounds for believing that the rent is due and (2) the exact amount owed. The lessor must post a bond.

A copy of the *distress warrant* (the order of seizure) is given to each defendant, along with a copy of the bond. The goods subject to seizure may include anything on the premises belonging to the tenant (including any assignees' or subtenants' goods) or goods that have been removed within the 30 days prior to seizure. If any of the goods seized are subject to a prior lien, the lessor's proceeds may be based only on the interest the tenant actually had in the personal property. Any sublessee is liable only to the extent that he or she owed money to the original tenant.

The seizure of a tenant's property arises from enforcing a landlord's lien, which is a statutory right. The landlord's lien relates back to the beginning of the tenancy, not merely to the time the rent became delinquent.

If seizure of the tenant's property is made for rent due, and any irregularity or unlawful act is performed during the proceeding by or for the landlord, the tenant may sue to recover damages from the landlord. However, the distress warrant itself is still lawful, and the tenant still owes the rent, despite any improper enforcement actions.

Prevention of Forfeiture

If a tenant who has been served with a "pay or quit" notice pays the arrears before his or her case comes to trial, the tenant will hold the tenancy just as he or she did before the proceedings began, without a new lease or conveyance. This could be looked upon as a sort of "right of redemption," similar to a debtor's right to recover property prior to a foreclosure sale. However, a tenant may exercise this right only once in any 12-month period.

Rent Control

In 1950, the Virginia General Assembly declared that federal rent control is no longer necessary in the state.

RESIDENTIAL LANDLORD AND TENANT ACT

Title §55, Chapter 13.2 of the Code of Virginia, the Residential Landlord and Tenant Act, was established to

- simplify and revise the laws for the rental of dwelling units;
- simplify and revise the rights of landlords and tenants;
- encourage the parties to maintain and improve the quality of housing; and
- provide a single body of law for landlord and tenant relationships.

Limitations

As the title implies, the act concerns itself with residential property. Not everyone or every residential property is subject to the act. The act does *not* apply to the following:

- Nonresidential rentals
- Residence at an institution if incidental to detention or the provision of medical, geriatric, educational, counseling, religious, or similar services
- Occupancy under a possession agreement by the purchaser of a property, i.e., an option contract
- Occupancy by a member of an organization in a portion of a structure operated for the organization
- Occupancy in a hotel, motel, or similar location for not more than a 30-day period if occupied continuously
- Occupancy by an employee of a landlord whose right to occupancy is a requirement or benefit of employment (such as a property manager)
- Occupancy by an owner of a condominium unit or holder of a proprietary lease in a cooperative
- Occupancy in HUD-regulated housing, where regulation is inconsistent with the statute
- Occupancy by a tenant who pays no rent
- Property owners who are natural persons (or their estates) who rent no more than ten single-family residences. Also, the act does not apply to owners who do not rent more than four single family residences and condominium units that are located in any city or any jurisdiction that has either an urban county executive or county manager form of government.

All apartments, regardless of the number owned and rented, are subject to the Residential Landlord and Tenant Act. Duplexes are considered to be apartments if there are common areas and/or utilities (such as one furnace.)

Application Fees

The landlord may charge a prospective tenant a fee at the time the tenant applies to lease a dwelling. If the fee exceeds $20 and the tenant does not rent the property, the landlord will refund all fees in excess of the landlord's expenses and damages (costs incurred for preparing the dwelling for occupancy, holding an unoccupied unit, etc.) within 20 days. If the application fees were made by cash, certified check, or money order, the excess will be refunded within ten days. The landlord may withhold $20 of the application fee to cover the cost of paperwork if it is specifically stated that this is a non-refundable application fee.

Unsigned or Undelivered Leases

If a written lease is not signed by either the lessor or the lessee, but the agreed rent is paid and accepted, the rental agreement is binding on both parties. Similarly, even if a lease is never delivered but the rent payments are accepted, the lease remains binding.

Security Deposits

The landlord may require the tenant to provide a security deposit at the time the property is leased. The security deposit is to protect the landlord against unpaid rents or damage—other than normal wear and tear—caused by tenants and/or pets during the lease period.

The security deposit may not exceed an amount equal to two months' rent. The deposit must be returned to the tenant within 45 days after the tenant vacates the property. If the landlord intends to withhold a portion of the security deposit to cover damages or losses, the tenant must be provided a written itemized list of such deductions. The landlord is required to make a final inspection of the dwelling within 72 hours of the termination of the lease. The landlord must notify the tenant of the date and time of the inspection, and the inspection must be at a reasonable time. The tenant has the right to be present during the landlord's inspection, but must advise the landlord in writing of the intent to be present.

When security deposits are held for 13 months or longer (in the case of renewed or multiyear leases), the landlord must pay interest to the tenant at 1% less than the federal discount rate, in effect on January 1 of each year, from the effective date of the agreement. Pet deposits are treated the same as a security deposit.

Landlord's Obligations

The landlord has certain obligations under the law; they are descibed below.

Disclosure of Ownership. The landlord must disclose to the tenant the name and address of the property owner or anyone authorized to manage the property or otherwise act on behalf of the owner. The disclosure must be in writing and provided to the tenant prior to the beginning of the tenancy. If the property is sold, the tenant must be supplied with the name, address, and telephone number of the purchaser. If the property is being converted to a condominium or cooperative, or if the tenant will be displaced due to the demolition or rehabilitation of the property within the next six months, the tenant is entitled to written notice of the situation.

Confidentiality. The landlord cannot release any financial or other information about a tenant to a third party without the tenant's written consent. The landlord is permitted to release information regarding the amount of rent paid for the tenant's unit and the tenant's record of payment. A contract purchaser of rental property may have access to all tenant information, however, without the tenant's consent.

Maintenance. Landlords must ensure that the premises comply with building and housing codes affecting health and safety. A landlord must maintain the property in a fit and habitable condition and keep common areas clean and safe. Electrical, plumbing, sanitary, heating, air conditioning, and other facilities and appliances supplied by landlords must be kept in good and safe working order, and all necessary repairs must be made. A tenant may accept appliances in "as is" condition, and the tenant may be responsible for maintenance under certain conditions if agreed to in writing. Landlords are responsible for providing adequate trash removal service, running water, and reasonable amounts of hot water (except when the hot water is supplied by the tenant or by a direct public utility connection).

If a landlord fails to maintain the property, the failure is considered to be a violation of the terms of a lease. The landlord could even be in violation of the law. A tenant whose landlord fails to properly maintain the premises must notify the landlord of the violation in writing. The landlord then has 30 days to correct the problem. Emergency situations warrant quicker action on the part of the landlord.

Tenants who choose to remain in a property, even though a violation has not been corrected, should continue to make rental payments within five days of the rental due date. However, the payments should be deposited with the general district court. To terminate a lease, a tenant must file a claim with the general district court.

House Rule Changes. During the period of occupancy, the landlord may adopt additional minor changes to the rules and regulations. However, changes to "house rules" may not alter the terms and conditions of the lease. For instance, a change in the hours the swimming pool is open or a requirement that parking decals be displayed on vehicles would be appropriate house rule changes; a change in the number of persons permitted in each unit would not be an appropriate midlease change. The landlord must give reasonable written notice of any rule changes.

Rule changes that substantially alter the rental agreement are only valid if the tenant agrees in writing to the changes. The tenant may refuse to accept the changes and insist on being bound only by the conditions of the original lease. However, at the expiration of the rental agreement, the tenant must either accept the changes or vacate the property.

Right to Access. The landlord must give the tenant reasonable notice of intent to enter the property, except in the case of an emergency. The tenant cannot deny a landlord's reasonable request, provided the landlord does not abuse the right. If the landlord abuses the right of access, the tenant may seek an injunction from the circuit court.

Tenant's Obligations

In addition to the lease provisions, the tenant has additional responsibilities under the law, as described below.

Condition of Property. A tenant must keep the leased premises as clean and safe as conditions permit. Garbage must be removed regularly. The facilities and equipment (including heating, plumbing, electrical, sanitary, air conditioning, and appliances) must be used in a reasonable manner. Tenants may not destroy or remove any part of the premises or permit anyone else to do so, either through negligence or deliberate act.

Behavior. Tenants must conduct themselves in a manner that will not disturb neighbors. Each tenant is expected to abide by all reasonable rules and regulations established by the landlord. A landlord may also serve notice to a guest of a tenant banning them from the premises for conduct violating the terms and conditions of the rental agreement, local, state, or federal law.

Violation of Rental Agreement. If a tenant violates the terms of a lease, the landlord must notify the tenant of the violation in writing and allow the tenant 21 days to correct the violation. If the tenant fails to take corrective action, the lease will terminate at the end of 30 days.

If repairs, replacement, or cleaning will correct the violation, the landlord may enter the property, correct the problem, and charge the tenant for any costs incurred. Under normal circumstances, the landlord must give the tenant 14 days' written notice prior to entering the premises. In an emergency, however, the landlord may enter and correct the violation as promptly as necessary.

Nonpayment of Rent. If rent payments are not received when due, the landlord may take the following actions:

- *Five Day Pay-or-Quit Notice.* The landlord may issue a written notice giving the tenant five days to pay the rent or vacate the property.
- *Unlawful Detainer Warrant.* The landlord may begin eviction proceedings immediately after issuing this warrant. The tenant remains obligated to pay the rent.
- *Eviction.* If full payment of rent is not received within five days, the landlord may file suit to have the tenant evicted. The landlord may not remove or exclude the tenant from the property or deny essential services until such time as the court takes eviction action.

Note: Recent legislation has passed to expedite the process for removing tenants from rental property. The unlawful detainer process now requires an initial hearing within 21 days, and the execution of the writ of possession by the sheriff should occur within 15 calendar days from the date received.

Returned Checks. If the tenant issues a check that is returned for insufficient funds, the landlord may give notice requiring payment in cash, cashier's check, or certified check within five days. If payment is not received, the landlord may proceed as with nonpayment of rent.

Security Devices. Tenants may install security equipment at their own expense. At the request of the landlord, the property must be restored to its original condition on termination of the lease. Tenants must provide the landlord with complete operating instructions, along with keys, codes, and passwords for any equipment installed.

Absence from the Property. If a tenant plans to be absent from the property for more than seven days, the landlord may enter the property for the purpose of protecting it. If the terms of the lease require tenant notification of extended absences, and if the tenant fails to advise the landlord, the tenant may be responsible for any damage that occurs during the absence.

Automatic Renewal Clauses

Many leases contain *automatic renewal clauses*. The clause specifies that the lease will automatically renew under the same terms and conditions unless either party gives written notice within a specific number of days prior to the termination date. Any changes, such as a rent increase, must be agreed to in writing by the tenant. Failure to agree to any changes constitutes notice to vacate. In the event that all terms and conditions including rent, remain unchanged, the renewal of a rental agreement is considered to be a new agreement.

Early Termination by Military Personnel

Military personnel who are transferred must be allowed to terminate a valid lease by giving the landlord at least 30 days' written notice and a copy of the official orders. Early termination cannot take place more than 60 days prior to the date necessary to comply with the orders.

The landlord may charge one month's rent as damages if the tenant occupied the property for less than six months *or* half of one month's rental if the tenancy was more than six months but less than one year.

Subleases

If the lease allows a tenant to sublease, the landlord must approve or disapprove the sublessee within ten days of written notification. Failure to respond within this time constitutes approval of the sublessee.

Disposal of Abandoned Property

Personal property left on the premises after the termination of a lease may be considered abandoned. The landlord may dispose of the abandoned property as he or she sees fit or appropriate, provided ten days' written notice has been given to the tenant. Any funds received from the sale of the abandoned property may be used to offset debts owed by the tenant, including the cost of moving and storing the abandoned property. Excess funds are treated as a security deposit.

Prohibited Lease Provisions

Virginia law does not permit the following provisions in residential leases:

- An agreement to waive any rights granted by Virginia law
- A confession of judgment or *cognovit* clause—an agreement by the tenant to permit an attorney to enter a confession of judgment against him or her in the event of a lawsuit arising out of the lease
- An agreement to pay the landlord's attorney fees (with certain exceptions)
- An agreement to limit the landlord's liability to the tenant or indemnify the landlord for the liability or any attendant costs
- An agreement to waive rights pertaining to the 120-day conversion or rehabilitation notice.
- An agreement for occupancy in public housing to restrict lawful possession of firearms unless required by federal law.

Any of these provisions, if included in a residential lease, is unenforceable. The inclusion of an unenforceable provision does not, however, void the lease.

Retaliatory Action

A landlord may not retaliate against a tenant who sues or otherwise seeks to enforce his or her legal rights or rights under the lease. Rent increases, a decrease in service, or termination of the lease are all barred retaliatory actions.

The tenant is protected from retaliation if the landlord has notice of any of the following:

- The tenant has complained to the government about building code violations or conditions dangerous to health or safety.
- The tenant has made a complaint to or filed suit against the landlord for violation of any provision of the Residential Landlord and Tenant Act.
- The tenant has organized or has become a member of a tenants' organization.
- The tenant has testified against the landlord in court.
- The tenant has complained about possible Fair Housing Law violations.

The act does not prevent a landlord from increasing rent in order to bring the property into line with prevailing market rentals for similar property. A landlord is also free to decrease services. The changes, however, must apply equally to all tenants.

MANAGEMENT RESPONSIBILITY

A property manager shares the owner's responsibility for ensuring that landlord-tenant relations comply with the Residential Landlord and Tenant Act. As the owner's agent, a property manager could be liable for any violations, especially fair housing and tenants' rights issues.

Questions

1. G, who lives in Virginia, is acting as resident agent for T, who lives in Los Angeles. T owns an apartment building in Alexandria. When a tenant is injured on the premises and decides to sue T, G is on an extended vacation and cannot be located when the notices are served. Who will receive these notices?
   1. The sheriff
   2. The president of the tenants' association
   3. T, the owner
   4. The Secretary of the Commonwealth

2. H owns the Cherry Run apartment complex, which has fallen into disrepair. H decides to repair and renovate the buildings and convert them to condominiums. How much notice is required to terminate the tenants' month-to-month leases?
   1. 30 days
   2. 60 days
   3. 90 days
   4. 120 days

3. A tenant rents farmland, a barn, and a house. The buildings are destroyed by a fire caused by lightning. Must the tenant still pay rent and abide by all the terms of the lease?
   1. Yes; based on common law principles governing ground leases.
   2. Yes; any damage to or destruction of the leased premises is the tenant's responsibility.
   3. No; destruction of the improvements terminates a ground lease.
   4. No; if the tenant is not at fault, he or she is entitled to release from the lease or a reduction in rent until his or her use of the land is restored.

4. A one-year lease period begins on April 1, 2001. The tenant stops paying rent on July 1; the notice to quit is received on August 1; and the landlord's lien is recorded on December 15. When does the landlord's lien attach to the tenant's property?
   1. April 1, 2001
   2. July 1, 1999
   3. August 6, 1999
   4. April 1, 2000

5. Four months before her lease expires, V abandons her apartment, stops paying rent, and disappears. V leaves her furniture and an expensive entertainment center behind. If the landlord sells the apartment's contents at a "garage sale," which of the following is true?
   1. V's obligation to pay rent for the lease term ends if the sale nets an amount equal to the outstanding rent.
   2. Because the landlord failed to obtain a distress warrant, V is relieved of all obligations under the lease and is entitled to damages.
   3. V may be entitled to damages for the landlord's unlawful seizure, but because the seizure was for rent due, V is not relieved of the obligation to pay the outstanding rent.
   4. The landlord acted improperly, no seizure of a tenant's property is lawful until the lease has ended.

6. A prospective tenant applies for a lease in the Seven Hills apartment building and pays the mandatory $125 application fee. If the tenant decides not to sign a lease, what happens to the application fee?
   1. The fee may be kept by Seven Hills.
   2. The fee must be returned to the prospective tenant within 20 days.
   3. The fee must be returned to the prospective tenant, less a 10 percent charge to cover paperwork.
   4. All sums in excess of the landlord's actual expenses must be returned to the prospective tenant.

7. A landlord, who is subject to the Residential Landlord and Tenant Act, charges $750 per month for an apartment. What is the maximum amount the landlord can require as a security deposit?
   1. $750
   2. $1,000
   3. $1,500
   4. $2,250

8. *B* entered into a one-year lease on July 1, 1999, with the right to continue on a month-to-month basis after the lease expires. *B* gave the landlord a 1 month rent security deposit. In accordance with the terms of the lease, *B* gives proper notice and vacates the property on October 31, 2000. How much interest will accrue on *B*'s 1 month rent security deposit?
   1. None
   2. 4 month's interest
   3. 12 month's interest
   4. 16 month's interest

9. During a crime wave, a tenant decides to install a burglar alarm in a rented house. Does the tenant need to inform the landlord?
   1. No; the tenant has full right of possession during the lease.
   2. No; only tenants in multiunit apartment buildings are required to inform a landlord about a security system.
   3. Yes; the tenant must also give the landlord instructions and passwords.
   4. Yes; but the cost of the system may be deducted from the rent.

10. Sgt. *T* rented an apartment at Happy Villas five months ago. He has now been reassigned to a different air base with orders to move in 30 days. His landlord may charge him for damages of
    1. 1 month's rent.
    2. 7 month's rent.
    3. ½ of 1 month's rent.
    4. nothing because he is military.

13 Fair Housing and Ethical Practices

The Virginia Fair Housing Law, Title 36, Chapter 5.1 [§36-96.1] states that it is the policy of the commonwealth to provide for fair housing throughout the commonwealth, to all its citizens *regardless of race, color, religion, national origin, sex, elderliness, familial status, or handicap*. All discriminatory practices in residential housing transactions are prohibited.

Virginia's fair housing law has been ruled substantially equivalent to the federal fair housing law. It is an exercise of the state's police power for the protection of the peace, health, safety, prosperity, and general welfare of the people of Virginia.

All *inhabitants* of Virginia are protected by the Virginia Fair Housing Law, whether or not they are also citizens of the commonwealth. See Code of Virginia Title 36, Chapter 5, at the following Web address

 WWWeb.Link
http://leg1.state.va.us/cgi-bin/legp504.exe?000+cod+36-96.1)

Protected Classes

The Virginia Fair Housing Law prohibits discrimination in housing and real estate activities on the basis of

- race,
- color,
- religion,
- national origin,
- sex,
- elderliness,
- familial status, or
- handicap.

Definitions

Certain terms in the fair housing law have specific legal definitions.

Dwelling. A *dwelling* refers to all or part of any building or structure designated or intended for use as a residence by one or more families. The term also includes vacant land offered for sale or lease for the construction or location of any residential building or structure.

143

Elderliness. For purposes of the fair housing law, an "elderly" person is any individual who has attained his or her 55th birthday.

Familial status. The fair housing law protects families against discrimination. A *family* is defined as a parent or other person who has legal custody of one or more individuals under the age of 18 who live with the parent or other person. The definition also extends to persons with custody of a minor with the written permission of a parent or guardian. The term also includes pregnant women and people who are in the process of securing legal custody of a minor.

Handicap. A person is considered "handicapped" if he or she suffers from a physical or mental impairment that substantially limits one or more of his or her major life activities. Having a record of such an impairment, or being regarded as having such an impairment, also constitutes handicaps under the fair housing law. The law does apply to individuals in a recognized drug treatment program. The statute does not apply to persons who use or are addicted to illegal substances. Transvestites are specifically excluded from the definition of handicap.

EXEMPTIONS

As with the federal law, there are some exemptions in Virginia, and they are

- A single-family residence sold or rented by the owner is exempt from the statute, as long as the owner owns no more than three homes at the time and, in the case of a sale, has not sold more than one rental property in the past 24 months. This exemption applies only if an owner does not employ the services of a real estate licensee and no discriminatory advertising is used.
- Rooms or units in one-to-four family structures are exempt if the owner occupies one of the units and does not use discriminatory advertising.
- Religious organizations, institutions, associations, or societies may limit the sale or rental of property they own or operate for other than commercial purposes to persons of the same religion. Such organizations may give preference to their members, as long as membership in the organization is not restricted on the basis of race, color, national origin, sex, elderliness, familial status, or handicap.
- Private, state-owned, or state-supported educational institutions, hospitals, nursing homes, religious organizations, and correctional institutions may, for personal privacy reasons, require single-sex occupancy of its owned and operated single-family residences, rooms, and units. Single-sex restrooms in such dwellings or buildings are not illegal.
- Private membership clubs that provide lodging that they own or operate for other than commercial purposes may give preference to their members.

Advertising for Shared Dwellings

An individual who intends to share his or her living quarters with another may advertise on the basis of sex, but only on the basis of sex. For example, an ad could say, "Females only need apply," but it could not say "Christian females" or "white females."

Single-Family Occupancy

Certain restrictive covenants and zoning laws exist that restrict housing in an area to single-family housing. According to Virginia Fair Housing law, a family care home, foster home, or group home in which no more than eight persons reside who are mentally ill, retarded, or developmentally disabled, together with resident counselors or staff, is considered single-family occupancy for zoning purposes. For purposes of restrictive covenants, there is no maximum number of residents.

A condominium unit owners' association may, if permitted by the bylaws, restrict the number of occupants in any unit, as long as the limitation is reasonable and not more restrictive than the local zoning ordinance.

Housing for Elderly Persons

It is legal to discriminate on the basis of age to permit housing for elderly persons. Housing is exempt from the familial status protection if it is provided under a state or federal program designed to assist the elderly, or if it is intended for and solely occupied by persons at least 62 years of age, or if it has at least one person 55 years of age or older in 80 percent of the occupied units. Qualified housing in this second category must provide the elderly with important housing opportunities and adhere to published policies and procedures that demonstrate the intent to provide such housing.

Criminal Background

People who have been convicted of the illegal manufacture or distribution of controlled substances are not protected by the fair housing law.

Rental applications may require the disclosure of any criminal convictions, and applicants may be required to consent to and to pay for a criminal background check. A building manager or property owner may refuse to rent a dwelling to an individual who has a record of prior criminal convictions involving harm to persons or property, and whose presence would pose a threat to the health or safety of others.

Similarly, the law's protections do not make it unlawful for an owner to deny or limit residential rentals to persons who pose a clear and present threat of substantial harm to others or the premises.

In Practice

Local counties, cities, and towns may enforce legislation adopted prior to 1991 that is *more restrictive* than either the state or the federal law. Any amendments to the local legislation, however, must conform to the state's law. Because licensees often practice in more than one jurisdiction within the state, they must be aware of all local legislation that differs from federal and state laws.

Impact for Real Estate Licensees

It is illegal for real estate licensees to be involved in discriminatory housing practices in any way. While licensees should be aware of the exemptions in order to fully comply with the law, it is of more vital importance that they comply with the law's nondiscriminatory intent. The law [§36.96.2A] states that

> ..this exemption shall not apply to or inure to the benefit of any licensee of the Real Estate Board, regardless of whether the licensee is acting in his personal or professional capacity.

UNLAWFUL DISCRIMINATORY HOUSING PRACTICES

In Virginia, it is illegal for anyone to commit any of the following discriminatory acts on the basis of a person's race, color, religion, national origin, sex, elderliness, familial status, or handicap:

- Refusing to sell or rent a dwelling to any person who has made a bona fide offer to do so, or refusing to negotiate the sale or rental of a dwelling
- Discriminating against any person in the terms, condition, or privileges of the sale or rental of a dwelling, or in providing services or facilities
- Making, printing, or publishing any notice, statement, or advertisement with respect to the sale or rental of a dwelling that indicates an actual or intended preference, limitation, or discrimination
- Falsely representing that a dwelling is not available for inspection, sale, or rental
- Denying membership or participation in a multiple listing service (MLS), real estate brokers' organization, or any other service, organization, or facility related to the business of selling or renting dwellings
- Including any discriminatory restrictive covenant in the transfer, sale, rental, or lease of housing, or honoring any discriminatory restriction
- Inducing or attempting to induce the sale or rental of a dwelling by representations regarding the entry or prospective entry into the neighborhood of protected persons
- Refusing to sell, rent, or negotiate with anyone on the basis of their own handicap, or that of anyone who will be residing in the dwelling, or anyone associated with them
- Discriminating in the terms, conditions, or privileges of the sale or rental of a dwelling, or in its services or facilities on the basis of an individual's handicap, or that of anyone associated with the individual

In Practice — The use of words or symbols associated with a particular religion, national origin, sex, or race is considered prima facie evidence of an illegal preference. The use of such words or symbols may not be overcome by a general disclaimer that no discrimination is intended.

Special Rule Regarding Handicapped Persons

Handicapped individuals, that is, persons with disabilities, must be permitted to make reasonable modifications, at their own expense, of existing premises in order to make the premises fully accessible to the individual. A landlord may make modification of rented premises conditional on the tenant's agreement to restore the premises to their original condition (reasonable wear and tear excepted) if it affects the value of the property.

It is unlawful to refuse to make reasonable accommodations in rules, practices, policies, or services in order to afford handicapped individuals equal opportunities to use and enjoy a dwelling. For instance, a "no pets" policy should be flexible enough to accommodate service animals, such as a seeing-eye dog or an assistance monkey.

New multifamily dwellings, that is, those with four or more units, must be designed and constructed in such a way that the public use and common areas are readily accessible to handicapped persons. All ground-floor unit doors must allow passage by persons in wheelchairs and contain light switches, electrical outlets, and environmental controls that are accessible by persons in wheelchairs. Kitchens and bathrooms must be designed for full maneuverability. In buildings with elevators, all units must meet the accessibility requirements.

Lending Institutions   The fair housing law also applies to lending institutions and other businesses involved in residential real estate transactions. It is unlawful to discriminate in the availability, terms, or conditions of real estate financing on the basis of race, color, religion, national origin, sex, elderliness, familial status, or handicap. Discrimination on the basis of financial qualification is permitted, however.

If any lending institution is found to be engaging in unlawful discriminatory practices, the fair housing law forbids state, county, city or municipal treasurers, or other government officials from depositing public funds in the institution. Existing deposits of public funds must be withdrawn from offending lenders, although the action may be deferred for one year to avoid financial loss to the state, county, city, or agency. If the lender corrects its practices, there is no prohibition against the deposit of public funds.

The Virginia Fair Housing Law also applies to those who are involved indirectly in the sale or rental of real property, such as newspapers and other publications. Appraisers cannot include any discriminatory information in appraisal reports.

ENFORCEMENT OF THE FAIR HOUSING LAW

Persons who feel that their rights under the fair housing law have been violated may take action against the party alleged to have discriminated. Complaints must be filed with the Real Estate Board (REB), which is empowered to initiate and receive complaints, investigate alleged violations, and resolve conflict either by conference and conciliation or by issuing a charge and referring the matter to the Attorney General for action.

A complaint must be filed with the REB within one year of the occurrence or termination of the alleged discriminatory practice.

In any action brought under the Virginia Fair Housing Law, the burden of proof is upon the complainant. The REB must acknowledge receipt of the complaint and advise the claimant of time limits and choices of forums for hearing the complaint.

Accused persons must be notified of the allegation and of their legal rights within ten days. Proceedings must commence within 30 days after receiving the complaint. The investigation must be completed within 100 days. While the investigation may take longer than 100 days in some circumstances, no investigation may take more than a year from the date of the complaint.

The REB may issue subpoenas, interview witnesses, and request the production of documents in the course of its investigation. During the investigative period, it is possible for the complainant and respondent to enter into a conciliation agreement, subject to REB approval.

If reasonable cause exists to believe that a discriminatory housing practice has occurred or is about to occur, the REB must seek resolution by conciliation or forward the charge to the attorney general for civil action. If no reasonable cause exists, the case will be dismissed.

Penalties

If the case results in civil action by the Attorney General, the court may

- award preventive relief by temporary or permanent injunction, restraining order, or other necessary order;
- award other appropriate relief, including compensatory or punitive damages;
- assess civil penalties (in cases involving zoning or land use ordinances, patterns, or practices of discrimination or the breach of a conciliation agreement) of up to $50,000 for a first violation and up to $100,000 for any subsequent violation; and
- award the prevailing party reasonable attorney's fees and costs.

Whether or not a complaint has been filed with the REB, a civil action may also be initiated by an injured person in a U.S. district court or state court within two years after the occurrence or termination of an alleged discriminatory housing practice. If a civil action is filed at the same time a complaint is filed with the REB, the REB will delay action until the court rules. If a conciliation agreement is breached, a civil action may be filed within two years of the breach.

Actions Against Licensees

If any real estate licensee is found guilty of violating the fair housing law, the REB will take appropriate steps to consider suspension or revocation of the license, or take other disciplinary action.

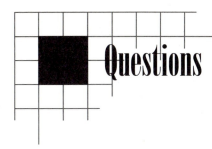

Questions

1. Which of the following is protected by the Virginia Fair Housing Law?
   1. Marital status
   2. Familial status
   3. Source of income
   4. Dietary restriction

2. All of the following are protected by the Virginia Fair Housing Law's provisions for the handicapped or elderly **EXCEPT** a
   1. 55-year old recovered heroin addict.
   2. 62-year old cocaine user.
   3. paralyzed veteran.
   4. mentally ill person.

3. An owner may discriminate on the basis of religion in selling or renting his or her own house in which of the following situations?
   1. The ad clearly states that religion is a criterion.
   2. The broker is fully informed of the religion criterion.
   3. The owner already owns four other properties rented to persons of the same religion.
   4. The owner is a religious organization or institution.

4. M was looking for someone to share her house. She placed the following advertisement in the local paper: "Share lovely town house. Large wooded lot, near transp, shops, and recreation. $650 per mo. Nonsmoker, female." Which of the following is TRUE?
   1. The ad is a violation of the fair housing law because it discriminates against people who smoke.
   2. The ad violates the fair housing law's prohibition against sexual discrimination.
   3. The ad is legal because M is sharing her own home.
   4. The newspaper is now subject to a civil action for publishing a discriminatory ad.

5. A building manager receives a lease application from T, a prospective tenant. The application discloses that T served time in prison for income tax evasion. T now has regular income from a manufacturing job and otherwise meets the building's qualification standards. Can the building manager lawfully refuse to rent an apartment to T?
   1. No; the fair housing law prohibits discrimination on the basis of prior criminal record.
   2. No; T's criminal conviction did not involve harm to persons or property.
   3. Yes; the fair housing law permits a building manager to refuse to rent to any convicted criminal.
   4. Yes; the fair housing law does not apply to actions by building managers.

6. When a young couple just recently immigrating from El Salvador attempted to rent an apartment, they were told that no units were available when in fact there were at least four available at that time. The rental company was guilty of
   1. nothing; they have the right to say what they please.
   2. nothing; they have the right to limit rentals to U.S. citizens.
   3. unlawful discriminatory housing practice of false representation.
   4. discrimination based on age.

7. A "no pets" policy would have to be waived in all of the following cases **EXCEPT**
   1. M has two small cats that have lived with her for 10 years.
   2. H is legally blind and needs a seeing-eye dog.
   3. J is hearing impaired and requires the service of a small dog that responds to alarms, doorbells, etc.
   4. D suffers from mild paralysis and needs the assistance of a spider monkey.

8. Two people apply for a mortgage loan from Mighty Mortgage Company: R, a 65-year-old blind male with no income or savings; and S, a 35-year-old black female with no debts and a six-figure income from her law practice. Based on these facts alone, if both R and S are turned down, Mighty Mortgage has most likely committed unlawful discrimination against:
   1. R only
   2. S only
   3. Both R and S
   4. Neither R nor S

9. Investigations of fair housing complaints must be completed within how long after a complaint is filed?
   1. 30 days
   2. 60 days
   3. 100 days
   4. 1 year

10. A civil action brought by the attorney general for a first violation of the Virginia Fair Housing Law could subject a guilty party to a monetary civil penalty of
    1. up to $10,000 for a first offense.
    2. up to $25,000 for a first offense.
    3. up to $50,000 for a first offense
    4. actual damages and legal fees only.

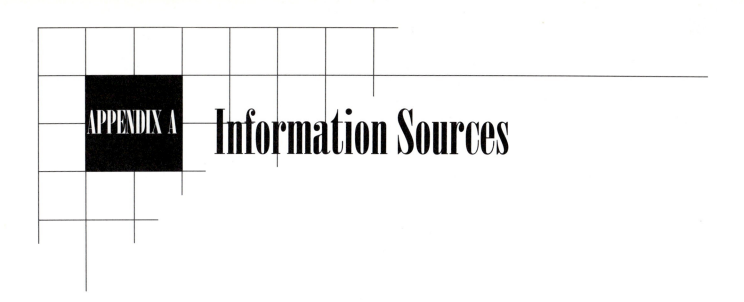

The Virginia Legislative Information System

The Virginia Legislative Information System (LIS) provides an easy way to locate sources of information in many areas. "Bookmarking" or making the LIS a "favorite" Web site will quickly give you access for individual research. The sample problem below shows one way to navigate the LIS.

Sample Research Problem

What happens to a brokerage firm when a principal broker dies or is disabled?

1. Go to the Legislative Information System Web site at **http://leg1.state.va.us**

2. Under Searchable Database, click on Code of Virginia
   (direct address: **http://leg1.state.va.us/000/src.htm**)

   The Code of Virginia Searchable Database provides space for a "search phrase" or provides an opportunity to browse the Table of Contents.

3. Click on Table of Contents
   (direct address: **http://leg1.state.va.us/cgi-bin/legp504.ex?000+cod+TOC**)

4. Select from Table of Contents Title 54.1 — Professions and Occupations
   Title 54.1 offers a "search for in this title only" and lists Table of Contents
   (direct address: **http://leg1.state.va.us/cgi-bin/legp504.exe?000+cod+TOC5401000**)

5. Select Chapter 21 — Real Estate Brokers, Salespersons and Rental Location Agents
   (notice that references are made as §§54.1-2100 through 54.1-2144)

   Chapter 21 offers a "search for in this chapter only" and lists Table of Contents
   (direct address: **http://leg1.state.va.us/cgi-bin/legp504.exe?000+cod+TOC54010000021000000000000**)

6. Click on §54.1-2109 and see:
   §54.1-2109. Death or disability of a broker.
   "Upon the death or disability of a licensed real estate broker..".

Figure A.1   Page 1 of the Virginia LIS Website

**Figure A.2   Title 54.1, Chapter 21
Real Estate Brokers, Sales Persons and Rental Location Agents**

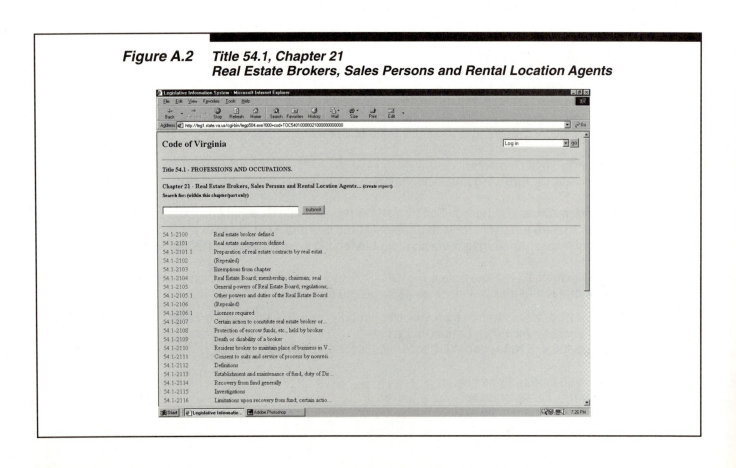

The very long direct http addresses are confusing and difficult to read and/or remember. By accessing the Legislative Information System you will have immediate access to either the Code of Virginia or the Virginia Administrative Code. From this point, use a "search phrase" or pull up the appropriate section from the Table of Contents.

Other Sources for Real Estate Information

Department of Professional and Occupational Regulations
3600 West Broad Street
Richmond, Virginia 23230-4917
(804) 367-8500
www.state.va.us/dpor

The Virginia Real Estate Board
3600 West Broad Street
Richmond, Virginia 23230-4917
(804) 367-8509
www.state.va.us/dpor

The Virginia Fair Housing Office
3600 West Broad Street
Richmond, Virginia 23230-4917
(804) 367-8530
www.state.va.us/dpor/fairhs01.htm *or*
www.fairhousing.vipnet.org

The Virginia Association of REALTORS®
10231 Telegraph Road
Glen Allen, Virginia 23059-4578
(804) 264-5033 or toll-free (800) 755-8271
www.VARealtor.com

Virginia Housing Development Authority
601 S. Belvidere Street
Richmond, Virginia 23220-5604
(800) 227-VHDA (8432)
www.vhda.com

Virginia State Bar
707 E. Main St., Ste. 1500
Richmond, Virginia 23219-2800
(804) 775-0570
www.vsb.org

Virginia State Taxation
www.tax.state.va.us

Sex Offender Information
www.state.va.us/vsp/vsp.html

Lead-based Paint Information
www.epa.gov/lead

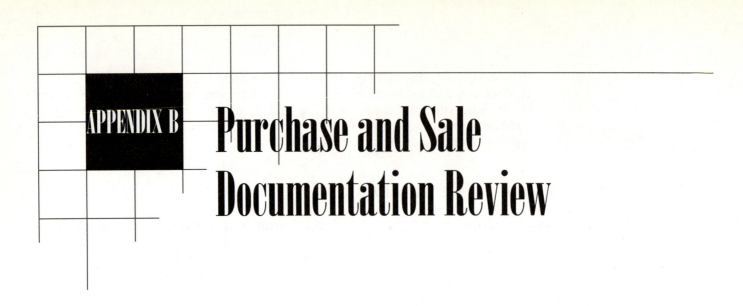

Appendix B: Purchase and Sale Documentation Review

Required Documentation for Purchase and Sale of Residential Real Estate in Virginia

Agency Disclosure

"Exclusive Right to Represent" (Listing Agreement): with Seller Client

"Exclusive Right to Represent Buyer Agency Agreement": (with Buyer Client)

Although oral agreements are legal in Virginia, it is, recommended that all brokerage relationships be established in writing with signatures of both client and broker.

If seller or buyer is NOT a client but is a customer, that is, no brokerage relationship exists between broker and principal, disclosure must be provided to the customer unless that party has their own agent:

"Disclosure of Brokerage Relationship" (Form to be Signed by Customer)

Documentation Required from Seller

"Virginia Residential Property Disclosure" or "Residential Property Disclaimer"

"Lead-based Paint Disclosure" (for properties built prior to 1978)

"Condominium document packet" (if property is a condominium)

"Property Owner Association packet" (if property located in a POA act development)

Documentation Required from Buyer

"Offer to Purchase/Contract" (if using Regional Sales Contract must include "Virginia Jurisdictional Addendum")

"Disclosure of Dual or Designated Representation" (if both parties to the transaction are represented by same broker)

"Lead-Based Paint Disclosure" and acknowledgement of receipt of EPA "Hazards of Lead-Based Paint" pamphlet.

APPENDIX C Practice Examination

1. Salesperson S represents Seller K and Salesperson B represents Buyer J in the same transaction. S and B both work for Broker N. In this situation, S is known as a(n)
   1. associate broker.
   2. subagent.
   3. single agent.
   4. designated agent.

2. Who of the following MUST hold a real estate license in Virginia?
   1. An attorney preparing an abstract of title
   2. A local multiple listing service company
   3. An officer of a limited liability company that specializes in commercial property
   4. A business executive selling her company's surplus acreage

3. The duties that an agent owes to his or her client are established by
   1. statute.
   2. common law.
   3. the agent's broker.
   4. the agent's client.

4. All of the following are ways to terminate a brokerage relationship EXCEPT
   1. default by either party.
   2. death of the salesperson.
   3. expiration of the agreement.
   4. mutual agreement by the parties to terminate.

5. Property disclosure and disclaimer forms must contain notice to purchasers regarding Megan's Law advising them of the source for information on
   1. registered sex offenders.
   2. agency representation.
   3. known property defects.
   4. stigmatized property.

6. If the seller gives the buyer the required disclosure/disclaimer statement three days after the contract is signed, when can the buyer terminate the contract?
   1. Within 15 days of date sent, if e-mailed
   2. Within 10 days, if hand carried
   3. Within 5 days of postmark, if mailed
   4. Under the doctrine of caveat emptor, the buyer cannot terminate the contract.

7. If a married woman with three children dies intestate, how would her property be distributed?
   1. To her husband under laws of dower and curtesy
   2. One-third to her husband, the remaining two-thirds to her children equally
   3. One-half to her husband, the other half to her children equally
   4. Two-thirds to her husband, the remaining third to her children equally

155

8. J is an unmarried homeowner of a $475,000 mansion. What is the total maximum value of J's homestead exemption?
   1. $4,750
   2. $5,000
   3. $237,500
   4. $475,000

9. When D died, he left his wife $10,000 and all of the rest of his property to his two children. D's wife renounced the will in order to claim her elective share of his augmented estate. She will now be entitled to
   1. all of his estate.
   2. one-half of his estate.
   3. one-third of his estate.
   4. none of his estate, but she may continue to live there.

10. H, M and R are joint tenants. M sells his tenancy to T. Which of the following is TRUE of this situation?
    1. H, R and T are now joint tenants.
    2. H, R and T are now tenants in common.
    3. H and R are tenants in common, with a joint tenancy with T.
    4. H and R are joint tenants with a tenancy in common with T.

11. S and J are tenants in common, and J dies intestate. What happens to J's interest?
    1. It passes to J's heirs.
    2. It passes to S as a sole owner.
    3. It passes to J's heirs with S as a joint interest.
    4. It passes to J's heirs if the property is sold.

12. K owns an individual unit in a condominium building and wants to sell it. Which of the following documents does K need to show prospective buyers before K can sell the unit?
    1. A list of any past suits or judgments against the condominium association
    2. A copy of the balance due on K's deed of trust loan
    3. A copy of the current bylaws and rules and regulations
    4. A plat map indicating the location of the condominium building

13. A and B have recently signed a contract to purchase a town house in a development governed by a Property Owner Association. They will be able to cancel this contract if they:
    1. change their minds.
    2. cancel any time prior to closing.
    3. cancel within 3 days of receiving the POA disclosure packet.
    4. cancel within 14 days of receiving the POA disclosure packet.

14. The following is what kind of legal description?
    All those certain lots, pieces or parcels of land, situated in the city of Roanoke, Virginia, known, numbered and designated on the Plat of Hampton Square and recorded in the clerk's office of the Circuit Court of the City of Roanoke, Virginia, in Map Book 26, page 7, as Lots No. 9 and 10.
    1. Metes-and-bounds
    2. Rectangular survey
    3. Government survey
    4. Lot-and-block

15. What is the most common method of describing real estate in Virginia?
    1. Combination of metes-and-bounds and government survey
    2. Combination of metes-and-bounds and lot-and-block
    3. Combination of lot-and-block and government survey
    4. Combination of rectangular survey and government survey

16. If a contractor records a mechanic's memorandum of lien on September 15, 2000, how long does he or she have to file a suit to enforce it?
    1. Until October 15, 2000
    2. Until December 31, 2000
    3. Until March 15, 2001
    4. Until September 15, 2001

17. If all of the following liens are recorded against a property and the owner forecloses, which will be paid first?
    1. Real estate tax lien
    2. Mechanic's lien
    3. Deed of trust lien
    4. Vendor's lien

18. *P* owns a house in severalty and wishes to sell it. His broker tells him that his wife, *N*, will need to sign the contract even though she does not own the property. Why would this be the case?
    1. *N* is required to sign the contract under the Statute of Frauds.
    2. *N* is required to sign the contract to convert the equitable title into legal title.
    3. *N* is required to sign the contract so that the title is "marketable."
    4. *N* is required to release any future interest in the property she might hold.

19. An implied warranty against structural defects on new construction continues for how long?
    1. 6 months after the date of transfer of title or the buyer's taking possession
    2. 1 year after the date of transfer of title or the buyer's taking possession
    3. 2 years after the date of transfer of title or the buyer's taking possession
    4. 5 years after the date of transfer of title or the buyer's taking possession

20. All of the following are requirements for a valid deed **EXCEPT**
    1. the signature of the grantee.
    2. consideration.
    3. accurate legal description of the property.
    4. delivery and acceptance of the deed.

21. *F* buys *T*'s home for $149,500. Which of the following is a correct statement of the grantor and recordation taxes to be paid?
    1. *F* will pay $224.25; *T* will pay 224.25.
    2. *F* will pay $224.25; *T* will pay $74.75.
    3. *F* will pay $299.00; *T* will pay $149.50.
    4. *F* will pay $149.50; *T* will pay $299.00.

22. *M* was very careful to execute a will leaving her beachfront condominium to her favorite niece, *S*. *S* will receive title to the property
    1. after the will has gone through probate court.
    2. anytime she wants to file with the clerk's office.
    3. immediately after the will is read.
    4. as soon as she pays the next month's condo fee.

23. The Virginia requirement that a deed of trust be recorded and all settlement proceeds be distributed within 2 days of the date of settlement is covered under what statute?
    1. Fair Lending Act
    2. Residential Deed of Trust Act
    3. Statute of Frauds
    4. Wet Settlement Act

24. All of the following information is found on a title report **EXCEPT**
    1. easements and covenants.
    2. buyer's full legal name.
    3. status of taxes.
    4. existing lenders.

25. A gap in the chain of title could be caused by any of the following **EXCEPT**
    1. a deed for one transfer of the property was never recorded.
    2. the seller was divorced in a foreign country.
    3. the name of the party on the deed was changed but never recorded.
    4. the property was sold to a relative for $1.00 with a recorded deed.

26. Under Virginia Real Estate License Law an "independent contractor" is
    1. anyone practicing real estate in Virginia.
    2. a salesperson who must pay federal taxes on estimated quarterly basis.
    3. a licensee representing a client other than as a standard agent.
    4. a person contracted with to add a deck to the property.

27. How is the selection of Real Estate Board members made?
    1. Elected by the public
    2. Selected by Virginia Association of REALTORS®
    3. Appointed by the governor
    4. Volunteers from real estate community

28. H completes his real estate salesperson course on June 20, 2000. He then takes and passes the Virginia licensing exam on July 15, 2000. How long does H have to apply for his license before being required to retake the exam?
    1. Until December 20, 2000
    2. Until January 15, 2001
    3. Until June 20, 2001
    4. Until July 14, 2001

29. If a licensee is found guilty of a violation of the license law or rules and regulations, the Real Estate Board may take all of the following disciplinary actions **EXCEPT**
    1. impose a prison sentence of no more than one year.
    2. levy fines.
    3. deny license renewal.
    4. suspend or revoke a license.

30. The Real Estate Board's activities include which of the following activities?
    1. Arbitrates disputes between salespersons and brokers
    2. Issues real estate licenses
    3. Recommends commission rates and commission splits
    4. Approves standardized listing agreements and sales contracts

31. K's license is about to expire, so she signs up for some continuing education classes. She takes 2 hours of Virginia real estate laws and regulations, 2 hours of ethics and standards of conduct, 2 hours of real estate taxes, and 2 hours of escrow requirements. Assuming K successfully completes these courses, will she have met her renewal education requirements?
    1. Yes; because she has completed at least 8 hours of continuing education.
    2. No; because she has failed to take a course on federal real estate laws.
    3. No; because she has failed to take a course on the Americans with Disabilities Act.
    4. No; because she has failed to take a course on fair housing laws.

32. J accidentally let his salesperson's license expire, but two months later is ready to renew it. How much money does J need to send to the Real Estate Board for his renewal fee?
    1. The current annual fee for a salesperson renewal
    2. The current annual fee for reinstatement
    3. The current annual fee for renewal plus the current fee for reinstatement
    4. The current annual fee for renewal plus reinstatement plus $100 fine

33. Salesperson R is getting married and will be changing her last name. What must she do to inform the REB?
    1. Notify the REB within 30 days of the wedding
    2. Notify the REB within 45 days of the wedding
    3. Notify the REB within 60 days of the wedding
    4. Notify the REB before her license renewal deadline

34. Salesperson R decides to leave Broker K's firm and work at Broker M's firm. How should the Real Estate Board be notified of this change?
    1. R should file a "Change of Brokerage" form with the REB.
    2. K should give R's license to M.
    3. M should apply to the REB to have R's license transferred to him.
    4. R and K should file a "Termination of Brokerage" form with the REB.

35. C has a Virginia salesperson's license, but she is currently holding it in inactive status. She decides to sell her home with the help of a local brokerage firm. Should she disclose her license status to potential buyers?
    1. Yes; because disclosure is required regardless of an inactive license status.
    2. No; because the local brokerage firm will be earning the commission from the sale.
    3. No; because disclosure is not required when a licensee sells his or her own home.
    4. No; because disclosure is not required when a license is inactive.

36. Salesperson *W* finds a buyer for a home he has listed. The buyer gives *W* an earnest money cashier's check for $2,000. What should *W* do with the check?
   1. Keep it until closing
   2. Deposit it in his escrow account within 3 business banking days
   3. Deposit it in his escrow account within 5 business banking days
   4. Immediately give it to his broker

37. The name of the broker must appear in all advertising **EXCEPT** a(n)
   1. newspaper Open House ad placed by salesperson.
   2. For Rent ad placed by salesperson on grocery store bulletin board.
   3. cable T.V. ad paid for by salesperson.
   4. salesperson selling as For Sale By Owner with disclosure that owner is licensed.

38. If the Real Estate Transaction Recovery Fund falls below $400,000, how much money may the Real Estate Board assess each licensee?
   1. $20 from each salesperson; $40 from each broker
   2. $20 from each inactive licensee; $40 from each active licensee
   3. $20 from each salesperson and broker, inactive or active
   4. $40 from each salesperson and broker, inactive or active

39. All of the following actions are considered improper delivery of instruments **EXCEPT**
   1. failing to promptly deliver complete and legible copies of any written contracts to each party in a transaction.
   2. failing to maintain all signed documents for a period of 3 years.
   3. failing to deliver a complete and accurate statement of money received and disbursed by a licensee.
   4. failing to provide timely, written notice of any material change in the transaction to all parties.

40. Which of the following statements is TRUE regarding institutional financing in Virginia?
   1. Mortgage loans, rather than deeds of trust, are the instruments primarily used in residential sales transactions.
   2. VA and FHA notes require notarization to be valid.
   3. Late charges on a loan may not exceed 3 percent of the installment due.
   4. Due-on-sale clauses are prohibited in Virginia.

41. One of the primary functions of the Virginia Housing Development Authority (VHDA) is to:
   1. build housing for low/moderate income people.
   2. research new methods of housing development.
   3. provide financing for residents of Virginia
   4. enforce Fair Housing and RESPA regulations.

42. A foreclosure of a deed of trust could be achieved without court action or sale of the property through which of the following?
   1. Strict foreclosure
   2. Deed in lieu of foreclosure
   3. Trustee sale
   4. Equitable foreclosure

43. *G* has just purchased a rental property that has 4 months to go on the current lease. The present tenants now have to right to
   1. continue their lease under current terms.
   2. move out immediately.
   3. sue the former owner for breaking the terms of their lease.
   4. demand repainting and recarpetting by the new owner.

44. *F* entered into a 1-year lease on October 1, 2000, with the right to continue on a month-to-month basis after the lease expires. *F* gave the landlord a security deposit. In accordance with the terms of the lease, *F* gives proper notice and vacates the property on December 31, 2001. How much interest will accrue on *F*'s security deposit?
   1. None
   2. 2 month's
   3. 12 month's
   4. 15 month's

45. The Virginia Residential Landlord and Tenant Act protects the rights of both landlords and tenants and applies to
    1. all properties advertised for rent.
    2. hotels offering two-week rentals.
    3. all apartment building rentals.
    4. occupancy by a property manager employed by the landlord.

46. If a tenant leaves 1 couch and 2 chairs in his apartment after the lease has ended, is the landlord allowed to sell it?
    1. Yes; provided the tenant is given ten days' written notice.
    2. Yes; within one week of the lease's termination date.
    3. No; Virginia includes a nonabandoned property clause in all leases.
    4. No; the furniture remains the property of the tenant.

47. Which one of the following is protected by Virginia's Fair Housing Law?
    1. A 58-year-old AIDS victim
    2. A 45-year-old homosexual
    3. A 35-year-old transvestite
    4. A 51-year-old veteran

48. *T* will be in violation of the Virginia Fair Housing Law if he refuses to rent his 2-bedroom apartment for any of the following reasons **EXCEPT**
    1. the couple applying are from Nigeria.
    2. the couple has 2 small children.
    3. the applicant is 65 years old.
    4. the applicants do not have adequate income.

49. All of the following apartment building accommodations for handicapped persons are considered reasonable requests **EXCEPT**
    1. allowing a blind person to have an assistance monkey in a "no-pets" building.
    2. allowing a paralyzed person to install railings in his or her bathroom.
    3. removing walls along a corridor of a common area to make the hallway wide enough for wheelchair access.
    4. giving first-floor unit preferences to a wheelchair-bound person.

50. If an alleged fair housing discriminatory act has taken place, how long after the occurrence of the act does the injured party have to file a complaint with the REB?
    1. 3 months
    2. 6 months
    3. 9 months
    4. 1 year

Answer Key

Chapter Quizzes

Chapter 1
1. (3)
2. (1)
3. (4)
4. (4)
5. (3)
6. (3)
7. (3)
8. (1)
9. (4)
10. (4)

Chapter 2
1. (2)
2. (1)
3. (2)
4. (3)
5. (3)
6. (3)
7. (2)
8. (4)
9. (3)
10. (2)

Chapter 3
1. (3)
2. (1)
3. (2)
4. (1)
5. (3)
6. (4)
7. (2)
8. (4)
9. (4)
10. (2)

Chapter 4
1. (4)
2. (1)
3. (2)
4. (4)
5. (4)
6. (1)
7. (2)
8. (3)
9. (2)
10. (1)
11. (3)
12. (1)
13. (2)
14. (3)
15. (3)
16. (2)
17. (3)
18. (2)
19. (2)
20. (4)

Chapter 5
1. (4)
2. (4)
3. (3)
4. (4)
5. (4)

Chapter 6
1. (1)
2. (2)
3. (4)
4. (2)
5. (1)
6. (3)
7. (3)
8. (3)
9. (2)
10. (4)

Chapter 7
1. (4)
2. (1)
3. (1)
4. (3)
5. (1)

Chapter 8
1. (3)
2. (4)
3. (2)
4. (4)
5. (1)
6. (2)
7. (3)
8. (3)
9. (2)
10. (2)

Chapter 9

1. (4)
2. (2)
3. (3)
4. (3)
5. (3)
6. (1)
7. (2)
8. (3)
9. (2)
10. (4)

Chapter 10

1. (4)
2. (1)
3. (4)
4. (1)
5. (3)
6. (1)
7. (2)
8. (3)
9. (2)
10. (2)
11. (3)
12. (2)
13. (1)
14. (3)
15. (3)
16. (2)
17. (4)
18. (4)
19. (2)
20. (2)
21. (4)
22. (3)
23. (1)
24. (2)
25. (4)
26. (4)
27. (2)
28. (4)
29. (4)
30. (1)

Chapter 11

1. (3)
2. (2)
3. (2)
4. (2)
5. (2)
6. (4)
7. (1)
8. (2)
9. (1)
10. (3)

Chapter 12

1. (4)
2. (4)
3. (4)
4. (1)
5. (3)
6. (4)
7. (3)
8. (4)
9. (3)
10. (1)

Chapter 13

1. (2)
2. (2)
3. (4)
4. (3)
5. (2)
6. (3)
7. (1)
8. (2)
9. (4)
10. (3)

Appendix C: Practice Exam

1. (4)
2. (3)
3. (1)
4. (2)
5. (1)
6. (3)
7. (2)
8. (2)
9. (3)
10. (4)
11. (1)
12. (3)
13. (3)
14. (4)
15. (2)
16. (3)
17. (1)
18. (4)
19. (2)
20. (1)
21. (3)
22. (1)
23. (4)
24. (2)
25. (4)
26. (3)
27. (3)
28. (4)
29. (1)
30. (2)
31. (4)
32. (2)
33. (1)
34. (3)
35. (1)
36. (4)
37. (4)
38. (3)
39. (2)
40. (2)
41. (3)
42. (1)
43. (1)
44. (4)
45. (3)
46. (1)
47. (1)
48. (4)
49. (3)
50. (4)

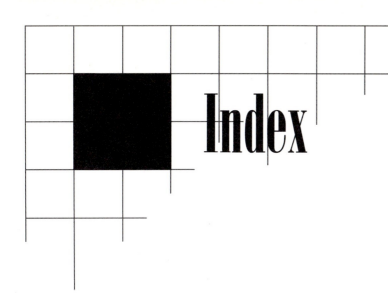

Index

A

Abandoned property, 139
Abandonment, 32
Active license, 98
Actively engaged, 93
Adverse possession, 82-83
Advertisements, 45, 109-10, 129, 144
Agency
  brokerage relationship, 7
  buyer's agent disclosure, 7
  definitions, 4-5
  disclosed dual, 9, 10
  disclosure requirements, 7-9
  duties to client, 6
  duties to customer, 6
  imputed knowledge, 9
  property management, 7
Agent, 2
Answer key, 161-62
Application fees, 136
As-built survey, 55
Assessment, 58-59
Associate broker, 3, 93
Association, 100
Attachment, 63
Auction, 129
Augmented estate, 32
Augmented Estate and Elective Share Act, 31
Automatic survivorship doctrine, 37

B

Behavior, 138
Boundary survey, 55
Branch office licenses, 98
Broker, 97
  compensation, 16
  definition of, 2
  escrow accounts, 107-9
Brokerage, 105-7
  definitions, 2-3
  relationship, 5, 7, 113
Building codes, 22
Business entity license, 100-101
Business name, 105
Business place, 105
Buyer agency
  agreement, 9, 20-21
  disclosure, 7
  representation, 17
Buyer's recourse, 26
Bylaws, 43

C

Caveat emptor, 129
Chain of title, 88
Claims procedure, 111
Clerk fees, 82
Client, 2, 5, 93
  duties to, 6
Code of Virginia, 1, 66, 93
Commercial broker's lien, 64
Commission, improper, 114-15
Common elements, 40
Common source information company, 3
Community property, 38
Competence, 80
Complaint procedure, 117-18
Concurrent licenses, 98
Condemnation, 30
Condemnation Act, 30
Condominium, 16
  ownership, 41-44
Confidentiality, 7, 136
Conflict of interest, 114, 129
Consent to suits and services, 99-100
Consumer Real Estate Settlement Protection Act, 87
Contingencies, 17
Continuing education, 102-3
Contract, 66-67
  procedures, 67, 78
  regional sales, 68-77
Control, transfer of, 46
Conventional loans, 125
Cooperative, 16
  ownership, 40-41
Co-ownership, 37-38
Corporation, 39, 100
Correction deed, 88
Credit line deeds of trust, 126
Criminal background, 145
Customer, duties to, 6

D

Death, 110
Deceased person's property transfer, 83-84
Declarant, 41
Declaration of cooperative, 40
Deed of trust, 17, 89
  credit line, 126
  deferred purchase-money, 127
  tax on, 82
Deferred purchase-money deed of trust, 127
Delivery of instruments, 115-16
Department of Professional and Occupational Regulation, 1, 105, 110
Deposits, 45
Descent, 31-32
Desertion, 134
Designated agency, 3, 5, 113
Designated representative, 9, 11
Destruction of premises, 134
Devise, 37
Disability, 110
Disbursement of proceeds, 129-30
Disciplinary action, 116
Disclaimer
  seller, 22
  statement, 25
Disclosure, 16
  agency options, 15
  brokerage relationship, 7-9, 113
  buyer agent, 7
  condemnation, 30
  designated representation, 9, 11
  dual agency, 9, 10
  eminent domain, 30
  exemptions, 26
  licensee, 106-7
  ownership, 136
  Property Owner's Association Act, 47-48
  seller, 17, 22
  statement, 23-24
  time for, 22
Discriminatory practices, 146-47
Dispute settlement, 54
Distress warrant, 134-35

163

Dual agency, 3, 5, 113
  disclosure, 9, 10
Due-on-sale clauses, 126
Dwelling, 143

E

Earnest money deposits, 45
Easement by prescription, 34
Easements, 33-34
Elderliness, 144
Elderly housing, 145
Eminent domain, 30
Enforcement, 147-48
Equitable title, 78
Escow account, 107-8
Escrow funds, 116
  protection of, 108-9
Estates in land, 31
Estate tax liens, 63
Examination, 97
  practice, 155-60
Exclusive right to represent agreement, 9
Exclusive right to sell agreement, 9, 18-19
Expiration date, 15

F

Fair housing, 143-46
Fair housing law, 15
  enforcement of, 147-48
Fair Housing law, 15
False description, 54
Familial status, 144
Federal Housing Administration loans, 128
Fiduciary responsibilities, 6
Financial records, 108
Financing, 124
Firm, 2, 93
Foreclosure, 128-30
Forfeiture, prevention of, 135
Full search, 88
Fund maintenance, 110-11

G–H

Grantee, 80
Grantor, 80
Grantor tax, 81-82
Habendum clause, 80
Handicapped persons, 144, 146-47
Holographic will, 83
Homestead exemption, 32-33
Home warranty, 78
House location survey, 55
House rule changes, 137

I–J

Improper brokerage commission, 114-15
Improper dealing, 115
Imputed knowledge, 11
Inactive license, 98-99
Inactive status, 94
Incompetence, 113-14
Independent contractor, 3, 5, 94
Informal Fact Finding Conference, 117
Information sources, 153
Inheritance tax liens, 63
Institutional advertising, 109-10

Institutional financing, 125-26
Interest-bearing accounts, 108
Interest rates, 130
Interval ownership, 44
Intestate distributions, 31-32
Joint tenancy, 37-38
Judgment lien, 89
Judgments, 62-63
Just compensation, 30

L

Landlord
  lien, 64
  obligations, 136-37
Land trust, 38
Late charges, 125
Lead-based paint, 16
Lease, 59, 133-35
  prohibitions, 139
  termination, 133
  unsigned or undelivered, 136
Legal description, methods of, 53-54
Legislative Information System, 151-53
Lending institutions, 147
License
  automatic suspension, revocation, 118
  business entity, 100-101
  discriminatory housing and, 145-47, 148
  exemptions, 4, 103-4
  fees, 104
  liability, 26-27
  obtaining, 105
  operating without, 96
  reciprocal, 99-100
  renewal of, 101-103, 104
  requirements for, 96-99
  who must have, 3-4, 95-96
Licensee, 3, 94, 113
Liens
  commercial broker's, 64
  estate, inheritance tax, 63
  judgment, 62-63, 89
  landlord's, 64
  mechanics', 61-62, 90
  tax, 58-61
  vendor's, 63-64
Limited liability company, 101
Limited search, 88
Lis pendens, 63
Listing agreement, 9, 14, 18-19
Listing forms, 14-17
Location change, 106

M–O

Maintenance, 137
Management responsibility, 140
Managing broker, 3
Marital estates, 31-32
Marketable title, 67
Mechanics' Lien Disclosure Act, 61
Mechanics' liens, 61-62, 90
Megan's Law, 26
Military personnel, lease termination and, 139
Ministerial acts, 5
Misrepresentation, 26-27, 115
Monetary limitations, 112
Mortgage, transfer fees, 82
Multiple listing service, 14, 16

Net listing, 14
New construction, 59
  warranty, 78
New home builders, 22
Nolo contendere, 113
Non-institutional advertising, 109-10
Nonresident, appointment of agent, 133
Office supervision, 106
Omissions, 115
Origination fee, 125
Ownership
  disclosure, 136
  name, 106

P

Partnership, 100
Penalty, 112
Physical survey, 55
Plat maps, 55
Power of attorney, 67, 81
Premises, destruction of, 134
Principal, 2, 116
  to transaction, 94
Principal broker, 2, 94
Proceeds, residue of, 129-30
Project instrument, 44
Promissory note, 130
Property, absence from, 138
Property condition, 137
Property management, 7, 108
Property Owner's Association Act, 16, 46-49
Protected classes, 143
PSI Real Estate Licensing Examination Service, 105
Public offering statement, 42, 45
Purchase contracts, 124
Purchase-money financing, 126-27
Purchase and sale documentation, 154

R

Real estate, 94
  description, 53
Real Estate Board, 40, 93, 94-95
Real Estate Board Rules and Regulations, 1, 14
Real Estate Cooperative Act, 40
Real Estate Transaction Recovery Fund, 110-12
Reciprocity, 99-100
Record keeping, 116
Recordation tax, 81
Records provision, 113
Recovery limitation, 111-12
Referral agent, 99
Registration fees, 104
Releases, 127
Renewal
  clause, automatic, 139
  of license, 101-102
Rent
  control, 135
  failure to pay, 134
Rental agreement violation, 138
Rental location agent, 104
Rental property sale, 133
Resales
  of condominium unit, 43-44
  of time-share unit, 46
Rescission, 41, 45, 48-49
Residential Landlord and Tenant Act,

135-40
Residential Property Disclosure Act, 16, 17, 27
Retaliatory action, 139-40
Returned checks, 138
Revocation, of license, 118
Right to access, 137

S
Sales
    condominium unit, 42
    contract, 68-77
    cooperative interest, 40-41
Salesperson, 2, 97
Secured debts, 33
Security deposits, 136
Security devices, 138
Seizure, of tenant property, 134-35
Seller
    disclaimer, 22, 26-27
    disclosure, 17
    responsibilities, 16
Selling price, 15
Settlement agent, 87
Sexual offenders, 26
Shared dwellings, 144
Signage, 106
Single-family occupancy, 145
Sole proprietor, 3, 94
Special assessments, 60-61
Sponsal consent, 67
Standard agency, 3, 4, 94
Standards of conduct, 112-16
Statute of frauds, 17, 67
Statute of limitations, 46
Statutory lien rights, 43
Stigmatized property, 27
Structural defect, 78
Subdivision plat, 55, 56
Sublease. 139
Subordinate licensees, 116
Supervising broker, 3, 94, 116
Surveys, 55-56
Suspension, of license, 118

T
Taking, 30
Tax liens, 58-61
Tenancy
    in common, 37, 38
    by the entirety, 38
    in partnership, 39
Tenant
    holdover, 133-34
    obligations, 137-38
    property seizure, 134-35
Termination, 43
    of affiliation, 106
    date, 7
Theft, 16
Time-share ownership, 44-46
Title, 67
    examination, 88-89
    issues, 89-90
Title insurance, 62, 89
Title report, 89, 128
Transfer, 106
    of control, 46
    fees, 82
    taxes, 81-82
    valid conveyance, 80-81
Trustee, 128-29
Trustee's deed, 129

U–W
Undivided percentage interest, 42
Unity of interest, 37
Unsecured debts, 33
Unworthiness, 113-14
Usury, 130
Vacation ownership, 44
Vandalism, 16
Vendor's lien, 63-64
Veterans Administration loans, 128
Virginia Administrative Code, Chapter 18, 1
Virginia Housing Development Authority, 127-28
Voting rights, 42
Warranties, 78
Wet Settlement Act, 130
Will, 83-84